D1245246

1,000,000 Books

are available to read at

www.ForgottenBooks.com

Read online
Download PDF
Purchase in print

ISBN 978-1-330-00294-0
PIBN 10001264

1 MONTH OF
FREE
READING

at
www.ForgottenBooks.com

By purchasing this book you are eligible for one month membership to ForgottenBooks.com, giving you unlimited access to our entire collection of over 1,000,000 titles via our web site and mobile apps.

To claim your free month visit:
www.forgottenbooks.com/free1264

English
Français
Deutsche
Italiano
Español
Português

www.forgottenbooks.com

Mythology Photography **Fiction**
Fishing Christianity **Art** Cooking
Essays Buddhism Freemasonry
Medicine **Biology** Music **Ancient
Egypt** Evolution Carpentry Physics
Dance Geology **Mathematics** Fitness
Shakespeare **Folklore** Yoga Marketing
Confidence Immortality Biographies
Poetry **Psychology** Witchcraft
Electronics Chemistry History **Law**
Accounting **Philosophy** Anthropology
Alchemy Drama Quantum Mechanics
Atheism Sexual Health **Ancient History**
Entrepreneurship Languages Sport
Paleontology Needlework Islam
Metaphysics Investment Archaeology
Parenting Statistics Criminology
Motivational

Young People's Story
of
American Literature

Revised Edition

By

Ida Prentice Whitcomb

Author of "A Bunch of Wild Flowers for the Children,"
"Heroes of History," "Young People's Story
of Art," "Young People's Story
of Music," etc.

With Numerous Illustrations

New York
Dodd, Mead and Company
1936

FOREWORD

A STORY is not necessarily bound by historical perspective; and in the following " Young People's Story of American Literature," the aim has been three-fold: First, to bring into clear outline such biographical and dramatic elements as appeal to young people and stimulate them to seek further.

Second, to incite the youth and maiden in committing to memory poetic selections. These faithfully garnered will prove a rich treasure.

Third, to interest the student in visiting the shrines of our own land as eagerly as those abroad.

In collecting materials for the book, the writer has been enabled through great courtesy to visit many of the places mentioned, and has noted much of local value in a desire to add colour to the story. Every shrine visited has made more vivid the personality associated with it.

So the " Firstly, Secondly, and Thirdly," are in brief: To seek companionship of the best books; to memorise choice poems; and to make pilgrimages to the homes of American authors.

The writer acknowledges, with thanks, the permission given by Houghton, Mifflin and Company to reprint extracts from the works of Whittier, Low-ell, Longfellow, Holmes, Thoreau, Stedman, and others; by Charles Scribner's Sons to quote from the poems of Rev. Dr. Henry Van Dyke, Eugene Field, and Sidney Lanier; by Small, Maynard and Company to quote short extracts from the poems of Rev. John B. Tabb; by Lothrop, Lee and Shepard Company to quote from the poems of Paul Hamilton Hayne; by D. Appleton and Company to quote from the poems of William Cullen Bryant; and by Little, Brown and Company to quote " Poppies in the Wheat," copyright 1892, by Roberts Brothers, and also some short quotations from other poems of Helen Hunt Jackson.

CONTENTS

CHAPTER   PAGE

I THE EVOLUTION OF THE BOOK I

II BEGINNINGS OF THE STORY 4

III JAMESTOWN AND CAPTAIN JOHN SMITH 6

IV OTHER WRITERS OF THE VIRGINIA COLONY . . . 13

V PILGRIM AND PURITAN CHRONICLERS 16

VI EARLY THEOLOGIANS 24

VII DIARISTS AND POETS 34

VIII BENJAMIN FRANKLIN 41

IX REVOLUTIONARY LEADERS 55

X THE NATION-BUILDERS 63

XI GLANCES BACKWARD AND FORWARD 72

XII WASHINGTON IRVING 76

XIII JAMES FENIMORE COOPER 90

XIV WILLIAM CULLEN BRYANT 101

XV SPASMODIC POEMS AND SONGS 114

XVI JOHN GREENLEAF WHITTIER 124

XVII WAR LITERATURE 140

XVIII BANCROFT AND PRESCOTT 156

XIX MOTLEY AND PARKMAN 165

XX NEW INFLUENCES IN PURITAN NEW ENGLAND . . . 175

XXI RALPH WALDO EMERSON 180

XXII HENRY DAVID THOREAU 196

XXIII NATHANIEL HAWTHORNE 205

XXIV HENRY WADSWORTH LONGFELLOW 220

XXV JAMES RUSSELL LOWELL 240

CONTENTS

CHAPTER   PAGE

XXVI Oliver Wendell Holmes 256

XXVII Edgar Allan Poe 275

XXVIII Other Southern Writers 291

XXIX Western Literature 304

XXX A Group of Eastern Authors 318

XXXI Woman in American Literature—Part First . . 335

XXXII Woman in American Literature—Part Second . 343

XXXIII Nature Lovers—Essayists—Historians 361

XXXIV Novelists 369

XXXV Poets 386

Afterword 402

ILLUSTRATIONS

The Orchard House: Home of the Alcotts . . . *Frontispiece*

FACING
PAGE

Evolution of the Book: Cairn, Oral, Hieroglyphics 2
Evolution of the Book: Pictograph, Manuscript, Printing Press 4
Monument to Capt. John Smith, Jamestown, Va 10
Gov. John Winthrop 18
Cotton Mather 18
John Eliot 18
Jonathan Edwards 18
National Monument, Plymouth, Mass 36
Thomas Jefferson 44
Alexander Hamilton 44
Benjamin Franklin 44
Samuel Sewall 44
Page from Poor Richard's Almanac, September, 1738 . . . 52
Washington Irving 78
J. Fenimore Cooper 78
Fitz-Greene Hallock 78
William Cullen Bryant 78
Sunnyside: Home of Washington Irving 86
Monument to J. Fenimore Cooper, Cooperstown, N. Y. . . . 96
William Cullen Bryant Memorial, Bryant Park, New York . . 108
John Howard Payne's "Home Sweet Home," East Hampton, L. I. 118
Home of John Greenleaf Whittier, Amesbury, Mass 130
William Lloyd Garrison 142
Daniel Webster 142
Henry Clay 142
Harriet Beecher Stowe 142
Lincoln Emancipation Statue at Washington, D. C. 150
Francis Parkman 160
John Lothrop Motley 160
George Bancroft 160
William H. Prescott 160
School of Philosophy, Concord, Mass 176
Ralph Waldo Emerson 184
Nathaniel Hawthorne 184

ILLUSTRATIONS

FACING
PAGE

Henry David Thoreau 184
Louisa M. Alcott 184
Home of Ralph Waldo Emerson, Concord, Mass 192
The Thoreau Cairn and Thoreau Cove, Lake Walden . . . 198
Old Manse, Concord, Mass 208
The Wayside: Home of Nathaniel Hawthorne, Concord, Mass. 216
Henry Wadsworth Longfellow 222
James Russell Lowell 222
Oliver Wendell Holmes 222
John Greenleaf Whittier 222
Craigie House: Home of Henry W. Longfellow, Cambridge,
    Mass 232
Elmwood: Home of James Russell Lowell, Cambridge, Mass . 248
Edgar Allan Poe 276
Sidney Lanier 276
Paul H. Hayne 276
Rev. John B. Tabb 276
Poe's Cottage at Fordham, New York City 284
Samuel L. Clemens 308
Francis Bret Harte 308
Eugene Field 308
Henry Cuyler Bunner 308
Edward Clarence Stedman 320
Bayard Taylor 320
Thomas Bailey Aldrich 320
Walt Whitman 320
Edward Everett Hale 330
Frank R. Stockton 330
William Dean Howells 330
F. Marion Crawford 330
Celia L. Thaxter 340
Sarah Orne Jewett 340
Helen Hunt Jackson 340
Mary Mapes Dodge 340

"Books are keys to wisdom's treasure;
Books are gates to lands of pleasure;
Books are paths that upward lead;
Books are friends, come, let us read!"
—POULSSON.

FOREWORD OF REVISED EDITION

Now, in 1922, a new edition of "Young People's Story of American Literature" is issued. What a wonderful broadening of vision since the beginning of our colonial period over three hundred years ago!

To-day there is more thoughtful and artistic authorship than ever before. Essayist and dramatist, biographer and historian, scientist and philosopher, novelist and poet, are writing; the illustrator is busy with brush and camera—and everybody reads. The demand is great and our literature is worthy of consideration.

Let us study its trend from the characteristics of a few representative authors, for it is better to be familiar with the work of a few rather than to have scant acquaintance with that of the many.

Which are the best we may not know, for it is never possible to give correct perspective of contemporary writers. Keenest critics fail in judgment of their own age.

Amy Lowell says:

"To-day can never be adequately expressed largely because we are a part of it and only a part";

while John Jay Chapman thus voices his views:

"A historian cannot get his mind into focus upon anything as near as the present."

I

THE EVOLUTION OF THE BOOK

AN English author rightly traces the origin of the book to the depth of some Asiatic forest, where centuries agone a rude savage stood, thorn in hand, etching upon a leaf — perhaps torn from a giant palm — a symbol by which to commemorate either joy or struggle in his simple life; and thus the tree became the parent of the book — the word "book" being derived from the beech with its smooth and silvery bark, found by our Saxon forefathers in the German forest, and the leaf explains itself.

Another more pictorial illustration of the origin of the book, we find in a series of six panels, painted by Mr. John W. Alexander, of New York, in the new Congressional Library, at Washington.

In the first of these expressive frescoes, prehistoric man erects upon the seashore a rough cairn of boulders. The task is laborious, but he must needs make his record.

In the second, the Oriental story-teller dramatically relates his tale to a group of absorbed listeners: this typifies oral tradition.

Again we look, and the Egyptian stone-cutter chisels his hieroglyphics upon the face of a tomb.

His cutting is vigorous and incisive — *his* tale is made to live.

Yet another, and a graceful American Indian paints upon a buffalo-skin the pictograph, which represents the war-trail or the chase.

We next glance into the dim scriptorium where the monastic scribe patiently illuminates his manuscript; and as the final evolution, Gutenberg eagerly scans the proof that has just come from the printing-press — *his* gift to the world.

So from prehistoric age to twentieth century, leaf, cairn and altar, oral tradition, hieroglyphic and pictograph, waxed tablet, illuminated manuscript and printing-press — have *all* had part in leading up to the book — the ultimate triumph of modern thought.

And the book is the vehicle of literature; and the literature that it holds is the reflection and reproduction alike of the intellect and deed of the people.

Honest John Morley says: —

" Poets, dramatists, humorists, satirists, historians, masters of fiction, great preachers, character-writers, political orators, maxim-writers — *all are* literature."

The story of literature is a curious and varied one that has unravelled century by century as Egypt, Assyria, Persia, China and India, Greece and Rome, and the more modern countries, have in turn added their records.

CAIRN

ORAL TRADITION

EGYPTIAN HIEROGLYPHICS

Our subject is *American* literature. This, how-ever, being but a branch of *English* literature, we join in the ranks and inspiration of that long and splendid procession, which, for twelve hundred years, has been marching along.

Our environment, it is true, has been different: another land and climate and social organisation, with democratic political problems to solve; but all the same, we, too, claim ancestral right in Chaucer and Spenser and Shakespeare and Milton — and English literature is indeed our glorious heritage.

And as we consider the work of our up-to-date author, seated in his library — running his fingers lightly over the keys of his typewriter — let us not forget the gratitude due to that primitive savage, who, in the fragrant woodland, traced *his* inspira-tion upon the leaf of a tree, and thus took the *first* step in *the evolution of the book.*

II

AMERICAN literature — where does it begin? Surely not among the prehistoric mound-builders whose instruments and ornaments are unearthed to-day. They builded their homes, tilled their soil, and worked their mines, but thus their record sadly ends: " They had no poet and they died."

Next, in historic sequence, we glance at the Indian, who is becoming to-day more and more to the American author a theme of romance. What was *his* contribution to the literature of an aboriginal age? It was scanty indeed — but it formed a beginning; for his speech and songs of magic and love displayed bold courage and an eloquent symbolism that we may not overlook.

The following, taken from Dr. Schoolcraft's " Indian Tribes " is an expressive illustration: —

" My love is tall and graceful as the young pine waving on the hill, and as swift in his course as the noble, stately deer; his hair is flowing and dark, as the blackbird that floats through the air, and his eyes like the eagle's, both piercing and bright; his heart, it is fearless and great, and his arm, it is strong in the fight, as this bow made of iron wood which he easily bends. His aim is as sure in the fight and chase as the hawk which ne'er misses its prey.

4

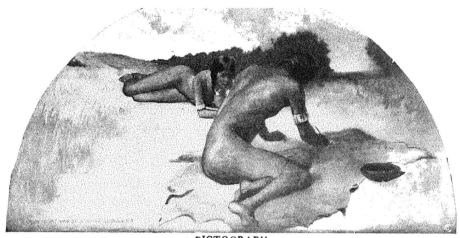

PICTOGRAPH

MANUSCRIPT BOOK

PRINTING PRESS

Ah, aid me, ye spirits! of water, of earth, and of sky, while I sing his praise."

Leaving behind us the mound-builder and the Indian, we next consider *true* American literature, which is divided into three periods: Colonial, Revolutionary, and National.

The Colonial began in America when in " Merrie England" the golden " Elizabethan Age " was at its height: when Shakespeare was unfolding his marvellous creations, and when Spenser sang of his " Fairie Queene," England disporting itself alike in drama and pageant.

Colonial literature here forms striking contrast to the brilliant period abroad, and it must have small space in our scheme, compared to that we must give to Revolutionary and National; and yet there is revealed in it to-day an increasing interest. We hear much of Colonial Dames and houses and architecture and historic data.

Truly these colonists " builded better than they knew," and our first duty must be to trace the earlier foot-prints which they made.

III

JAMESTOWN AND CAPTAIN JOHN SMITH

COLONIAL literature has two divisions: one treats of "Jamestown and the Cavalier"—the other of "Plymouth, the Pilgrim, and the Puritan." We consider "Jamestown and the Cavalier" first, for this was the earlier.

It was in the winter of 1606, that a party of romantic aristocrats, unruly gallants, mechanics and farmers, and beggars pushed thither by friends — adventurers all — set out in a pigmy fleet of three ships from England for America. They were under a charter to a London Company to seek here gold mines and precious stones.

Four months they sailed over three thousand miles of unknown sea, and finally in April, 1607, were driven by storm into a large river, its shores blooming with dogwood and redbud, and on a bright day, they landed on the bank at a perilous spot; and James River and Jamestown were later named in honour of their illustrious English King.

This was the region which the chivalrous Sir Walter Raleigh — the dauntless sailor — had previously penetrated in one of his futile attempts to colonise North America; and though he had not conquered, he had succeeded in christening the land Virginia, in gratitude to his " Virgin Queen," and this name yet binds Virginia to the Mother Country.

And as at Jamestown our forbears disembarked — the dense wilderness behind, the wide ocean before — how little they realised the boundless future! With the exception of Gosnold and Captain John Smith, they knew nothing of leadership, but many of them were manly men who loved liberty and adventure. The struggle was bitterly waged against famine and the Indians; but out of all, the Virginia colony was established—the *first permanent English settlement* in North America.

There may have been imaginative, resourceful spirits among these pioneers, but what wonder that they had scant leisure for literary pursuits — for drama or pageant or smooth narrative. No poet or novelist could assert himself. These were days of *action* not *thought;* and yet in compacts and journals and letters home, we may discover, even at this remote date, the beginnings of our story of American literature — for we at once descry the picturesque figure of the redoubtable John Smith — soldier, captain, governor, saviour and historian, of the colony.

He stands at the gateway of American literature just as the old tramp-explorer, Sir John Mandeville, stood three hundred years before, at the gateway of English literature.

A born fighter was this Lincolnshire boy, who very early ran away from home, " foreign countries for to see." He fought in France, the Netherlands, and Italy; he fought the Spanish, Tartars and Turks; and blazoned on his escutcheon were the heads of three Turkish champions that he had severed in single combat.

He encountered shipwreck and slavery; and a veritable knight-errant of English chivalry, he returned to London, at the age of twenty-five — a battle-scarred hero.

Then catching Gosnold's enthusiasm, he was seized with a mania for colonisation, and being just in time, he started in 1607, with the motley crew for Jamestown. They *sailed* for the riches of the South Sea — they *found* as their " El Dorado " only cotton and tobacco; but dependable Captain Smith endured hardships and disappointments with optimism.

In his little pinnace, *Discovery,* he explored the Virginian bays, so carefully surveying the coast, that among his works he published, in 1612, " A Map of Virginia, with a Description of the Country, the Commodities, People, Government, and Religion "— a voluminous title, but it was a fashion in those days to make a title a summary of the contents of a book.

Captain Smith bartered so skilfully with the Indians that he kept the colony from starvation. His services were of unquestioned value: at one time governor — at another barely escaping the gallows — his zeal being always greater than his discretion.

After hundred of settlers had been added to the colony, he was removed; returning afterwards to explore the New England shores, he received from King James the title " Admiral of New England." All told, he was in America less than three years.

Captain Smith's life did not seem adapted to literary achievement, but he wrote two booklets here which gave him a place in colonial literature. His other works belong to the long, quieter years that followed his going back to England.

It is strange to think of the hardy soldier, seated in his aboriginal hut of logs and mud, and on an improvised desk with goose-quill pen, recounting his deeds. His apology is, that he " admired those whose pens had writ what their swords had done." He explained that he could not " write as a clerk, but as a soldier," and he begs his friends and well-wishers to accept the results!

There being no printing-press in America, his first writings appeared in London, in 1608 — the year that Milton was born. Eight volumes, large and small, related to Virginia, giving account " of Such Occurrences and Accidents of Note as hath Happened " there. In fact, Captain Smith must not only have interested others in book-making but also tempted many to the colony.

His best book, " A General History of Virginia," is a rough-hewn recountal of the initial contact with the wilderness, made by the adventurous pen of one who was *always* the *centre* of the *adventures!* His fault was boastfulness — but had he not a right to glory in his great deeds?

In speaking of Virginia, he quaintly says: —

" There is but one entrance into this country, and that is at the mouth of a goodly bay eighteen or twenty miles broad. . . . Within is a country that may have the prerogative over the most pleasant places known, for earth and heaven never agreed better to frame a place for man's habitation. The mildness of the air, the fertility of the soil, and the situation of the rivers are as propitious to the use of man, as no place is more convenient for pleasure, profit, and man's sustenance, under any latitude or climate. So, then, here is a place, a nurse for soldiers, a practice for mariners, a trade for merchants, a reward for the good, and that which is most of all, a business to bring such poor infidels to the knowledge of God and His Holy Gospel."

Recall these words to-day! Think of his Old Point Comfort — of the many that have since found comfort within its harbour; and of its Military School which has become truly " a nurse for soldiers "; of Hampton Roads and " its practice for mariners "; of " the trade for merchants," at Newport News and Norfolk; and best of all, of the gracious Hampton Institute, with its civilising and Christianising influences. Was not Captain Smith,

MONUMENT TO CAPT. JOHN SMITH, JAMESTOWN, VA.

with everything else, gifted with prophetic vision?

Besides, he first gave the Indian to American literature, for you remember that he lived long before Cooper and Longfellow. For the race in general, he had no respect. He dubs the Indian as inconstant, crafty, cautious and covetous, quick-tempered, malicious and treacherous. He made an exception, however, in his Pocahontas story; it may be a myth but it is his finest bit of colouring.

How vivid is the picture of his capture by Powhatan — his rescue by the beautiful maiden; of her bringing corn to the famished colonists, and her later royal reception in London as the daughter of an Indian king. It is the first dramatic tale that comes into American literature.

John Smith began his literary work when Shakespeare was. writing; he, too, was a dramatist, but in a different way. While some of his descriptions border on the marvellous, he is always able to make up in romance what he lacks in history, and his compositions have done more to preserve his fame than his brave doings.

His enemies accused him of exaggeration, saying that "He writ too much, and done too little." But whatever he "writ" and whatever he "done," his chivalrous narrative is a most valuable literary relic.

We do not like to think that Captain John Smith, our earnest chronicler, " died poor and neglected in England,"— but so it is told.

The " English Drayton " in a " spirited valedictory " to the three ship-loads of heroic fortune-hunters who had sailed from England, in 1606, prophesies for them a literary future : —

> " And as there plenty grows
>   Of laurel everywhere,—
>   Apollo's sacred tree —
>   You it may see
>   A poet's brows
> To crown, that may sing there."

IV

OTHER WRITERS OF THE VIRGINIA COLONY

AND there were other attempts besides that of Captain John Smith to leave to posterity a literary record. William Strachey, secretary of the colony, wrote and sent to London, in 1610, a manuscript, telling of a fierce storm and shipwreck off the Bermuda Islands —" the still vex'd Bermoothes "; and this thrilling description, it is thought, may have furnished a plot to Shakespeare in " The Tempest."

George Sandys, treasurer of the colony, working sometimes by the light of a pine knot, made a most imaginative translation of Ovid's " Metamorphoses."

And there were later adventurers and annalists: among them, Colonel William Byrd, a wealthy and brilliant man, and an amateur in literature, who, in 1736, when writing the history of his experience in running a dividing line between Virginia and North Carolina, gives a pleasant picture of colonial life; but he says :—

" They import so many negroes hither, that I fear the colony will, some time or other, be known by the name of ' New Guinea.' "

Bacon's Rebellion was one of the most striking

13

episodes in these anti-Revolutionary times; and in 1676, " The Burwell Papers " described it, and in these appeared some elegiac verses on the death of Nathaniel Bacon.

So Virginia, the " Cradle of the Republic," became, also, the " Cradle " of a literature associated with noble names.

Many of the colonists came from the titled ranks of English society. They were the originators of the " F. F. V's," or " First Families of Virginia," and strongly bound both to royalty and the Established Church. Instead of building many towns, these planters spent a manorial existence on their broad estates, devoting their free and careless hours to fox-hunting, horse-racing, and cock-fighting.

Robert Beverly, in his " History of Virginia," published in 1705, emphasises Southern hospitality. Indeed, this was one of the strongest traits in the character of the planter. Families of ample means sent their sons abroad to be educated; and the courthouse rather than the school was the nucleus of social and political life.

It was proposed early in the seventeenth century to build a University, and some Englishmen donated the money for the purchase of the land; but a terrible Indian massacre interfered. So William and Mary College was not begun at Williamsburg until 1660, and did not receive its charter until 1693. It was closely fashioned after Oxford, in England; and

James Blair, its founder, and author of "The Present State of Virginia," was a man alike of force and intellect. And many more old chroniclers there were who wrote about Virginia, the State destined later on to be "The Mother of Presidents." Doubtless, their documents are historically valuable but they would form curious reading for us.

And what may we find in Jamestown to-day to help us recall our earliest colonial literature? Only a few indefinite relics. Captain Smith selected this as "a fit place for a great city," but it proved too marshy and unhealthful. The land, however, has been recently set apart by the "Virginia Antiquarian Society," in order to preserve the ruins.

Among them, there is seen under water the remains of a powder-house built by Captain Smith. There are, also, some graves in an ancient burial-ground. The most attractive thing is an old church tower, which legend says stands upon the spot where, under a sail stretched between the trees, the colonists first worshipped. Near this to-day is a statue of valorous John Smith, whose pluck and daring laid the foundation of our earliest literary structure. The inscription reads: "So thou art brass without but gold within."

V

PILGRIM AND PURITAN CHRONICLERS

JAMESTOWN and Plymouth were the rallying-points of very distinct ideals in this dawn of American civilisation, and the contrast was typical even in the landing of Cavaliers and Pilgrims.

The former arrived in Virginia, amid the blossom and fragrance of the Southern spring-time, while the Pilgrims, in 1620, thirteen years later, disembarked in the dead of winter on the bleak New England coast — *so* bleak that in a few months there were but forty-four survivors of the hundred who had come on the *Mayflower.*

Stern men were these Pilgrims! Having earlier opposed the Established Church, they had been " harried out of England, by King James I, and after toilsome years in Holland, the little company set sail for America — not seeking gold and gems like the Cavaliers but just 'Freedom to worship God.'" And with the Puritans who landed with Winthrop, in 1630, they were for nearly two centuries masters of the religious, political, and literary life of New England.

These devout Old Testament heroes laboured with desperate zeal, for time was too solemn to be frittered away. Narrow and bigoted, of restrained speech, they had come to *enjoy* religious liberty — *never* to *give* it! Those who dared differ from them must follow their example and seek other lands. In truth, these fanatical nation-builders commended the persecution of witches, and forbade Friends and Baptists to join them.

Yet with all their fanaticism and all their mistakes — they planted " a Government by the People, a Church without a Bishop, a State without a King." Perhaps they did this more securely, because their vision was bounded by theology, law, and education.

Plymouth, Massachusetts, was their first settlement, and hardly were their primitive cabins built here before the rectangular meeting-house topped the hill; and on its flat roof small cannon were placed, making it at once a military as well as religious post. Summoned to church by the drum-beat, it was compulsory *to go,* and none were freemen until they became church members.

Every man carried his gun, and with the Indian ever in the foreground, spiritual warfare was too often converted into earthly conflict. The Bible was the text-book; the sermon might easily be from two to four hours long, and the prayers, too, were lengthy and profound.

At first, the congregation did not sing, for singing turned the mind from God; but Rev. John Cotton investigated the subject under several heads, and citing as an illustration that Paul and Silas sang Psalms in prison, it was finally decided that the *Puritans* might sing, too.

Several divines assisted in making a metrical version of the Book of Psalms. In doing this, they were faithful to the original Hebrew, and the version was inharmonious, without poetic grace, the apology being: —

"We have respected rather a plaine translation then to smooth our verses with the sweetness of any paraphrases and soe have attended conscience rather than elegance. . . . That soe we may sing in Sion the Lord's songs of prayse according to his owne will; until hee take us from hence and wipe away all our teares, and bid us enter our Master's ioye to sing eternall Hallehuiahs."

The " Bay Psalm Book " was one of the very first books printed in America. It came from the Cambridge Press, in 1640. When it was used the Psalms were lined off, two lines at a time, and this was followed by the command " Sing! " To-day the " Bay Psalm Book " is a curiosity of literature. Here is one of the paraphrases: —

> " How good and sweet, O see
> For brethren 'tis to dwell
> As one in unity!
> It's like choice oyl that fell
> The head upon
> That down the beard unto
> Beard of Aaron."

18

GOV. JOHN WINTHROP

COTTON MATHER

From an old wood cut.

JOHN ELIOT

JONATHAN EDWARDS

It may be added that attendance at service was the only amusement shared by the sanctimonious Pilgrims, and from it came strength for the weekly conflict. To them, " Remember the Sabbath day, to keep it holy " held a meaning quite unknown now. New Englanders may well be proud of such ancestry, and yet congratulate themselves that they did not belong to the earlier generations.

Literature in these days was the handmaid of religion, and attendance at school was as obligatory as at church. Settlements of fifty families were compelled to establish a school — if there were a hundred, it must be a grammar-school.

In 1636, Cambridge College was founded. It did not receive — like William and Mary, in Virginia — rich gifts from English donors; but the four hundred pounds with which it was started were gotten in New England. Two years later, by bequest of John Harvard, a young Charlestown minister, the college had an endowment fund of three thousand five hundred dollars, and three hundred volumes constituting his entire library.

In 1639, it was ordered that " the college agreed upon formerly to bee built at Cambridg shal bee called Harvard Colledge," in honour of its first benefactor; and in 1650, the institution was chartered " for the education of the English and Indian youth of the country in knowledge and godlyness."

Nearly a hundred years after John Harvard's

death, the alumni of Harvard University erected a monument to his memory in the burial-ground of Charlestown, dedicated with an address by Edward Everett.

Yale College was founded in 1700, and its library was begun at a meeting of Connecticut ministers, each depositing forty books upon a table, declaring as he laid them down: " I give these books for the founding of a college in this colony."   A commemorative stone may be seen at Saybrook, Connecticut, the original site of the college.

We are reminded of Burges Johnson's words: —

"The little Yankee colleges, God bless them heart and
       soul —
   Each little lump of leaven that leaveneth the whole;
   What need of mighty numbers if they fashion, one by one,
   The men who do the little things a-needing to be done?"

And from the " stern and rock-bound " New England coast — the land of the evening lamp and the winter fire — has come to us a more abundant literature than from the " Sunny South."   Weighty tomes there are with cumbersome titles that belong to the seventeenth and eighteenth centuries; and while our literature of to-day concerns itself chiefly with the nineteenth and twentieth centuries, we must, in order to get the continuity of our subject, take from the top shelf of the dark closet a few of these dusty recordings, and glance at the men who penned them.

Governor Bradford — himself a *Mayflower* passenger — was an inveterate diarist. He ruled the Province from 1621 to 1657, and it is said that he managed the affairs with the discretion of a Washington. He was the skilful diplomat who — during a famine when a chief sent to the colony a bundle of arrows tied in a serpent's skin — returned the skin crammed with powder and bullets.

Governor Bradford appears here not because of his political wisdom, but as the author of his unique " History of Plymouth Plantation." This was not written in Captain John Smith's boastful style, but just as a quaint, vigorous, straightforward chronicle, inspired by piety.

It describes feelingly the persecution in England; the departure for Holland; the setting forth from Delfthaven; the perils encountered on the furious ocean; the compact and the landing; the desolate wilds and famine; the sufferings and death-roll of the first winter; troubles and treaties with the Indians; the building of the State on a sure foundation; — all ending in peace and liberty.

This picturesque but ponderous year-book would have made Governor Bradford a forerunner in letters, but he can hardly be ranked as " The Father of American Literature," as he has sometimes been styled. There are fine passages but little perspective. The following which refers to leaving Holland has always been accounted a gem. —

"So they lefte yt goodly and pleasant citie which had
been ther resting-place near 12 years; but they knew they
were pilgrimes, and looked not much on those things, but
lift up their eyes to ye heavens, their dearest countrie, and
quieted their spirits."

The manuscript of this famous "History of Plymouth Plantation," consisting of two hundred and
seventy pages, disappeared from Boston in colonial
days, and came into the possession of the Lord Bishop
of London. In 1897, on request, he generously restored it to the Commonwealth of Massachusetts.

On Plymouth's hallowed "Burial Hill," stands a
marble obelisk, in memory of Governor William
Bradford, Zealous Puritan and Sincere Christian,
Governor of Plymouth Colony, 1621-1657.

Edward Winslow (1595-1655), was another well-
known Plymouth diarist. His, however, was a day-
book, not a year-book. He was greatly interested
in the Indians, specially in the courteous Massasoit.
He became governor and was three times in office.

Governor John Winthrop (1588-1649), also recorded doings colonial. He was an aristocratic
Englishman of marked wisdom, who, having been
elected in England as Puritan leader of the Massachusetts Bay Colony, set sail with his charter and
about a thousand followers, in 1630. They settled
on the site of modern Boston.

Governor Winthrop, the leading spirit, was historian. His noted "Journal," called "A History

of New England," was a faithful reflection of the life of the country. It is in a smoother, more polished style, but not so picturesque as that of Governor Bradford. It began before leaving England and was continued forty years.

All these antiquated chronicles — important though they be in keeping alive our history — would prove tedious reading now-a-days; but Hawthorne, Longfellow and Whittier, by their magic touch, have transformed some of them into unforgettable tales.

> "A rock in the wilderness welcomed our sires,
> From bondage far over the dark rolling sea;
> On that holy altar they kindled the fires,
> Jehovah, which glow in our bosoms for Thee."

VI

WE have referred to Rev. John Cotton, in connection with the " Bay Psalm Book." He was a robust preacher, who, fleeing from Boston, England, on account of Bishop Laud's persecution, came over to the village of Trimountain, which in his honour was named Boston, and which as has been said was later the capital of Governor Winthrop's colony; and it is a curious fact that while he fled to escape persecution, he waged fiercest war against the Baptist — Roger Williams.

He wrote perhaps half a hundred books, but the only thing by which we recall him is his little ninepaged " Catechism," entitled " Spiritual Milk for Babes." This was first published in England, while he was pastor there in Boston; but it was many times re-issued in America, for it became " *the* Catechism " in an age of catechism-making. It was bound with the " Primer " so that the youngest New Englander might imbibe " spiritual milk " while learning the alphabet; and the Primer, too, was a sort of sacred book, many Biblical facts being inculcated in its study.

Indeed, with the very first letter "A" was the gloomy announcement: —

> "A. In Adam's fall,
>   We sinnéd all."

and the following are some of the other rhymes: —

> "G. As runs the glass
>   Man's life doth pass.
>
> J. Job feels the rod
>   But blesses God.
>
> N. Nightingales sing
>   In time of spring.
>
> S. Samuel anoints
>   Whom God appoints.
>
> Z. Zaccheus he
>   Did climb a tree
>   Our Lord to see."

And so with nearly every letter is impressed some lesson either from the Bible or history or Nature; and those simple, rhythmic lines were dear to those who learned their "New England Catechism" "by heart." When we realise what both Pilgrims and Puritans stood for, it was most natural that even the children should be trained in *theology!*

Another of these early divines was Thomas

Hooker (1586-1649), the founder of Hartford. He usually preached over two hours and wrote many pamphlets with ponderous titles. It seems sad that so much brain-energy was expended in literature scarcely read to-day — for there were great theologians among the makers of the new nation.

The Mather family was far and away the most illustrious clerical-literary one, in the seventeenth and eighteenth centuries. Ten of its members were ministers — three of them very famous. Sturdy, indomitable supporters of Calvin's theology, their ceaseless sermons and treaties ended only with their lives.

First, there was the father Richard, the English divine, with stentorian voice and majestic manner, who came to New England, in 1635. Next was his son Increase (1639-1723), who, entering Harvard at twelve, was in turn preacher, diplomat, and educator. He later became the sixth President of Harvard College. He was as full of superstition as of piety, and devils were to him so real that he took a most active part in the persecution of witches.

Increase Mather wrote nearly one hundred works, but we name just one — his quaint, weird " Essay for Recording Illustrious Providences." It is a curious mixture of religious awe and sentiment, full of ghosts and demons and thunders and lightnings and persecution.

The last and most renowned of the family was Cotton Mather (1663-1728). *He* was so pious that as a mere child he composed forms of prayer for his school-mates — and he made them use them, " though they cuffed him " in return. As a boy, too, he undertook serious vigils to make himself holy, and always led the life of an ascetic.

This youthful prodigy entered Harvard at eleven. At twelve, he knew Hebrew, and had already mastered leading Greek and Latin authors. He had a marvellous memory and could be theological in several languages, specially the dead ones: he quoted from classic writers quite as readily as from English ones.

His principle was never to waste a single minute, and prominently displayed in his study to meet the visitor's eye, was the phrase " Be Short." He began to preach at seventeen, and later was associated with his father over North Church, Boston; and he retained this pastorate until his death, in 1728 — and during these forty-three years, he dominated over all his listeners. His style was like that of Dr. Johnson. While he fully justified the persecution of the witches, he was a life-long worker among Indians, prisoners, and sailors.

He was born and he died in Boston, and was never one hundred miles away from this town, named as has been told for his maternal grandfather, Rev. John Cotton. It is said that he possessed one of the largest libraries in America. He was such an incessant writer that his own three hundred and eighty publications alone would have made him a good-sized bookcase in those days; indeed, he was himself " a walking library."

The work that lives is his " Magnalia Christi Americana," or " Ecclesiastical History of New England." This is called " The Prize Epic of New England Puritanism." It was published in London, in 1702, and widely read in the eighteenth century. It is a fantastic store-house of both useful and useless knowledge, relating to New England life, and in its day it stood forth as a remarkable book. Dear old credulous Dr. Mather! how the surprising stories of " Magnalia " interested the Puritan households!

And Mrs. Harriet Beecher Stowe has told how as a child she ardently *believed* every one. She read, and re-read, till she felt that she, too, belonged to a consecrated race, and her soul was filled with a desire to go forth and do some valiant deed.

If ever a man was imbued with the idea that he had a *divine mission — that* man was Cotton Mather.

Next, in our category, we place John Eliot (1604-1690), " The Apostle to the Indians." Educated at Cambridge, England, he appeared in New England, in 1631. This was at a time when the Puritans were most incensed against the " Salvages " or " Devil-Worshippers " as they called the Indians, and they were already beginning to crowd them out of the land. But colonial threats could not prevent Eliot from an interest in a race that he thought descendants of the "Lost Tribes of Israel," and in the spirit of an old Bible prophet, he determined to devote his life to their conversion.

Among his other writings, he assisted in the paraphrasing of the "Bay Psalm Book"; but his wonderful literary monument is the translation of the Bible into Algonquin. We remember that the strange Indian language had no written form — so Eliot had to create one. After patiently accomplishing this most difficult task, he set himself to the still greater one of translating the Bible *into* the written language which he had created.

And Eliot's Bible is an inestimable contribution to philology, and ranks its maker among the foremost literary men of America. This — the first Bible printed here — appeared a little later in the seventeenth century than the English translation so familiar to us. That was issued by order of King James I, and made by forty-seven scholars; John Eliot's work was unaided, and his Bible is in our day the only relic of a tribe and language of the past. There are probably but four copies in existence.

Well did this faithful missionary deserve his title! Twenty-four of his converts assisted in establishing small churches of natives in both Plymouth and Massachusetts Bay Colonies. Even on the day of his death, he lay upon his bed, teaching a dusky lad his letters.

Hawthorne gives Eliot this beautiful tribute: —

" I have sometimes doubted whether there was more than a single soul among our forefathers who realised that an Indian possessed a mind and a heart and an immortal soul. That single man was John Eliot! "

We have noted how the Puritans established — but would not grant — liberty, and the story of Roger Williams (1606-1683), forms an excellent illustration. He was an impetuous, warm-hearted Baptist clergyman of Salem, who dared assert that every one had a right to worship God in his own way. Indeed, Governor Winthrop relates in his " History of New England " : —

" Notwithstanding the injunction laid upon Roger Williams not to go about to draw others to his opinion that he did use to entertain company in his house and preach to them."

And he had to suffer for his fearless modern views. Driven from Massachusetts, he fled to the South, and founded a settlement on Narragansett Bay, which he named Providence, in the firm belief that God had directed him there.

Roger Williams's literary theme is " Christian Liberty," in defence of his constant controversies with the Puritans — the most memorable being the one with Rev. John Cotton.

Side by side with these worthies, but in a later age, appears that most profound theological philosopher, Rev. Jonathan Edwards (1703-1758).

He was born at East Windsor, Connecticut, and at six commenced the study of Latin. He was such a pious child that he was allowed to join the Church when very young — a thing unusual in those days. As his studies progressed, he proved to be such a marvel of youthful brilliancy that he was entirely beyond the comprehension of his teachers. He loved the woods and stars — in fact was interested in all natural sciences — specially in electric experiments, even prophesying Franklin's later achievements.

At fourteen, he said that he read Locke's " Essay on the Human Understanding " " with more pleasure than that felt by the greedy miner when gathering nuggets of gold and silver." He graduated at seventeen from Yale College, and for a while remained there as tutor. He planned to spend thirteen hours daily in study, and framed seventy resolutions for his conduct which he aimed to keep until the end. Modest and lovable, enduring a life of many privations, and never in robust health, Jonathan Edwards is a rare type of moral heroism.

For twenty-three years, he was minister over the Northampton Church. Here his sympathy was aroused in the work of young David Brainerd, the consecrated toiler among the Indians. Brainerd died at the home of his pastor friend, and the latter wrote his life.

The congregation at Northampton was, at first, strongly attracted to this young preacher; but with time it grew weary of his vivid, harrowing sermons, in which he portrayed forcibly the terrors of Calvinism — and more and more the people differed from their pastor on these theological tenets. It is strange that much as he delighted in the new era of scientific theories and discoveries, he held so rigidly to the orthodox views of his fathers.

Finally, he was dismissed from Northampton; and yet so far-reaching was his fame that one hundred and fifty years later, a bronze tablet in his memory was placed on the wall of the old church, and here we may see it to-day.

Jonathan Edwards left Northampton for Stockbridge, where for eight years he laboured as a missionary among the Indians. He had a wife and ten children to care for and he was very poor — *so* poor that he wrote his books on the backs of letters and newspaper margins; when riding or walking, he would pin bits of paper on his coat — one for every thought that he wished afterwards to write down. Sometimes he would be seen fluttering all over with scraps, for he was always either thinking or writing.

And it was at Stockbridge that he wrote " The Freedom of the Will," a work which enrols him among the finest metaphysical writers of the eighteenth century. But though a marvel in bold thinking, it is scarcely read now — and it has lost its force, because so few consider the subject from his point of view. He wished in it to show how far God governs the will, and how far people choose for themselves. His theory is — that the will is not self-determined, for if it were, God would not rule over all.

In appreciation of Jonathan Edwards's literary acumen, he was elected, in 1757, President of Princeton College; and after holding office less than three months, he died of small-pox, and was buried in the graveyard at Princeton.

His theology made a lasting impression on the New England thought of the eighteenth century. A gentleman of forceful spirit, of mighty intellect, and sternest orthodoxy — such was Jonathan Edwards.

The following are some of his " resolutions ": —

" Resolved, To do whatever I think to be my duty, and most for the good of mankind in general."

" Resolved, To live with all my might while I do live."

" Resolved, Never to lose one moment of time, but to improve it in the most profitable way I can."

" Resolved, Never to do anything which I should be afraid to do if it were the last hour of my life."

" Resolved, To maintain the strictest temperance in eating and drinking."

VII

DIARISTS AND POETS

SAMUEL SEWALL (1662-1730), the most famed colonial diarist, is known as "The Puritan Pepys." A graduate of Harvard, he became in 1671, Chief-Justice of Massachusetts, and his colonial mansion pointed out with pride in Newburyport High Street reveals the aristocratic environment in which he lived. As a judge, he at one time condemned the Salem witches, but later on, confessed to "the blame and shame of his decision."

He was perhaps the earliest pronounced abolition-ist of Massachusetts; for in his day there were a few slaves in this Northern State, and in 1700, published a tract entitled "The Selling of Joseph." This was the first argument written in America against the slave-trade.

But it is as "The Puritan Pepys" that one may claim more pleasing and intimate acquaintance with Judge Sewall than with the more religious colonial writers. Like the amusing English diarist, he walks about his narrow world, noting its fashions and follies, its petty humours and flirtations — photo-graphing his Boston as Pepys did his London.

Though he calls himself a Puritan, we catch but

34

glimpses of his exceeding piety. His " Diary," with some breaks, runs for fifty-six years (1673-1729); and it furnishes the daily gleanings of his career from the time that he was a young Harvard instructor until a courtly, dignified judge. Matters, small and great, are found in picturesque variety.

He chronicles descriptions of his relatives, friends and acquaintances, his four courtships, and two marriages. We learn of his horror of wigs and fondness for funerals. May-poles are set up; Indians and pirates assert themselves; and we turn eagerly from theological doings to scan a picture of secular happenings in the colonies of two hundred years ago, in Judge Sewall's three, goodly volumes.

What would he have thought of the comments of the twentieth century reader upon what he deemed, his *private* " Diary "1 Many, however, think it about the only readable book of the day, and withal, it holds its own with the great diaries of the world.

Time moves on — and brings before us another journal of a wholly different character, but of unique interest. This is the " Journal " of John Woolman (1720-1722). Woolman was in turn clerk, school-teacher, tailor, preacher, anti-slavery agitator, and above all, a sincere and lovable Quaker.

Let us add to the value of his work the estimate of others: Coleridge was fascinated by it; Crabbe calls it " a perfect gem "; Charles Lamb wrote, " Get the writings of Woolman by heart"; and Channing deems it " the sweetest and purest autobiography in the language." Whittier, in editing the book, was " solemnised by the presence of a serene and beautiful spirit."

At this time, verse-making was a feature of colonial literature. People busy cutting down forests and striving for material comforts, had no leisure to cultivate either fancy or imagination, and the solemn Puritans frowned alike on love-song and on jest; and yet there were two poets of whom they boasted. One was Mistress Anne Bradstreet (1612-1672), the first authoress and first poetess in the New World.

She was born in England of gentle blood, carefully educated, and married at sixteen. Then leaving an atmosphere of wealth and refinement for a home in the Massachusetts wilderness, she and her husband, who later became Governor Bradstreet, embarked for America, in 1630, with John Winthrop's party.

It is singular that in her verse there is seldom a reference to her New England surroundings. Often real flowers bloom and real birds sing — but we catch the fragrance of *English* flowers and the warble of the lark and nightingale. She sometimes makes a good line but it is rarely sustained — yet the following stanza is well put : —

NATIONAL MONUMENT, PLYMOUTH, MASS.

"The fearful bird a little nest now builds,
    In trees and walls, in cities and in fields,
    The outside strong, the inside warm and neat,
    A natural artificer complete."

Mistress Bradstreet's poems were published without her knowledge, in England, in 1650, and bore the fulsome title: "The Tenth Muse lately Sprung up in America." We wonder what London thought of this collection — for it was *the age of Milton!* When the copy was shown Mistress Bradstreet, she expressed with pretty simplicity her feelings at seeing "the ill-formed offspring of her feeble brain," and she blushed as many a later poet has done at the printer's errors.

The Bradstreet mansion is yet pointed out at North Andover, Massachusetts. Here its honoured mistress brought up eight children, lightening the burden of daily life with the consolation of literature.

In one way or another, Richard Henry Dana, Oliver Wendell Holmes, and Wendell Phillips, claimed descent — and perchance a touch of genius — from "The Tenth Muse."

But the one famous poem in New England, two hundred and fifty years ago, was "The Day of Doom," by Michael Wigglesworth (1631-1715). The author who was a genial man came as a young boy from England. He graduated at Harvard and entered the ministry; but ill-health interfered with his preaching, as he intimately confides to the reader in this introduction to his popular poem: —

> " I find more true delight
> In serving of the Lord
> Than all the good things upon earth,
> Without it can afford.
> Thou wonderest perhaps
> That I in Print appear,
> Who to the Pulpit dwell so nigh
> Yet come so seldom there,
> And could my strength endure,
> That work I count so dear,
> Not all the riches of Peru
> Should have me to forbear."

But as his " strength " did *not* " endure," he gave to New England a perpetual poetical sermon, the text of which was " The Day of Doom," and it is conspicuous as the earliest prolonged poem.

This appealed tremendously to the zealous Puritan because it pictured in such terrific colouring the Calvinistic doctrine of " the Elect " transported rejoicing to heaven, while the wicked were consigned to the pit of woe. It was like one of those mediæval representations of the " Last Judgment."

The first edition printed in sheets was widely circulated. Lowell terms it " The solace of every fireside." The elders pondered it, while children were obliged to commit it to memory with their catechism, and for a whole century Michael Wigglesworth's direct and forceful — yet monotonous verses

— in their sing-song metre, held extraordinary sway over the readers — even causing many *to shudder!*

In citing a few landmarks of colonial literature, we have done it topically rather than historically. We have discovered that in the seventeenth century, the theological writers of New England — who were indebted for their style to their knowledge of the grandeur and poetic beauty of the Bible — seemed to overshadow all other inspirations. But in the eighteenth century, this solemn literature that had grown up about the meeting-house and the fireside was getting away from week-day life.

A growing commercial prosperity was now giving influence to social conditions; and the colonies strewn along the Atlantic coast, at first independent of one another, were allied in common themes: *politics* rather than *theology* began to dominate statesmanship.

There had been before a fashion for writing mortuary verses and epigrams; and to these were now added essays and newspapers and other periodical literature. There was increasing interest in almanac-making. Indeed, the almanac came to be a perfect encyclopædia, full of snatches of respectable literature which tempted one to seek further.

Books of Nature and travel, too, made their appearance: as example of the latter, in 1704, Sarah Kemble Knight gave to the world her graphic description of *five months'* adventures on a horseback trip from *Boston* to *New York*.

This colonial epoch as we have said opened when the glorious " Elizabethan Era " was at its zenith. It closed at about the time that the " Wits " of Queen Anne's reign were prattling in " Tatler " and " Spectator," and the trio of eighteenth century novelists were weaving their fictions. But while centuries of scholarly thought and life had been expended upon authorship in America, no drama or novel or story appeared in colonial literature — not one such book that we would mark to-day as of the highest literary standard.

Plymouth, Massachusetts, which was designated by the Pilgrims as " the howling wilderness " holds to-day more definite landmarks of their arrival there, in 1620, than does Jamestown of the coming of the Cavaliers, in 1607. This is a most interesting region for the student to visit. Not many miles distant is the imposing monument at Cape Cod, recently dedicated, on the site of the first landing-place.

And who can forget the beautiful panorama of Plymouth Harbour, the world-famed rock, Pilgrim Hall, the colonial houses, and Burial Hill; and crowning all, the noble national monument to the forefathers, upon which stands " Faith." In one hand, she holds a Bible — with the other, she points heavenward. This memorial was placed here by a grateful people, in appreciation of labours, sacrifices, and sufferings, in the cause of religious liberty!

VIII

BENJAMIN FRANKLIN (1706-1790)

LOWELL calls Jamestown and Plymouth " the two great distributing centres of the English race in America." From each flowed a stream of colonial literature which presently united into a swift, deep current. This current is symbolic of the new, broader thought that in the eighteenth century was at work, developing our story into its second or Revolutionary Period.

The first chapter of this era must be granted to Benjamin Franklin, because he served his country so faithfully in politics and literature; and though much of his life belongs to colonial days, his was alike a formative and very modern influence.

The youngest son of a tallow-chandler, he was born in Boston, in 1706, and his childhood was passed under Puritan influences. He had meagre book-learning, for before he was ten, his father took him from school to assist him in the shop; and as Ben cut wicks, filled dipping-moulds, and ran on errands, he was always either wishing that he might be a sailor, or wondering how he might secure an education.

His father, observing his bookish turn of mind,

apprenticed him at twelve to his brother James, and he learned easily to set types. He was even then an omnivorous reader, and every penny that he could spare was spent on literature, and there was no variety from which to choose. Of the six hundred books published during the first twelve years of his life, about five hundred were on religious subjects, and fifty more were almanacs.

As far as we know, not a copy of Shakespeare had made its way into Boston — but all the same, Benjamin read everything that he could lay his hands upon. " Plutarch's Lives " and " Pilgrim's Progress " specially interested him; and prowling one day among such classical and theological works, he came across a copy of " Spectator," really a novelty in the town.

This was fortunate, for he was just trying to form his own style by studying the uses of common words rightly placed.

He was delighted with the essays; read and re-read them; made outlines from them; and presently caught the trick of composition and ventured to write himself. His expression was not so light and graceful as that of Addison and Steele — but full of common sense and blunt humour.

In 1721, the brother started " The New England Courant," and Benjamin, now fifteen, determined to become a contributor; so he stuck one of his own essays anonymously under the printing-house door. It was accepted, others followed, and people liked them. In short, the writer proved " the brains " of the establishment.

Perhaps he grew too wise for his proprietor brother but for some reason they quarrelled, and " B. Franklin " as he briefly subscribed himself — whenever he *did* sign his name — slipped away on a sloop bound for New York and continued his journey to Philadelphia. He reached the latter, dirty and hungry, his pockets stuffed out with shirts and stockings — and he had but just one " Dutch dollar " with which to begin business.

With a roll under each arm and eating a third, he walked up Market Street, and a girl standing on her father's stoop, laughed as she saw the runaway pass; and this was Elizabeth Read, his future wife.

Franklin obtained work in a printer's office where he remained two years. Clever, industrious young fellow that he was, he even now attracted influential people. Sir William Keith, Governor of the Province, persuaded him to go to London in order to secure a good printing outfit, promising his patronage; it was a fruitless errand — the promised letters were not sent, and Franklin soon found himself three thousand miles from home, without either money or friends.

For eighteen months, he spent in London a kind of vagabond life as a journeyman-printer. Yet he held himself well and was so temperate that his companions nicknamed him " The Water-American "; but this knocking about proved fit preparation for a broad career. Wiser for his experience, he returned, in 1726, to Philadelphia which ever after was his home.

A born printer, publisher, and editor, he began business by shrewdly advertising his proficiency in all three. He also opened a stationer's shop, and like the young Jonathan Edwards in *spiritual* matters, *he,* too, drew some " resolutions " in regard to managing the *temporal* affairs of his life, some of them being on temperance, silence, frugality, and industry. The one on "resolve " is as follows: —

> " Resolve to perform what you ought,
> Perform without fail what you resolve."

Franklin bought out " The Pennsylvania Gazette," the first American magazine. He was interested in science and began to show himself a man of affairs.

In 1730, he married Elizabeth Read, and for many years she stood by him in the humble stationer's shop, aiding him by her frugality; and presently our forefather of American editors, publishers and printers, drew about him many prominent people. He was already outgrowing his environment, and transferring the literary centre from Boston to Philadelphia.

Think of some of the things that he did, that early converted this town into the foremost of American cities. He organised here the first regular fire and

THOMAS JEFFERSON

ALEXANDER HAMILTON

BENJAMIN FRANKLIN

SAMUEL SEWALL

police forces of which our country could boast; invented the Franklin stove to give out more heat with less wood. He helped to establish hospitals. He formed a debating club called "The Junta," the members of which kept their books at the rooms, and so easily out of it grew the first circulating library. He set on foot an academy, now the University of Pennsylvania; and he always worked by the principle that if he wished a thing *well done,* he must *do* it *himself.*

Then he started his "Poor Richard's Almanac," which, as we shall later see, helped the Philadelphians in forming regular, saving, and industrious habits. He became clerk of the General Assembly and postmaster of Philadelphia.

Finally, in 1748, when he was forty-two years old, he retired from business; for he had gained a competence and desired more leisure — which " leisure " he defined as " a time for doing something useful." His journalism and scientific investigations were already giving him world-wide fame, and he wished to accomplish even greater results in both.

As postmaster of Philadelphia, he had felt the necessity of a centralised system for all the colonies. To further his purpose, he travelled in a gig with his daughter Sallie throughout the " Thirteen Colonies," and in 1755, was appointed Postmaster-General.

In order to understand his later work as statesman

and diplomat, we must briefly glance at the growing unrest that confronted him. One result of the French and Indian War had been to teach the colonies a lesson of union against a common foe, and loyalty to England was at once giving place to patriotism. King George Third seemed to realise this and with high-handed measures tried to quell it — but he little understood the spirit of his subjects scattered along the shore beyond the wide sea.

Franklin had been twice to England — first as a journeyman-printer, and in 1757, as an agent from Pennsylvania to settle a dispute with the heirs of William Penn; and now, in 1765, as foremost American diplomat, he was sent again — this time to enlighten the Mother Country about her duty to the rebellious " Thirteen "— by protesting against the Stamp Act.

Somewhat later, we find our dignified advocate, standing before the court of the mightiest kingdom upon earth. What cared he for its pomp and pageantry as with calm demeanour and forceful argument he earnestly pleaded the cause of the colonies! and his address made such an impression that the obnoxious Stamp Act was repealed.

Among other things that Franklin did in London was to publish anonymously a most clever essay: " Rules for Reducing a Great Empire to a Small One." This was an imaginary edict issued by the

King of Prussia, in which by right of ancestry, he asserts a claim to tax England and make her laws. It was written that England might see herself from the American point of view.

An amusing incident occurred in connection with this. Franklin, a little later, was visiting an English lord — when the valet broke into the room, waving a newspaper as he excitedly exclaimed: " Here's news for ye! Here's the King of Prussia claiming a right to this kingdom! "

Franklin endeavoured by every persuasion to avert war, but this he could not accomplish, and naturally he made enemies and lost power beyond the seas. Dr. Johnson even pronounced him " a master mischief-maker." Finally despairing of future usefulness, he sailed for home, reaching there at just about the time when the first guns were fired at Lexington and Concord.

He was at once elected to the Revolutionary Congress, and on July Fourth, 1776, signed the Declaration of Independence; and when Harrison appealed for a unanimous vote in the Senate, it was Franklin who exclaimed: " We must all hang together — or assuredly we shall all hang separately! "

During his ten years' absence abroad, his wife had died, and his daughter Sallie had taken her place at the head of his household; but quiet days were not for him — yet another diplomatic mission awaited; for though seventy years of age, he was sent as commissioner to the court of France to win sympathy for our nation in her war with England.

The French were delighted to receive him. To them, he was ' the personification of ' the rights of man ' " — the very principles which they were preparing to assert in their own Revolution. Franklin's demands were met — France generously aiding the colonies with both money and ships. Mirabeau styled Franklin " The Genius that freed America "; and another called him " a modern Solon."

A friend of King Louis XVI. and Queen Marie Antoinette, and surrounded by admiring courtiers, he — even at Versailles — maintained dignified simplicity; but he seemed by nature a patrician and greatly enjoyed court life.

Popular enthusiasm for Franklin ran high! Everywhere he heard his proverbs repeated in French. Applauded in public, people gathered in the streets to see him pass; his face appeared alike in print-shops and in the boudoirs of court ladies. They wore bracelets and carried snuff-boxes adorned with his head, and discussed his merits about a Franklin stove in the salon. Poets rhymed sonnets in his praise; and when a medal was struck in his honour, the great Turgot wrote an inscription which translated reads: " He has seized the lightning from Heaven and the sceptre from tyrants."

And then at the close of the Revolutionary War, with his fellow-commissioners, Adams and Jay, he cordially conducted peace negotiations with England, and in 1783, signed the treaty, and when Thomas Jefferson was sent to France to replace him, Jefferson said: " I may *succeed* but can never *replace* him."

And the venerable diplomat returned and was welcomed by triumph and celebration as " The Father of Independence." He now becomes one of the framers and signers of the new Constitution. Indeed, his signature has been affixed to more of the early State compacts than that of any other man. It seemed as if no measure could be accomplished without his touch!

But with added honours, Franklin somehow grew more serious. He missed old companions and now at eighty years of age, felt the pains incident to infirmity and disease, and he said one day: " I seem to have intruded myself into the company of posterity when I ought to have been abed and asleep."

And yet he was cheerful and in the intervals of suffering, read and wrote and told many stories. He approached death without fear, saying that as he had seen a good deal of this world, he felt a growing curiosity to be acquainted with some other — but he was not a religious man.

He died at Philadelphia — the city of his love — on April seventeenth, 1790. Twenty thousand witnessed his burial; and from that day to this, probably millions more have done him reverence as they have stood before the plain, unobtrusive slab that marks his resting-place in the old burying-ground in the heart of Philadelphia.

When his death was announced, both the United States Congress and the French National Assembly went into mourning. A great man had fallen, and he still remains an electrical power in all the world.

Franklin had little sympathy with the narrow creeds of the day, and yet two things deeply influenced his life: an "Essay on Doing Good" by Cotton Mather, and Whitfield's rousing sermons. His conduct manifested the *work* side of *faith*. We might to-day call him "an apostle of social betterment"; for he turned his attention to the *present* life as the early New Englander to the *future*. He advised "honesty" — not because the Bible exhorts it — but because it "is the best policy."

His character was many-sided. He is compared to Washington — for he did at the King's court what Washington did on the field. His humour and practical sense resembled Lincoln's, but he lacked Lincoln's spontaneity. Like Lincoln, he had no systematic education.

He loved fellowship, and his wit and anecdote made him always a welcome addition to any assembly. He had an excellent habit of investigating everything that came in his way, and so he was master of whatever he touched in science.

His experiment was most valuable, in proving the identity of lightning and electricity — and he invented the lightning-rod. Every school-boy knows the story of " the kite-flying." Indeed, his scientific essays and discoveries gave him world-wide fame. Both Harvard and Yale conferred honours upon him; England made him a Fellow of the Royal Society; he was called in France, " the foremost scientist "— in Germany, " the modern Prometheus." Dr. Franklin was very proud of his " A.M." and " LL.D."

He was not an author by profession and could not be noted as a very literary man, for he was entirely destitute of ideals and poetic genius.

But he had a peculiar gift of combining clear expression with a bit of wisdom to catch the reader's eye, and a keen insight into human nature. One has said of him: " But seldom do the good notions of the world get jogged along by so sturdy and helpful a force as Benjamin Franklin."

He was a charming letter-writer, and he early marked the important influence played by the almanac in the colonial home. Suspended by a string from the chimney-side, it was studied almost as much as the Bible and catechism. He finally resolved to write one; and beginning in 1732, for a quarter of a century, " Poor Richard's Almanac " was printed yearly.

" Richard Saunders, Philomath," was the nominal author; but Dr. Franklin always stood behind " Richard " and preached, like the proverbial schoolmaster, a continued sermon in diligence and thrift. He thus ministered to the needs of every day — for he told the people *what* to do and they *did* it!

Dr. Franklin in his modesty disclaimed much originality in the selection of these proverbs — but he had most apt skill in putting them. Read over and over, committed to memory and quoted, these maxims were heard — even in the Sunday's sermon — indeed, they were the common law of living. The " Almanac " promptly passed into circulation, and every issue was eagerly awaited not only in Philadelphia but up and down the coast — as a " general intelligencer."

The pioneer claimed it; it sped across the ocean to be published in Europe in several languages; and all the twenty-five years, its annual sale was ten thousand copies; for apart from the calendar and absurd weather predictions, it was full of wisdom — not sparkling and elegant — but with whimsical gleanings of observation on human nature by our first American humourist.

As preface to the final copy in 1758, he gathered into a connected discourse many of the best proverbs and named it: " Father Abraham's Visit to the Fair," or " The Way to Wealth." This is perhaps the most widely read of all, not only in our own land, but in European countries.

And what wonder that one who held a brisk pen, and who lived from the day of the colonial diary

VII Mon.   September hath xxx days.

These Lines may be read backward or forward.

Joy, Mirth, Triumph, I do defie ;
Destroy me Death, fain would I die :
Forlorn am I, Love is exil'd,
Scorn smiles thereat ; Hope is beguil'd ;
Men banish'd bliss, in Woe must dwell,
Then Joy, Mirth, Triumph all farewell.

1	6	♂ ♃ ☿ ♌, fair.	1	♍	5	45	7	*As we must ac-*
2	7	London burnt.	2	17	5	46	7	New ☽ 2 day
3	A	14 *Sund. p.* Trin.	3	♎	5	48	7	at 7 aft.
4	2	windy,	4	14	5	50	7	*count for every,*
5	3	flying clouds.	5	28	5	51	7	*idle word, so we*
6	4	7* rise ♉ 23	5h	♏	5	52	7	☽ sets 8 14 aft
7	5	Day shorter 2 34	6	27	5	54	7	*must for every*
8	6	warm, and	7	♐	5	55	7	*idle silence.*
9	7	Vc.☉♃ pleasant	8	27	5	56	7	First Quarter.
10	A	15 Sund p. Trin.	9	♑	5	58	7	
11	2	△♄♀ cool	9h 25	5	59	7	Day 12 h long
12	3	☉ in ♎	10	♒	6	0	6	Eq. Day & Ni.
13	4	with rain.	11 23	6	1	6	☽ sets 1 30 mo
14	5	Days short. 2 46	12	♓	6	2	6	*I have never*
15	6	Twilight 1 24	1	13	6	4	6	*seen the Philo-*
16	7	clouds.	2	♈	6	5	6	Full ● 16 day,
17	A	16 *Sund p* Trin.	2h	14	6	7	6	at 6 aftern.
18	2	pleasant &	3	26	6	8	6	*sopher's Stone*
19	3	7* south 2 58	4	♉	6	10	6	*that turns lead*
20	4	warm.	5	20	6	11	6	*into Gold; but*
21	5	St. Matthew.	6	♊	6	13	6	*I have known*
22	6	□☉♄ dull	6h	14	6	14	6	☽ rise 9 30 aft
23	7	changeable weath	7	26	6	15	6	*the pursuit of it*
24	A	17 Sund. p. Trin.	8	♋	6	16	6	Last Quarter.
25	2	wind with	9	20	6	18	6	*turn a Man's*
26	3	△☌☿ rain,	10	♌	6	19	6	*Gold into Lead.*
27	4	then clear	11 17	6	20	6	☽ rise 1 30 mo.
28	5	☌♃☿ again:	11	♍	6	21	6	*Never intreat*
29	6	St. Michael.	12 13	6	22	6	*a servant to*
30	7	7* south 2 20	1	26	6	23	6	*dwell with thee.*

through the whole Revolutionary era, and was able to congratulate General George Washington as the first President of the United States, should naturally write a characteristic and captivating "Autobiography"!

Read his "Almanac"; appropriate the proverbs; ponder on "The Whistle"; on "Turning the Grindstone"; on "Father Abraham's Visit to the Fair"; indeed ponder his essays on many subjects; but if you would feel the perennial charm of his personality, read his "Autobiography."

Begun in 1771, it is left unfinished in 1788. It is as simple in style as "Robinson Crusoe" or "Pilgrim's Progress," and in it Dr. Franklin treats himself with perfect frankness, without a thought of compliment. By his "Autobiography" he is most widely known, for it has been translated into nearly every civilised language. Curious as it seems, it was first published in French, and did not reach a correct English edition until 1868, when the Hon. John Bigelow, another famous American diplomat, edited it with his own notes.

Even if Dr. Franklin was not a literary man by profession, he certainly led others to an interest in literary subjects. We remember what Sidney Smith, the brilliant English wit, said one day to his daughter: "I will disinherit you, if you do not admire everything written by Dr. Franklin."

But what he *wrote* was not a fraction of what he

did, and one might write books and books and not tell it all. And in many cities over our broad land, we find memorials to Franklin, side by side with those to Washington and Lincoln. Specially in our National Capital, he is seen on the avenue, in the Congressional Library, in Statuary Hall, and in the White House; and everywhere his old home Philadelphia records the honour which she pays to her adopted son; in public park and building, in portrait and historic scene, in architecture and sculpture — look where one will — the renown of Dr. Franklin is perpetuated.

SELECTIONS FROM "POOR RICHARD'S ALMANAC."

Many a little makes a mickle.
Little strokes fell large oaks.
A small leak will sink a great ship.
The cat in gloves catches no mice.
One to-day is worth two to-morrows.
An empty sack cannot stand upright.
Little boats should keep near shore.
Three removes are as bad as a fire.
Never leave that till to-morrow which you can do to-day.
Experience keeps a dear school, but fools will learn in no other.
Those have a short Lent who owe money to be paid at Easter.
Dost thou love life? Then do not squander time, for that's the stuff life is made of.
God helps them that help themselves.

IX

So Franklin broke with old traditions and opened the door to a broader literature; and now we ask what was the part played by other more serious literary nation-builders.

As the feeling in the colonies grew more and more foreign to England, times called for eloquent men — and they were ready! Fiery orators harangued, and their words fell upon eager minds. Balladists, wits, and prose-writers took up the liberty pen — not to win fame but freedom: so sword and voice and printed page worked together, until *American* independence and *American* literature were achieved!

The Revolutionary literary period preceded, attended, and followed the Revolution. First there were the balladists, who in war-time play havoc with metre and rhyme and sing as they march. Their songs were of a monotonous type but spirited, too, and set to popular airs. Among them was Francis Hopkinson's humourous " Battle of the Kegs," which put the British in a ridiculous light, and the " Return to Camp," sung to " Yankee Doodle."

And the " Sons of Liberty " organised in New York, and planted and re-planted their liberty-poles, which were again and again cut down by the British; and the " Daughters of Liberty " served the " Sons " with inspiring cups of tea.

The following is one of thirteen stanzas of a ditty created by the Stamp Act: —

" With the beasts of the wood we will ramble for food,
   And lodge in wild deserts and caves,
   And live poor as Job, on the skirts of the globe,
   Before we'll submit to be slaves! "

Philip Freneau (1752-1832), was called " The Poet of the Revolution," because in either satiric or graceful stanza, he recklessly recorded nearly every great event, and his four volumes of political bur-lesque were most popular. Sometimes, too, he struck a gentler note, and several of his lyrics contain lines of beauty and delicacy as in the last stanza of his " Wild Honeysuckle ": —

" From morning suns and evening dews,
   At first thy little being came;
If nothing once, you nothing lose,
   For when you die you are the same;
The space between is but an hour,
   The frail duration of a flower."

Freneau's " House of Night " and " Indian Bury-ing-Ground " are always remembered.

There was, also, a group of Yale graduates of rare and varied gifts, who, at this time, would seek immortality by founding an expressive national literature. Calling themselves " The Hartford Wits," they made this city their literary centre and indulged in extraordinary rhyme — both satiric and patriotic. The most famous of these " Wits " were John Trumbull, Timothy Dwight, and Joel Barlow.

John Trumbull (1750-1821), wrote " McFingal," a mock-heroic poem modelled after Butler's " Hudibras." It was published in detached parts during the war, or from 1775 to 1782. It is a striking parody on the Tory, or peace party.

In this, the great squire " McFingal," the Tory magistrate, whose

> " High descent our heralds trace
> In Ossian's famed Fingalian Race,"

and who can storm

> " In true sublime of scarecrow style "—

makes an absurd harangue in favour of peace — whereupon a fight ensues. He is tarred and feathered, and finally tied to a liberty-pole.

" McFingal " appeared at a propitious moment; even the rustic understood its import, and was impelled to rush into the ranks. Thirty editions followed one another, and Trumbull sprang into fame as " The Father of American Burlesque."

Timothy Dwight (1752-1817), while chaplain in

the army, composed his popular song " Columbia," beginning : —

" Columbia, Columbia, to glory arise,
    The queen of the world, and the child of the skies."

But this did not satisfy Dwight's ambition, for he believed that a true epic should mark the foundation of a literature. So seizing Pope's motto : —

" Fired at first sight with what the muse imparts
    In fearless youth we tempt the heights of art,"

he struggled with holy themes until in 1785, he produced " The Conquest of Canaan," in eleven volumes. Cotton Mather, with his text " Be Short," could hardly approve its nine thousand six hundred and seventy-one lines! However, this ambitious epic was dedicated to " His Excellency, George Washington, Esq., Commander, Saviour, and Benefactor of Mankind." How Dwight's grandfather, Dr. Jonathan Edwards, would have appreciated it! the Puritans revelled in it, comparing the writer to both Homer and Milton!

Though this stately epic is almost unreadable now — there are some passages worthy of interest as suggestive of both Canaan and Connecticut.

Patriot, classical scholar, theologian, celebrated President of Yale College — Dr. Timothy Dwight was a famous man — but *not* an *epic poet*.

The third of the trio was Joel Barlow (1753-1812). After serving as chaplain in the war, he became a financier and diplomat. He, too, wrote patriotic songs, and also attempted a national epic that was to rival " The Iliad." This was " The Vision of Columbus " (1787), later " The Columbiad."

In this, Columbus, taken from prison, is led up to a " Hill of Vision," where Hesper unfolds before him the history and future greatness of America. Stately and prodigious poem, it for a little electrified the people. They even named the guns for coast defence, " Columbiad."

Hawthorne later playfully suggested that " ' The Columbiad ' be set to music of artillery and thunder and lightning and become our national oratorio "; and in the new musical impulse that inspires our land, in the twentieth century, possibly this may yet be accomplished. But our *epic* is not *yet written!*

Still later, in far-off Switzerland, Barlow wrote and dedicated to Lady Washington a less pretentious poem, " Hasty Pudding." This is a lament that foreigners may not enjoy

> " The sweets of hasty pudding,
> My morning incense and my evening meal ";

and its setting is a realistic picture of New England

home life. "The Columbiad" is forgotten but "Hasty Pudding" is read to-day.

These "Hartford Wits" were artificial and imitative; but they were an impulse towards — even if they were not the founders of — a national literature.

And just now the English Tom Paine (1737-1809), plunged heart and soul into the cause. He was a successful pamphleteer, and pamphleteers did brave duty in these "times that try men's souls," as he wrote in his "Crisis." And this pamphlet literally *was* brought forward at *every* crisis. Read at the head of the troops, it quickened the marches!

No single effort was more powerful than "Common Sense," published in 1776, and undoubtedly it hastened the "Declaration of Independence." In this are the words: "The same tyranny which drove the first emigrants from home pursues their descendants still." But Thomas Paine's splendid work for liberty was marred by his "Age of Reason," which embodied an infidel belief.

We next glance at the orators whose fearless, passionate eloquence made war literature; and among the most inspired of these remonstrants were Samuel Adams, James Otis, Josiah Quincy, and Patrick Henry.

As there was no short-hand reporting in those days much that they said has come to us only in fragmentary passages; yet they are familiar to every schoolboy and have won world-wide respect.

Samuel Adams (1772-1803), aimed to keep the public aroused as " Father of the Town-Meeting." He was always talking politics, and as a contributor to several papers his *one* topic was " Freedom "; and this " Great New England Incendiary " *did* make George III. tremble upon his throne!

James Otis (1725-1783), was " The Silver-Tongued Orator," who, with well-modulated voice, piercing eye, and forceful manner, commanded wild applause. He wrote pamphlets on colonial rights; and it was after a five hours' address, that John Adams, the later President, called him " a flame of fire," and added that " then and there the child Independence was born." It seems strange but this " Flame of Fire " met instantaneous death by a flash of lightning.

And Josiah Quincy (1744-1775), leaped into the arena exclaiming —

" With the God of armies on our side, even the God who fought our fathers' battles, we fear not the hour of trial, though the hosts of our enemies should cover the field like locusts! if this be enthusiasm, we will live and die enthusiasts! "

And there was Patrick Henry (1736-1799), " The Firebrand of Virginia." It is claimed that his artistic and fervid eloquence alone would have bound the colonies. In proof of this, we might quote from many addresses. But his resonant words, in 1775, before the Virginia Convention, can never be lost from history: —

"Why stand we here idle? what is it that gentlemen wish? what would they have? is life so dear, or peace so sweet, as to be purchased at the price of chains and slavery? Forbid it, Almighty God. I know not what course others may take, but as for me, give me liberty, or give me death!"

And many other pre-Revolutionary utterances roused the patriots, not only in this crisis but in later ones — yet for want of space we may not quote them.

But as we pause before the monument at North Bridge, Concord, where

"The embattled farmers stood,
And fired the shot heard round the world,"

we must gratefully recall the balladists and " Liberty Boys " and " Hartford Wits "; and also give due honour to the orators, who heroically stood behind these " embattled farmers "!

X

THE NATION-BUILDERS

So poets sang their songs and orators fulminated with passionate speech, and as a result the Declaration of Independence was signed, the war was fought, the victory won.

But Revolutionary singers and orators while they could *inspire,* could not *organise* liberty; and in 1783, thirteen obstinate independent little colonies waited to be welded into union. It was a critical period; and many prophesied that all would end in strife and anarchy, such as in an earlier age arose in Greece and Italy.

But there came at once to the front real *makers* of a *nation,* splendidly endowed men of noble sentiment, ready to do their part! Never since in the history of our country has such a group appeared. Among them were Jefferson, Hamilton, Adams, Madison, Jay, and Washington. They did not write to gain renown — but to establish a strong, flexible government — and their splendid service is counted literature.

Of these men, Thomas Jefferson (1743-1826), the great Virginian, was a most cultivated scholar and advanced political thinker. Educated at Wil-

Iiam and Mary College, he became a scientist, linguist, educator, and reformer. Verily he did so many things well that he has sometimes been compared to Leonardo da Vinci. He was, however, not an orator but he held a reforming pen.

He has left his " Notes on Virginia " and a philosophical " Autobiography "; but his most graceful literary monument is his correspondence, for he was a voluminous letter-writer. And this was the " Golden Age " of letters when they were written as carefully as if they were to be published; and the epistolary labours of Thomas Jefferson and other statesmen are very valuable as historic and literary records. Alas! that in this day of cheap postage and rapid mails, this beautiful art of letter-writing is lost!

Thomas Jefferson bequeathed volumes and volumes to posterity but his masterpiece is the " Declaration of Independence," which Americans call " the most concise, logical, political document in the world." It is traced in brilliant rhetoric and proclaims splendid faith in the people. Just the first sentence reveals its character: —

"We hold these truths to be self-evident: that all men are created equal; that they are endowed by their Creator with certain inalienable rights; that among these are life, liberty, and the pursuit of happiness."

And John Hancock expressed the spirit of the

signers when appending his signature, he exclaimed: —

" I will write it large enough for George Third to read without spectacles! "

And Jefferson was the first clear exponent of democracy. He was always fearful that a central government would overthrow individual rights. *State* — rather than *United States* — rights he vindicated — democracy rather than aristocracy. His Anti-Federalist Party bitterly opposed the Federalists led by Alexander Hamilton; and even now, Thomas Jefferson's belief in the capacity of the people for government, helps to mould public opinion.

Jefferson was, in every sense, a leader. He organised a movement in favour of religious freedom, and founded the University of Virginia. He was the diplomatic successor of Franklin in France, and the third President of the United States. He was a delightful personality. His home at Monticello was perhaps second only in interest to that of Mt. Vernon, and its charming hospitality was felt all over the land.

Writer, educator, foreign minister, Anti-Federalist, Cabinet officer, and President — he ignored all when he wrote the inscription for his tombstone — the silent witness of his desire to be remembered as the author of the " Declaration."

On the Fourth of July, 1826 — just fifty years to a day from the adoption of the Declaration — Jefferson died. And this was a fated day for Presi-

dents; for John Adams, "the great pillar which sup-
ported it," also passed away, exclaiming just before
the end: " This is the glorious Fourth — God bless
it! "

On the slope of the Virginia mountains, at Monticello, there stands a monument upon which is inscribed: —

> Here was buried
> Thomas Jefferson
> Author of the
> Declaration
> of
> American Independence
> of the
> Statute of Virginia
> for
> Religious Freedom
> and Father of the
> University of Virginia.

Alexander Hamilton (1757-1814), was an ardent
Federalist, believing in a strong central government,
and so as has been said the political opponent of
Thomas Jefferson, the Anti-Federalist. Born in the
West Indies, he was a precocious lad, who, at the
age of seventeen, while a student at King's College
(now Columbia), delivered in New York a Revolutionary address which stamped him as a remarkable
youth, and his anonymous pamphlets also attracted
much notice.

" The little lion " he was called. Small and dark with fine figure, a dignified carriage, an eye that flashed fire, and a winning personality — it was not many years before he became the foremost statesman of the day. He distinguished himself in battle, and was long enough on Washington's staff to prove his patriotism. He was also employed on secret, delicate missions. Owing to a creative genius for finance, he established a protective tariff and a banking system, and in time was the first Secretary of the Treasury.

In the chaos succeeding the Revolution, a Constitution had been moulded for the United States by the wisdom of the nation-builders — in which the cleverness and force of Gouverneur Morris was very evident: but every point in it was instinct with Hamilton's suggestion.

And then the question arose — " Should this Constitution be adopted? " and as in our own day, the country was split by political parties, and the Constitution was sharply attacked by Jefferson and his followers.

Just at this juncture (1787-1788), there appeared in " The New York Independent Journal " a series of eighty-five essays entitled " The Federalist." They were written by Jay, Madison, and Hamilton — and *all* over the *one* signature " Publius." They were addressed to the people of the State of New

York, urging them to adopt the Constitution that upheld

> "The Fed'ral system which at once unites
> The 13 States and all the people's rights."

John Jay (1745-1829), the honoured Chief-Justice of the United States, contributed five of these; James Madison, "The Father of the Constitution," wrote twenty-nine, and on these is based his literary reputation; and Hamilton, the third of the great trio, wrote fifty-one.

All these essays were on profound themes and each is marked with sincerity and dignity. Guizot says of those contributed by Madison: —

> "There is not one element of order, strength, or durability in the Constitution which he did not powerfully contribute to introduce, and cause to be adopted."

The result was achieved; for in 1790, the Constitution was accepted by the "Thirteen States," and thus national existence was firmly established.

And "The Federalist" still remains an authority on the principles of government; and for it we are indebted to Hamilton more than to any other man. Even his unswerving opposer, Jefferson, declared him "The Colossus of the Federalists." And this challenged Constitution has adapted itself to the growing conditions of our phenomenal government, and with but few amendments still remains a monument to our " Master Nation-Builder."

Hamilton built his country home, " The Grange," on Harlem Heights, nine miles from the city. It was in the centre of a rolling region of field and forest and winding roads, with a glimpse beyond of silvery river and bay. Here, also, he planted thirteen gum trees as symbolic of the thirteen original States.

And it was on a fateful July morning, in 1804, that Hamilton left " The Grange " and crossed the Hudson to meet his death at the hands of Vice-President Aaron Burr; and he was borne to his grave in Trinity churchyard, amid the splendour of a great pageant. " The Order of Tammany," the most famous " Order of the Cincinnati," Federalist and Anti-Federalist, were all in line, and behind the bier two black men robed in white led Hamilton's charger; and Gouverneur Morris gave the impassioned funeral oration in which he said: " His sole subject of discussion was your freedom and your happiness.

To-day, at Convent Avenue and One-Hundred and Forty-first Street, in the great city, we find " The Grange " in good preservation, used as the rectory of St. Luke's Church; and an apartment house covers the site of the thirteen colonial trees. They had lived for many years, an object of interest to sightseers.

Downtown in Trinity churchyard, not far from

Hamilton's old city home, we read on his tombstone the following inscription: —

"Erected by the Corporation of Trinity Church, in testimony of their respect for
The patriot of incorruptible integrity,
The soldier of approved valor,
,The statesman of consummate wisdom, whose talents and virtues will be admired by a grateful posterity long after this marble shall have mouldered into dust."

And other nation-builders there were, but only one more to whom we shall allude, and this is George Washington, " The Father of his Country." He left, it is true, but small mark upon the writings of his day, but his letters and documents manifest a pious and patriotic spirit. His public utterances were always dignified.

In old " Fraunce's Tavern," corner of Broad and Pearl Streets, New York, we visit the room where, in 1783, he bade farewell to his officers, saying in parting: —

"With a heart full of love and gratitude, I most devoutly wish that your latter days may be as prosperous and happy as your former ones have been glorious and honourable."

His noblest literary production, however, is his more famous " Farewell Address," issued in September, 1796, on his retirement from the Presidency.

It is full of good advice and produced a profound sensation; and we close this period of Revolutionary strife with its tranquil note: —

"I have not only retired from all public employments, but I am retiring within myself, and shall be able to view the solitary walk, and tread the paths of private life, with a heartfelt satisfaction. Envious of none, I am determined to be pleased with all; and this being the order of my march, I will move gently down the stream of life until I sleep with my Fathers."

"WHAT CONSTITUTES A STATE?

Not high-raised battlement or laboured mound,
    Thick wall or moated gate;
Not cities fair, with spires and turrets crowned:
    No: — Men, high-minded men,
With powers as far above dull brutes endued,
    In forest, brake, or den,
As beasts excel cold rocks and brambles rude —
    Men who their duties know,
Know too their rights, and knowing, dare maintain;
    Prevent the long-aimed blow,
And crush the tyrant, while they rend the chain."

                    —*Alcaeus* (tr. Sir William Jones).

XI

GLANCES BACKWARD AND FORWARD

WE have considered the strivings of our colonial forbears and our heroic nation-builders, and there are yet other forces which combined to hasten the National era that is just before us.

For example, no sooner was the Revolutionary War over than patriotic Noah Webster exclaimed: " Let us seize the present moment and establish a national language "; and now, in 1783, he offered new literary implements in the form of a speller, grammar, and reader, which he called his " Grammatical Institute "— and the trio accomplished most successful educational results all over the United States. The speller alone, with its tempting fables, succeeding " The New England Primer," has appealed to more than sixty million young Americans.

And this professor, lexicographer, lawyer, and writer, had the excellent habit of jotting down every word whose meaning was not clear, and he was so often unable to find a definition, that he determined to prepare a compendium of the whole Enblish language; and with careful labour he commenced a Herculean task, and in 1828, " Webster's Dictionary " was published.

Just about this time, too, the novel that had been in a formative state began to materialise — the novel that in early New England was such a forbidden pleasure that anybody guilty of enjoying one, might be read from the pulpit; and pious old President Dwight moralised on the great gulf fixed between the novel and the Bible, explaining how contact with the former must needs imperil the soul.

For another reason, also, the American novel was belated, for before creative genius was born, England had been a perfect treasure-house of literary models suggestive for Americans; and except De Foe, hardly an English novelist had appeared before the eighteenth century trio — Richardson, Fielding and Smollett. There had been published in America a few silly, sentimental novels, written usually by women.

But the first significant novels were those of Charles Brockden Brown (1771-1810). A Philadelphian, he attempted to study law, but he was so fascinated with literature that he made it a profession. He tried both in Philadelphia and New York to establish two or three magazines. A mysterious, picturesque romancer, he loved complicated plots, filled with horror and mystery. Indeed, he much more enjoyed creating these in the novels that he wrote than the foolish, statuesque actors moving in them.

The first one, " Wieland," came out in 1798. To

make his novels interesting, he realised the necessity of giving them local colouring. He took his reader into the out-door country, and the Indian is seen in the wilderness. He was a careful observer of Philadelphia life, one hundred years ago, and his " Arthur Mervyn" gives a graphic description of the ravages of the plague there; and thus Brown becomes our earliest preacher of sanitary reform.

It seems strange that he accomplished so much with a dearth of literary companionship, and always hampered by ill health — his short consumptive career closing with thirty-seven years — but none may dispute his title, " Father of the American Novel."

Yet another influence to better literary work is found in the fact that strife is relaxed, and there is leisure to think and write on other subjects than politics. " The Americans as a people are to take pride in a literature of their own, and to realise that a National literature is a National force."

And our literary roll-call is hardly a hundred years old, so it seems as if it could not yet hold many masterpieces; but like everything else in our land, literature has made marvellous growth, and authors have grouped themselves according to congenial topics. Great cities have always proved literary centres; and in time Plymouth and Boston and Philadelphia gave place to commercial New York. Here originated much of that charming literature which graces the very commencement of the new era.

The slender little bookcase begins to lengthen as the works of the Knickerbocker writers appear, and from New York are sent the first volumes that give American literature a home in Europe. And of the " Knickerbocker Group " which claims our attention, no name is more widely known than that of Washington Irving.

XII

WASHINGTON IRVING (1783-1859)

JUST across William Street, from the oldest house in New York, built of little bricks brought from Holland, there stands to-day the magnificent Underwriters' Building, over the site where long ago stood the modest house in which Washington Irving first saw the light. He was the youngest of a large family, his birthday, April thirteenth, 1783, being just at the close of the Revolutionary War.

His mother said: "Washington's work is ended, the child shall be named for him!" and "The Father of his Country" and "The Father of American Literature" met just once. It was when little Irving was six years old that one day, walking with his nurse, they saw the procession escorting Washington to the Treasury — to take the oath of office as President.

His nurse, pushing through the enthusiastic crowd, exclaimed eagerly as she held forth her small charge: "Please your Honour, here's a bairn was named after you!" and George Washington, gently touching his head, bestowed a blessing upon his namesake.

Like many another genius, Washington Irving hated school. He was, however, willing to scribble

76

by the hour, and was always glad to trade essays for problems. Not being strong, his parents encouraged an out-of-door life — and how he loved to stroll!

His quests began with the Battery, a region rich in whimsical lore; about the pier-heads he wandered — later with dog and gun through Westchester County, captivated with hill and wood and the witchery of Sleepy Hollow, intently listening to every recital of old Dutch legends. He sailed up the Hudson, gathering folk-lore all the way; and as he looked and thought and listened he was creating a native vein, which afterwards he was to weave into scenes of romantic imaginings, to endow the banks of our American Rhine with priceless legends.

He began to study law at sixteen, in Judge Hoffman's office, but did not enjoy it — but he loved the play, which his Puritanical father regarded a wicked amusement; and often at night after family prayers he would climb down from his window, and joining his friend Paulding, would visit the old John Street Theatre.

His two older brothers, after graduating at King's College, edited " The Morning Chronicle," to which young Washington, at nineteen, contributed some sportive " Jonathan Oldstyle " papers, that in a small degree satirised the town foibles. But he could not do much; for year by year he seemed to grow more consumptive, until when he was twenty-one, it was decided to send him abroad for his health —

and in those days this was accounted *a grand tour!*

He wandered through England and on the Continent; saw Kemble and Mrs. Siddons; listened to the famous conversationalist, Madame de Staël; and was received by literary men — his own charm of manner proving always contagious. He specially enjoyed Westminster Abbey, St. Peter's, and the Coliseum; and meeting Washington Allston in Rome, he resolved that he, too, would be a painter — but in three days, he changed his mind. When he returned home after an absence of two years, his health was perfectly restored.

Irving never seemed ambitious to enter upon a career, and though when admitted to the bar, he *did* hang out his shingle at Number 3, Wall Street (his brother John's house), he is not known to have tried a case. He loved society, saying that he preferred to be a champion at tea-parties.

He now became secret partner in his brother's literary ventures and with his friend Paulding began the droll and sparkling and somewhat youthful " Salmagundi " papers, to vex and charm the town — " Salmagundi," by the way meaning " a mixture " or " hash." They were written in Addison's style — for Irving, like Franklin, read deeply into Addison.

The intention of the infallible editors was " to instruct the young, inform the old, correct the town, and castigate the age." And they *did* it — and just

WASHINGTON IRVING   J. FENIMORE COOPER

FITZ-GREENE HALLOCK   WILLIAM CULLEN BRYANT

at the full tide of success, they suddenly *ceased!*
To-day these papers are a humourous reflection of
New York manners, in 1708.

In 1809, appeared Irving's " Knickerbocker History of New York," full of half-humourous, half-real
scenes, descriptive of the city, from the beginning of
the world to the end of the Dutch dynasty.   Among
the amusing characters are William the Testy of brilliant achievement; Peter the Headstrong, with silver
leg and brimstone-coloured breeches; the central
figure being a caricature of Governor Wouter Van
Twiller of unutterable ponderings, who represented
the " Golden Age " of New Amsterdam history.

This illustrious old gentleman was shut up in
himself like an oyster.   He seldom spoke, except in
monosyllables — but then it was allowed that he
rarely said a foolish thing.   A model of majesty and
lordly grandeur, he was formed as if moulded by the
hand of some cunning Dutch statuary.

He ate four meals a day, giving exactly one hour
to each; smoked and doubted eight hours; slept the
remaining twelve.   In council, he presided with state
and solemnity, instead of a sceptre, swaying a long
Turkish pipe; and during any deliberations of importance, he would sometimes close his eyes for two
hours at a time that he might not be disturbed by
external objects.

This " Knickerbocker History," combining both
fact and fancy, is called by many the *first readable*

book in American literature. Indeed, some make its publication, in 1809, the *true beginning* of *American literature*. It was at once most popular, both here and abroad. All the world laughed — except the old Dutch burghers, who were insulted at the treatment of their ancestors; but the humour was so gentle that even with them, amusement soon followed annoyance, and New York was most proud in being invested with traditions like those clinging to Old World cities.

While engaged in this work, a crushing sorrow had come to the young author, in the death of Matilda, the daughter of Judge Hoffman, to whom he was engaged. He bore the blow like a man but he always mourned her and never married. He could not bear, in years to come, even to hear her name mentioned, and always treasured her Bible and Prayer Book. Her steadfast friend, Rebecca Gratz, the beautiful Jewess, Irving later described so enthusiastically to Scott that she became the " Rebecca " of his " Ivanhoe."

Irving was devoted to women and little children, and with his gently modulated voice, delightful smile, and almost courtly manner, he was to them a winning personage. He was much sought for in society, because he added unusual wit and geniality to conversation. One of his special admirers in Washington was Dolly Madison, whose picturesque ways, tactful sympathy, and extraordinary popularity, made her

even as " Mistress of the White House "— just
" Dolly."

Irving determined to take up arms in the War of
1812, and was appointed on the military staff of the
governor of New York — but all was over, before
he distinguished himself. In 1815, he again went
abroad to look after the interests of the firm of " Irving Bros." and as the writer of " The Knickerbocker
History," he was even more delightfully received
than before. He soon claimed Southey, Moore,
Byron, Coleridge, Campbell, Rogers, Jeffrey and
Scott, among his friends — and he flattered them by
his responsive familiarity with their works.

Three years later his firm failed; and now, for the
first time thrown upon his own resources, his manhood and genius came to the fore, and he determined
to support his family by adopting literature as a
profession, and he settled down in London to write
— rapidly when the fit was upon him — and again
waiting days for an inspiration.

And in 1819-20, " The Sketch Book " by " Geoffrey Crayon, Gentleman," counted as Irving's best
work, came out in numbers in pamphlet form. It
contained short, gracefully told stories, with unique
literary touch, in which the author gave free play to
his humour; and perhaps the most famed of these
sketches is " Rip Van Winkle."

This legend had existed in various European forms
but Irving brought it to America. He peopled the

rocky crags of the Catskills with mountain sprites, and there it was that the thriftless, lovable vagabond, Rip Van Winkle, watched Hendrik Hudson and his unruly crew play nine-pins, while he quaffed the magic liqueur that put him to sleep for fifty years.

Another scene— and this is laid in that land of Sleepy Hollow, where the people were always doling out wild and wonderful legends;— and sometimes in the golden pomp of an autumn day, we may yet imagine Ichabod Crane, jogging along upon choleric " Gunpowder," to win the heart of the country coquette, Katrina Van Tassel; or shudder at night as we recall the frenzied pedagogue encountering the " Headless Horseman," and being hurled into the dust by the impact of the pumpkin!

These two tales would have made " The Sketch Book " immortal, but there were many other sketches; one in which Irving represents the sad dreariness of Westminster Abbey — the " Empire of the Dead "— the beginning and end of human pomp and power. Again, he describes Stratford-on-Avon so delightfully that he sends thousands of literary pilgrims to visit Shakespeare's home.

Then there is the English " Christmas," in which we find the worthy old squire, the vast hall and laden board, the crackling fire and blazing logs — the banqueting and minstrelsy. Others there are — but we must linger only to beg the student to take a leisure hour now and again, to enjoy quietly the vague and exquisite pictures portrayed in " The Sketch Book."

" His ' Crayon,' I know by heart," said Byron. Sir Walter Scott read it aloud to his family till his sides were sore with laughter; and then in his quick appreciation, introduced Irving to his publisher Murray, and the latter speedily brought it out — " The Sketch Book." It was at once honoured on both sides the Atlantic and " Geoffrey Crayon " was popularised. " Bracebridge Hall," a glimpse of English country life, and " The Traveller," soon followed.

Spain has always possessed allurement for Americans; and in 1828, Irving went there to seek facts for a life of Columbus — and he was fortunate in finding illuminating documents that had been hidden away for many centuries. In his " Life of Columbus," he presented the human side of the intrepid discoverer; but Irving could not do all things, and his historic accuracy has been questioned. His " Conquest of Granada," narrates the subjugation of the last Moors in Spain, by Ferdinand and Isabella. The romantic assaults and other brilliant achievements of his knights recall vividly the mediæval days.

In those golden months, Irving lived within " The Alhambra," that wonderful palace where every mouldering stone held its chronicles. He raved over the exquisite architecture — he drew forth the rich legends. He revelled in its moonlight enchantment when the halls were illumined with soft radiance — the orange and citron trees tipped with silver — the fountains sparkling in the moonbeams — and even the blush of the rose faintly visible; and with artistic perception, he wove the old tales into " The Alhambra "— a veritable Spanish " Sketch Book," instinct with Spanish sights and sounds.

In 1829, Irving returned to London as secretary of legation; and among the honours conferred upon him was a medal at Oxford, of the " R. S. L." or " Royal Society of Literature "; and he received it amid shouts of " Diedrich Knickerbocker! " " Ichabod Crane! " " Rip Van Winkle! "

In 1831, after an absence of seventeen years, Irving returned to his native land — and such an ovation as he received! A public dinner was tendered him at the City Hotel, in New York, where a little later, he presided over one given to Dickens. Irving could never bear to preside, and after presenting Dickens in the most abrupt way, he terminated with the aside: " I've told you I should break down and I've *done* it! "

He was amazed at the growth of New York City and at the expansion of the country; and under a commission to the Indian tribes west of the Mississippi, he made an extended trip, embodying his experiences in a " Tour on the Prairies," and the description of this land known only to the trapper is interesting reading to-day. To this period, also, belongs " Astoria," arranged at the instance of his warm friend, Mr. John Jacob Astor, and giving, with other details, an account of the fur-trading settlement of the Astors in Oregon.

And he bought "Sunnyside," at Tarrytown, a little farm on the banks of the Hudson not far from his loved Sleepy Hollow — with a snug and picturesque house " as full of gables as Peter Stuyvesant's cocked hat." It was surrounded by ancient weather-vanes and soon was overrun with ivy from Melrose Abbey. At the right was Irving's library where he wrote his last books; at the left the dining-room with the old mahogany furniture, and from this room beyond was a lovely view of the river.

From here, ten years later, Irving was called by Daniel Webster — then Secretary of State under President Tyler — to become Minister to Spain, and he accepted; but Spain had lost its glamour, and his heart always yearned for " Sunnyside."

After four years, he went back there to spend his closing days amid the scenes of his early delight. Here his sister presided and the house " was well-stocked with nieces." It was " the best house to which an old bachelor ever came"; he had " but to walk in, hang up his hat, kiss his nieces, and take his seat in his elbow-chair for the remainder of his life."

And in this intellectual " Mecca," he was visited by Paulding and Willis and Dr. Holmes and Prescott

and Thackeray and Louis Napoleon and other celeb-
rities; and they strolled under the sycamore trees
and gazed away over the broad Tappan Zee, flecked
with its tiny craft.

Irving was annoyed when he heard that a railroad
might be run along the bank of the Hudson right under his home, and sincerely hoped that the project
might not be carried out; and he fully believed that if
the Garden of Eden were then in existence, the " pro-
gressive prospectors " would not hesitate to run a
railroad straight through it; and he heartily wished
— as others have done since — that he might have
been born when the world was finished! But when
all was completed, he yielded gracefully. Of course
he did! for was he not the optimist that once said:
" When I cannot get a dinner to suit my taste, I endeavour to get a taste to suit my dinner! "

At " Sunnyside," Irving wrote his later sketches
— one collection entitled " Wolfert's Roost "— and
in 1849, his " Life of Goldsmith "; and there was
such sympathy between Irving's spirit and that of the
gay, unthinking, struggling poet that the " Life " is
winsome and lovely. Thackeray styles Irving " The
Goldsmith of our Age."

Irving never forgot that George Washington had
touched him when a child, and now in old age, he
would touch the life of the great " Father of his
Country "; and with his " Life of Washington," he
concludes his literary career. His genius not being

SUNNYSIDE: HOME OF WASHINGTON IRVING

adapted to the minute details and accuracy which such a record requires, it is not perhaps a historical success. But like Columbus, Washington in his hands became as Prescott says:—

"Not a cold marble statue of a demi-god, but a being of flesh and blood like ourselves."

And Irving wrote many other things; yet we do not recall this "Story King of the Hudson" by his numerous works — but by the "Knickerbocker History," "The Sketch Book," "The Alhambra," and "The Life of Goldsmith."

He was a familiar figure in the city of New York and was asked to become its mayor, and he was the first president of the Astor Library. More than once he was offered a position in the President's Cabinet, but his cherished aim was a life of letters, and it was thought that he made two hundred thousand dollars with his pen. As he approached his eightieth year, ill health and much pain came to him, so that he was forced to lay down his pen but not his cheerful spirit.

He died on November twenty-eighth, 1859, and he had that very year completed his "Life of Washington." His funeral took place at Christ Church, Tarrytown, which for many years he had served as vestryman, and a large number from the guild of letters streamed by the altar to look upon his face; and at the close of a lovely Indian summer day, he was borne by a great concourse of friends to Sleepy Hollow Cemetery — and ever since the elequent trib- ute of a well-worn path leads to the modest slab that marks his grave.

Through the courtesy of the present owner, Wash- ington Irving's grand-nephew, the literary devotee may to-day visit the library at " Sunnyside," entering it from the square stone porch. It is a highly inter- esting little room, and holds Irving's great writing- table, his chair and portraits as he left them. Here the walls are lined with bookcases, containing choice editions, many of them presented by the authors.

The out-doors, too, has memorials of Irving, here is his river view and the broad meadow, the brook and the hill; here are the tall trees that he planted, where the " birds in the fulness of their revelry " still " flutter and chirp and frolic."

We visit the site of the old bridge, famed in goblin story, and watch the new one now under construction; and in Sleepy Hollow Cemetery, on a green knoll still shaded by trees, stands the haunted church with its antique Dutch weather-cocks.

In Christ Church, we find Irving's pew carefully set apart in the Baptistery, and over it is a mural in- scription and coat-of-arms with three holly leaves — and it is interesting that he who loved legend could claim an emblazoned one.

It appears that Irving's Scotch ancestors, the De Irvines, secreted Robert Bruce when fleeing from his enemies. One of them became his cup-bearer and was hidden with him in a copse of holly; and in memory of his escape, Bruce adopted three holly leaves and the motto, " Sub sole, sub umbra, virens." In return for De Irvine's fidelity, Bruce later conferred upon him both the badge and Drum Castle — and the Irvings have retained the holly leaves.

Irving did not try for great things. " My writings," he said, " may appear light and trifling in our country of philosophers and politicians, but if they possess merit in the class of literature to which they belong, it is all to which I aspire."

" Jonathan Oldstyle "—"Diedrich Knickerbocker " —" Geoffrey Crayon "— our beloved Washington Irving! Thackeray calls him: " The first Ambassador of Letters from the New World to the Old."

Lowell says: —

" But allow me to speak what I honestly feel,—
To a true poet-heart add the fun of Dick Steele,
Throw in all of Addison, *minus* the chill,
With the whole of that partnership's stock and good will,
Mix well, and while stirring, hum o'er, as a spell,
The fine *old* English Gentleman simmer it well,
Sweeten just to your own private liking, then strain,
That only the finest and clearest remain,
Let it stand out-of-doors till a soul it receives
From the warm lazy sun loitering down through green
        leaves,
And you'll find a choice nature, not wholly deserving,
A name either English or Yankee,— just Irving."

XIII

JAMES FENIMORE COOPER (1789-1851)

EACH early writer gave of his best to broaden our youthful literature: Charles Brockden Brown his crude, weird novels — Irving his storied sketches — and now Cooper is to bring his offering from both forest and ocean.

He was born in Burlington, New Jersey, on the fifteenth of September, 1789, and while a mere baby, his father, Judge Cooper, who owned thousands of acres of land in Central New York, removed to the wilderness of Otsego Lake. Here he built "Otsego Hall," a kind of feudal castle, over which he presided like the baronial lord of old, parcelling out his estate to other settlers, and a village was cut out and named Cooperstown in his honour.

And James, one of a family of twelve children, passed his boyhood on the edge of the vast, mysterious forest which sheltered alike Indian and wild beast. Fearless, high-spirited, and impressionable, he learned to love the sounds of woods and water. He became familiar with wigwam life and the tricks of the trapper. Fond of adventure, rifle in hand he would spend whole days with the pioneers, studying the secrets of the woodland and the craft of the savage.

Sometimes in the evenings he would listen to political discussions between Federalist and Anti-Federalist; for his father, Judge Cooper, was a Member of Congress and an ardent politician, and James always formed an independent opinion.

He went first to a village school and later to Albany to be tutored, and at thirteen entered Yale College, then under the leadership of President Dwight. The restraints of the college were not to the liking of such an unfettered youth, and in the third year he was dismissed for a boyish frolic. It was such a pity that he did not persevere until he had at least attained a thorough knowledge of English; for in maturer years, his ignorance in construction too often showed itself in careless literary work.

Judge Cooper, now feeling that his son needed discipline, sent him into the navy, and in 1806, he shipped before the mast for a year's cruise. Later he was promoted to a lieutenancy and for a time served on the quarter-deck of a man-of-war, and was also stationed at Oswego; and in his four years' experience, he learned much about ships and sailors, the Great Lakes, the sea and its imagery.

And then the handsome young naval officer offered himself to Miss de Lancey of " Heathcote Hall," in Westchester County, and when she accepted him, he promptly resigned his commission. After their marriage, they lived in different homes — the first being dubbed " Closet Hall " from its diminutive size. In the second, a picturesque cottage, Cooper began his literary career, and this is associated with the following incident:

One day while reading a stupid English novel aloud to his wife, he suddenly threw down the book, declaring that *he* could write a *better* one! His incredulous wife playfully challenged him; he took up the challenge, and presently produced his " Precaution." It was about English society, a subject of which he was perfectly ignorant — so it was weak and dull.

But through doing it, he discovered his own possibilities and a friend encouraged him to try again — using *precaution* in selecting a theme with which he was familiar — and he tried and succeeded. The title of this second novel was " The Spy "; and the scene was laid in Westchester County where he had heard many tales of plundered farm and hamlet, of plot and counterplot and bloody strife in the Revolutionary War.

Cooper was a frequent guest at " Bedford House," the home of the Jays; and here one afternoon seated upon the piazza, he had grown greatly interested in the story of a grave, sagacious, and nameless patriot, who had served the Jays as a spy during the war.

He took him for his hero; and for his occupation

and appearance, he selected a versatile peddler, who, " staff in hand and pack at back," frequently passed his door — and Harvey Birch, the faithful spy, as moulded by Cooper, was at once a master-spirit in fiction; and landmarks associated with Cooper's homes and with the war-lore of " The Spy " are to-day recalled in the neighbourhood of Mamaroneck and New Rochelle.

And if you would know with what different eyes Irving and Cooper looked out upon Westchester County scenes, read " The Legend of Sleepy Hollow " and then " The Spy." One spread over the land the halo of romance — the other developed local patriotism.

" The Spy " had wide circulation not only in America and England, but was translated into foreign languages; indeed, it was read even to Persia and the Holy Land, to Mexico and South America — and Cooper's surprise was unbounded.

After his real entrance upon literary pursuits, he made his home in New York for three or four years. It was here that he started the noted " Bread and Cheese Club "—so called because in electing members, "bread" was used for an affirmative and " cheese "' for a negative vote.

The deliberations were held in Washington Hall. Bryant, Halleck, Percival, and other well-known men belonged. Cooper was a conspicuous figure in " The Den," a celebrated lounging-place for authors

—" The Den " being a back room in Wiley's book-store in Wall Street. Cooper always numbered among his friends the best and most prominent citizens.

In his next novel, " The Pioneers," Cooper uses the wilderness as a background; and here we meet for the first time the primitive American Hawk Eye, or Natty Bumppo, a gentle, deliberate and manly child of Nature whom the Indians call Leather Stocking. It takes five tales to unfold his adventurous career, and through these he becomes one of the celebrated characters of fiction. " A Drama in Five Acts " Cooper termed them and as we read on, we grow very fond of this philosopher of the woods.

We must not take the books in the order in which Cooper wrote them — for he buried and resuscitated Natty Bumppo, but this must be our sequence; " The Deer Slayer "; " Last of the Mohicans "; " Pathfinder "; " Pioneers "; and " Prairie."

And after " The Pioneers," he wrote " The Pilot." This was the outcome of a dispute about Scott's " Pirate "— Cooper insisting that Scott could have written a better sea-tale, if he had ever been a sailor; and he wrote " The Pilot " to prove his point, and in it he caught a graphic portraiture. Long Tom Coffin, the Nantucket whaler, sturdy, homely and full of action, we recognise as the gallant Revolutionary hero, John Paul Jones. The action is splendid — the tale savours of salty tang as had the forest tales, of spruce and hemlock.

Cooper has sometimes been called " The American Scott." It is true that both were story-tellers but Scott had more humour; he never lingered over side issues like Cooper, but went slowly and surely to the heart of his story; Cooper could never make people talk while Scott indulged in long conversations; Scott created many prominent characters while Cooper has but few. But after writing " The Pilot," the conservative " Edinburgh Review " announced that the " Empire of the Sea " had been conceded to Cooper by acclaim.

In 1826, the second " Leather Stocking Tale," " The Last of the Mohicans," was published. Some consider this Cooper's masterpiece. Chingachgook and his son Uncas are manly, noble Indians; they are true to life as far as they go, but they are not representative Indians — but Cooper had a right, if he chose, to leave out the uglier types of the race.

In the same year, 1826, Cooper went abroad and remained seven years; and in Europe he wrote " The Prairie "— his most poetic of the " Leather Stocking " series —" The Red Rover," and other fine sea-tales. And it was wonderful how his swift popularity amazed the world! for his books were at once published on both sides of the Atlantic — not only in English but in many languages: among others,

French and German and Norwegian and Russian and Arabic and Persian. It is said that of all other American authors, only Mrs. Stowe with her " Uncle Tom's Cabin " reached such celebrity.

In 1833, Morse, the inventor of the telegraph, writes : —

" In every city of Europe that I visited, the works of Cooper were conspicuously placed in the windows of every book-shop. They are published as soon as he produces them in thirty-four different places. They have been seen by American travellers in the language of Turkey and Persia, in Constantinople, in Egypt, at Jerusalem, at Ispahan. England is reading Irving — Europe is reading Cooper."

It was the novelty of his subject that held all captive, and for a time he had the field to himself; and it is disappointing to approach another side of Cooper's character which embittered his closing years, and rendered his later works unpopular. This was his controversial spirit. Of a forcible, impetuous disposition, full of prejudice, he could never brook a hostile criticism.

A fearless fighter, there was to him no neutral ground. Every critical speech about our young Republic he attacked in word and writing, and on his return " lectured his countrymen gratis "; for he liked not their manners, their love of gain, and fondness for boasting and admiration. So in his books he strayed away from the path of the story-teller to

MONUMENT TO J. FENIMORE COOPER, COOPERSTOWN, N. Y.

lash both Europe and Africa, and naturally made many enemies.

In all this, he was most unjust to himself, for at heart he was a true patriot; he had a strong, kindly face and genial address — and was a lover of friends and home. Bryant says that "his character was like the bark of the cinnamon tree — a rough and astringent rind outside, and an intense sweetness within."

And now for over half a century, critics have been busy with Cooper's fame. It must be granted that he did express too freely his prejudices; that his perspective was bad; that he was deliberate even to tediousness; and that he wrote many books indifferently rather than a few well. Indeed, some of them are never read, and Mark Twain has striven to prove that he cannot write a story; and Lowell, the irate censor, after honouring Natty Bumppo and Long Tom Coffin says: "All his other men figures are clothes upon sticks." But allowing all this, we study an author from two points of view — his *own* day and *ours* — and Cooper is very much alive in his "Leather Stockings Tales" and a few of his sea-novels.

Himself a lover of forest, Cooper was like a strapping woodsman who stuck his axe into a dense wood of tangling branches, and the clearing grew until he descried Chingachgook and Uncas and Leather Stocking; and through them ever since has been interpreted for us the spirit of the wilderness; or again Turner-like, Cooper has ventured far out over the stormy wave, where amid clang of the tempest, the man-of-war grapples with the whistling hulk of the enemy; and later writers have learned from him to spin sea-yarns.

No: let the critics wage their war. Harvey Birch, Leather Stocking and Chingachgook and Uncas and Long Tom Coffin will live on and on in their wonderful world of action.

We must read Cooper in a leisure mood and we must continue reading. Julian Hawthorne wisely remarks: " We proceed majestically from one stirring event to another, and though we never move faster than a contemplative walk, we know like the man on the way to the scaffold that nothing can happen till we get there! "

Though the settings of the novels are in rough places, they are pure and patriotic books to give into the hands of youth and maiden. Every boy is himself a story-teller and an adventurer; and as generations of boys have pored over Cooper's romantic dramas, they have given them most uncritical popularity.

On Cooper's return from Europe, he mounted a house in Bleecker Street, New York City, with French furniture and French servants; but he finally went back to his ancestral home at Cooperstown for the rest of his life. It was a house of generous dimen-

sions, set among stately elms and maples, and of a
beautiful hospitality; and in the gathering twilight,
he would pace up and down the great hall, pondering
over chapters from his books — for his pen was
never idle.

On his death-bed he begged his family not to aid
in any preparation of his life — for he wished the
controversies forgotten. He died on the fourteenth
of September, 1851, and was buried in the neighbouring churchyard.

Afterwards the homestead was burned; and the
materials and furniture rescued from the ruins were
used in the picturesque cottage of his gifted daughter Susan. A bronze statue of the " Indian
Hunter," by J. Q. A. Ward — a facsimile of the one
in Central Park — now stands on the site of " Otsego
Hall."

But Cooper seems yet to permeate the village,
beautiful for situation. Whether we float upon its
lake in its emerald setting, or tread the woodsy way
— everywhere we find reminders of his genius; for
street and inn and boat and brook and falls bear the
name of some book or character evolved by him;
and upon a sculptured shaft overlooking Otsego
Lake, the rugged figure of Leather Stocking appears — an emblem of fearless energy.

Five months after Cooper's death, a commemorative meeting was held in New York. Daniel Webster — the representative statesman of the day — pre-

sided, and in his address suggested that Cooper's works, so truly patriotic and American, should find a place in every American library. Bryant, as very often on such occasions, was orator, and after speaking of Cooper's life and books, he said: —

"Such are the works so widely read, and so universally admired in all zones of the globe, and by men of every kindred and every tongue; books which have made those who dwell in remote latitudes, wanderers in our forests and observers of our manners, and have inspired them all with an interest in our history."

XIV

WILLIAM CULLEN BRYANT (1794-1878)

POETRY is a divine gift and true poets see visions; and we may enter into special intimacy with these seers and prophets as their varied inspirations suit our varied moods. Thus far our tale has been most prosaic — but now the poetic dawn is breaking — as with Irving, " Story King of the Hudson," and Cooper, " Novelist of Forest and Ocean," we associate William Cullen Bryant, " Father of American Song."

The parents both traced their ancestry from *Mayflower* Pilgrims — the mother directly from John Alden — and William Cullen, one of a family of seven children, was born at Cummington, Massachusetts, November third, 1794. Some think that he was not an unusual child, but he knew his letters before he was two and at five could repeat Watts's Hymns.

In the old Puritan home, children brought up in the fear of God were expected to study the Bible, and he was so familiar with his own, that at nine he had turned the first chapter of Job into classical couplets. He caught his early, stately forms of expression from the prayers that he heard in church

and at family worship.   Poetic little Puritan that he
was, he used one daring variation in his own inter-
cessions "that he might receive the gift of genius
and write verses that should endure."

The scholarly father was a country physician, and
looked carefully after his puny boy's education.
The mother did all the work for her family; she
cooked and washed and ironed and spun, and one
day "made for Cullen a coat!"

In the "St. Nicholas" of December, 1876, Bryant tells delightfully the story of his boyhood; and in
it he emphasises the awe in which boys in that day
held parents and all elderly persons, observing in
their presence a hushed and subdued demeanour, this
being specially marked towards ministers of the
Gospel.

Bryant's early education consisted in attendance at
a district-school, and being tutored by two clergymen.
Devoted to classical study, he in time became a fine
linguist. He belonged to a family addicted to
rhyming, and his own talent early blossomed into
verse. At ten, short poems appeared in the newspaper. His knowledge of metre was caught from
Pope's translation of "The Iliad"; and he told his
friend Dana, years later, that when a copy of Wordsworth's "Lyrical Ballads" fell into his hands, "a
thousand springs seemed to gush up at once in his
heart — and the face of Nature of a sudden changed
into a strange freshness and life."   Indeed, no other

American poet has equalled Bryant in boyhood achievement.

We hear little of his youthful sports, but we do know that whenever he could " steal an hour from study and care," he would wander in the woods; and he became the first laureate of the sky and forest and birds and brooks and meadows and granite hills of Western Massachusetts. Nearly every poem contains a bit of scenery.

Even as a youth, the mysteries of life puzzled him, and he tried by communing with Nature to learn her secrets; and it was this tendency to brood over life as a preparation for death that led to his " Thanatopsis," or " Glimpse of Death." This poem represents a lofty religious philosophy, redolent of Puritan faith — a striking conception of time and eternity —" a kind of requiem of the universe."

It was five or six years after he wrote it that his father found it with another poem in a drawer, and in his paternal pride, unknown to his son, he started literally post-haste to Boston one hundred miles distant to offer it to the publishers of " The North American Review"; and as Phillips, one of the editors, read it aloud to the others, one of them exclaimed:

" Ah, Phillips, you have been imposed upon — no one on this side of the Atlantic could write such verses!" But with " Thanatopsis " true poetry had come to América. It was the soul utterance of a youth of seventeen — the most famous thing written by one of that age in our land — and it is read to-day with reverent earnestness.

Bryant was in Williams College for less than a year and then was honourably dismissed. He would have entered Yale, but Dr. Bryant was unable to pay tuition bills; so regretfully his son took up the study of law, and worked very hard in order to support himself as soon as possible, and in 1815, he was admitted to the bar. It was while practising in Great Barrington that he fell in love with Fanny Fairchild, "Fairest of the rural maids!" and married her.

Shortly after his marriage, a paper-covered book of forty-four pages, containing eight of Bryant's poems, was issued by the Cambridge Press. Among these was the one " To a Waterfowl," embodying its lesson of faith, and " The Yellow Violet," one of the earliest tributes to an American flower; for Bryant was one of the first to announce in poetic way that the flowers and birds of America are unlike those of England.

The little volume included, also, " The Entrance to a Wood," conveying the promise of calm to him who lingers in its quiet haunts; " The Ages," read before Harvard College; and " Thanatopsis."

This book made him again prominent; but at the end of five years, he had realised from its sale but fourteen dollars and ninety-two cents. It is now most valuable as our first publication of creative poetry, and General James Grant Wilson tells us that not very long ago, he paid ten dollars for a single copy.

Young Bryant felt a growing distaste for law, and an increasing love for literature; and in 1825, he made his way to New York, which was then a literary as well as commercial centre. He came as a kind of adventurer, and obtained employment on a short-lived periodical, and in four years was principal editor of " The Evening Post." This position he held for over fifty years, never permitting journalism to interfere with his lyric muse.

When we think that Bryant lived during the administration of nineteen Presidents — from Washington to Hayes — and that during this time, the number of States increased from fifteen to thirty-eight, we may realise that editorial work on a leading paper for half a century of that period was most arduous; specially as he felt obliged to infuse into " The Evening Post " his Democratic principles, and further on, his equally ardent Republican ones. He was fond of travel and went abroad six times — sending to the paper descriptive letters and essays, later published in book form.

His best work belongs to middle life. After some years, his son-in-law, Parke Godwin, and his intimate friend, Hon. John Bigelow —" The Old Man Eloquent "— were associated with him on " The Post," each being his affectionate and scholarly biographer.

In regard to his friendships, it is a rare delight to listen to the reminiscences of General Wilson — himself a man of great literary charm — who enjoyed more or less intimacy with many of the "Old Guard" of American authors, and also the eminent and gifted in other lands. Among his recollections of Bryant is a story which the latter told him of his first coming to New York. Shortly after his arrival, he met Cooper, to whom he had been previously introduced; and Cooper invited him to dinner to meet Halleck adding, "I live at 345 Greenwich Street." "Please put that down," said Bryant, "or I shall forget the place." "Can't you remember '3—4—5'!" Cooper replied bluntly. Bryant *did* remember and for all the future, and the friendship made that day with Cooper and Halleck was severed only by death. To Halleck he was always devoted.

Among his other friends were Irving, Dana, Drake, Verplanck, and Willis. He had pleasure in Whitman but could not understand his poetry. Wordsworth was his English inspiration and Rogers's "breakfasts" his special delight.

Hawthorne thus describes Bryant's appearance when he met him in Rome: "He presented himself with a long white beard such as a palmer might have worn on the growth of a long pilgrimage." In all his friendships, there was a kind of Puritan veneer that never wore off; a quiet reserve and dignity seemed always to belong to him.

Bryant had several homes in New York — the last at Twenty-four West Sixteenth Street, where he lived for twenty-four years — but a ruralist at heart, country life attracted him most. He bought the old homestead at Cummington, among the hills that he loved, and he returned to it year by year; and in order to be nearer New York City, he purchased, in 1843, an estate at Roslyn, Long Island, and for thirty-five years, " Cedarmere " was his home.

The house stands in charming grounds, overlooking a lovely lake: the library with two bay-windows, affording a view of woods and water — with ample bookcases, and fireplace set round with old Dutch tiles. This room was Bryant's castle! No journalist work was allowed to enter, for it was here that he donned his singing-robes.

After his death, the homestead remained in the family, and several years ago, it was nearly destroyed by fire; but appreciative hands restored what was left of his household goods, and they are to-day in the present mansion.

It was at " Cedarmere," after the death of his wife, in 1865, and when he was over seventy, that Bryant made his monumental translation of " The Iliad " and " The Odyssey "; and he did this in a Homeric spirit for he seemed to understand blank verse and " the rush of Epic song." He shows, also, true fidelity to the text, and many rank this the best metrical version of Homer in the language; and like Pope, he made it on the back of old papers and letters.

And now to return to the creative works of our " out-of-door lover." He was reticent in verse, for although he lived to a good old age, all his poems are contained in one volume — but the finest belong to his younger days. All are short — for to him a *long* poem was as impossible as a continued ecstasy.

He revelled in solitude, and said that when he entered the forest, power seemed to come unbidden. His " Forest Hymn," was breathed in the depths of the shady wood, amid the brotherhood of venerable trees — and while we " meditate in these calm shades," we think only of his minor key; yet again his " Robert of Lincoln " is

> " Merrily swinging on briar and weed,"

singing

> " Bob-o'-link, bob-o'-link,
> Spink, spank, spink."

Sometimes Bryant voices the spirit of freedom; his note is decided but more restrained than Whittier's. We find it in his " Song of Marion's Men "; and in her hour of need, he sounds forth " Our Country's Call "; and from him comes the famous quatrain of "The Battle-Field " : —

Herbert Adams Sc

WILLIAM CULLEN BRYANT MEMORIAL IN BRYANT PARK,
NEW YORK CITY

"Truth, crushed to earth, shall rise again,—
   The eternal years of God are hers;
But Error, wounded, writhes in pain,
   And dies among her worshippers."

Then there is the bloom of summer in his verse; again

"The melancholy days have come, the saddest of the year";

and yet again, the frosts of winter, with his unusual "Little People of the Snow":—

"A joyous multitude,

. . . .

Whirled in a merry dance to silvery sounds,
That rang from cymbals of transparent ice,
And ice-cups, quivering to the skilful touch
Of little fingers."

Some have called Bryant "The American Wordsworth." He, too, dwelt by a lake — and he caught a Wordsworthian inspiration. But Bryant appeals more to the intellect, while Wordsworth dwells in the heart of man.

Bryant, with his deep-set eye, patriarchal beard — diminutive, erect and buoyant — was a striking personality in Broadway — going to and from the office of "The Post." He was for many years the honoured President of "The Century Club," and so its representative citizen, presenting to it many illustrious visitors from abroad. He was keenly interested in civic affairs and often presided as orator on commemorative occasions, as on the death of Cooper, Halleck, and Irving.

He gained wealth as others may gain it by the thrift inculcated in "Poor Richard's Almanac." On his eightieth birthday, thousands of congratulatory letters came to him from all over the land, and a loving-cup was presented him which may now be seen in the Metropolitan Museum.

For this Nestor of counsel — this patriotic journalist and poet — serene and philosophic — worked on, "Without haste, without rest," giving quietly and strongly of his best to the world; and yet this singer of "an unfaltering trust" seemed constantly in his life to exemplify those lines from his "Waiting by the Gate": —

"And in the sunshine streaming on quiet wood and lea,
 I stand and calmly wait till the hinges turn for me."

Bryant expressed grateful appreciation for the artistic impulse which the Italians had given to New York, in presenting so many statues of their renowned men; and he had profound sympathy for the life and work of the Revolutionist and statesman, Mazzini; — he who has been called "the brain," in connection with Garibaldi, "the sword," Cavour, "the genius," and Victor Emmanuel, "the banner" — of "Italy free"!

Mazzini's bust was to be unveiled in Central Park and Bryant was invited to give the oration. It was a warm June day, and he stood with bared head. The address was scholarly and looking up into Mazzini's face, he closed with these words: —

"Image of the illustrious champion of civil and religious liberty, cast in enduring bronze to typify the imperishable renown of the original! Remain for ages yet to come where we place thee, in this resort of millions; remain till the day shall dawn . . . when the rights and duties of human brotherhood shall be acknowledged by all the races of mankind!"

These were the last public words he was to speak; for at the close of the ceremonies, he was stricken by the heat of the sun and died, just a few days later, on the twelfth of June, 1878. The simple funeral took place at Roslyn, and village children dropped flowers into the grave.

In 1883, "The Century Company," influenced by Hon. John Bigelow, appointed a committee to perpetuate the name of "The Father of American Poetry," and two honours have been accorded him. The first of these was when "Reservoir Square" became "Bryant Park"; then after the completion of the New York Public Library, there was placed on the esplanade, at the back of the palatial building, a statue of Bryant made by the sculptor, Herbert Adams.

Like that of Mazzini, it is cast in enduring bronze. The hand holds a manuscript, suggestive of literary work. The poet gazes over his Park towards Irv-

ing, who, at the other end, is taking a view of his
modern Knickerbocker city. The statue was unveiled by Miss Frances Bryant Godwin, a great-
granddaughter of the poet. Mr. Bigelow was not
able to be present; and it was most fitting that in his
stead our optimistic philosopher and Nature-inter-
preter, Rev. Dr. Henry Van Dyke, should deliver
the address.

The base bears the following selection from one of
Bryant's later poems — and how truly it characterises
his stateliness of expression: —

"Yet let no empty gust
Of passionate feeling find utterance in thy lay,
    A blast that whirls the dust
Along the howling street and dies away:
Best feelings of calm and mighty sweep
Like currents journeying through the windless deep."

TO THE FRINGED GENTIAN

"Thou blossom, bright with autumn dew,
    And coloured with the heaven's own blue,
    That openest when the quiet light
    Succeeds the keen and frosty night;

Thou comest not when violets lean
O'er wandering brooks and springs unseen,
Or columbines, in purple dressed,
Nod o'er the ground-bird's hidden nest.

Thou waitest late, and com'st alone,
When woods are bare and birds are flown,

And frosts and shortening days portend
The aged year is near his end.

Then doth thy sweet and quiet eye
Look through its fringes to the sky,
Blue — blue — as if that sky let fall
A flower from its cerulean wall.

I would that thus, when I shall see
The hour of death draw near to me,
Hope, blossoming within my heart,
May look to heaven as I depart."

— Bryant.

TO A WATERFOWL

"Whither midst falling dew,
While glow the heavens with the last steps of day,
Far, through their rosy depths, dost thou pursue
Thy solitary way?

.   .   .   .

There is a Power whose care
Teaches thy way along that pathless coast,—
The desert and illimitable air,—
Lone wandering, but not lost. ˗

.   .   .   .

Thou'rt gone! the abyss of heaven
Hath swallowed up thy form; yet, on my heart
Deeply hath sunk the lesson thou hast given,
And shall not soon depart:

He, who, from zone to zone,
Guides through the boundless sky thy certain flight,
In the lone way that I must tread alone,
Will lead my steps aright."   *— Bryant.*

XV

SPASMODIC POEMS AND SONGS

SOME of our earlier writers live to-day in one or two poems or songs, and in the following chapter we have strung together just a few of these inspiring verses.

The first we seek in the " Knickerbocker Group," that fashionable coterie of young men, who, with Irving as their centre, were all aspirants for literary fame. Among them were Paulding, Willis, Dana, Drake and Halleck, and it is from Drake and Halleck that we gather our memorials. Their first meeting was on this wise: They were standing on the Battery, New York, admiring a rainbow that spanned the heavens, and a mutual friend introduced them.

Halleck, who was a great admirer of Campbell remarked: " It would be heaven to ride on that rainbow and read Campbell." Drake liked the words, clasped his hand, and a " David and Jonathan " friendship was formed only to be severed by Drake's early death.

They called themselves " Croakers," and their " croaks " gave a pleasant picture of New York society in the first part of the nineteenth century —

for they literally found " fun in everything."
" Croaker and Co." wrote " The American Flag "—
Drake all but the last four lines.

Drake's reputation, however, rests on his " Culprit Fay," which grew out of a discussion with
Cooper and Halleck — they insisting that a fairy
touch could not be given to our American rivers. In
three days Drake proved his point by his exquisite
poem — its scene laid on the banks of the Hudson,
the legendary abode of " Rip Van Winkle."

In this a fay has committed the crime of falling
in love with a mortal, and part of his punishment is
to light his lamp by the first spark of a shooting-star;
and Drake's theme is saturated with fairy lore as
we may feel in reading these lines : —

" The winds are whist, and the owl is still;
    The bat in the shelvy rock is hid;
And naught is heard on the lonely hill
But the cricket's chirp, and the answer shrill
    Of the gauze-winged katydid;
And the plaint of the wailing whip-poor-will,
    Who moans unseen, and ceaseless sings,
Ever a note of wail and woe,
    Till morning spreads her rosy wings,
And earth and sky in her glances glow."

Youthful, brilliant Drake — our " American
Keats "— was a born lyrist. He died at twenty-five
and Halleck wrote in his memory : —

> " Green be the turf above thee,
>   Friend of my better days!
>   None knew thee but to love thee,
>   None named thee but to praise."

And Halleck lived on. He, too, had a spark of genius yet he sang very little — but edited books of other authors. He was a great favourite, and came so prominently in touch with other literary men, finding such an affectionate biographer in General Wilson — that we are all familiar with his name. He was long an accountant for John Jacob Astor in New York, and on his death, the multi-millionaire left him a small estate; and so " passing rich on forty pounds a year," he returned to his old home, Guilford, Connecticut, where he cultivated his exquisite love for Nature.

On the eightieth anniversary of his birth, in 1877, his friends unveiled to him a bronze statue in Central Park, New York — the first one there dedicated to an American poet; and on this occasion Whittier paid to his friend this just encomium: —

> " In common ways with common men,
>   He served his race and time,
>   As well as if his clerkly pen
>   Had never danced to rhyme."

Halleck's chief title to poetic fame rests on " Marco Bozzaris." Its subject is a Greek leader

who fell, in 1823, in the war against Turkey for
Greek independence. Americans at that time were
interested not only in the struggle of brave little
Greece, but in our own recently achieved liberty; and
how many boys from that day to this have emphasised
the words: —

    " Strike — till the last armed foe expires;
      Strike — for your altars and your fires;
      Strike — for the green graves of our sires;
        God — and your native land! "

Certainly Drake's ode " The American Flag "
and his " Culprit Fay " and Halleck's " Marco
Bozzaris " are *three* of the *immortal* poems " that
were not born to die! "

And our flag has been the theme of yet nobler
song; and the dilapidated " Key Mansion " is still
preserved in Georgetown, D. C., as the home of the
author of our " Star-Spangled Banner." It was in
1814, during the British bombardment of Fort Mc-
Henry that Francis Scott Key started out one morning to attempt to secure the release of a friend, imprisoned on one of the British ships. A truce boat
was placed at his disposal, and on his arrival at the
scene of war, Admiral Cockburn promised that a few
hours later his friend should be free, but that in the
meantime, he, too, must be detained; for the Admiral
was just then preparing to attack the fort and could
not allow its defenders to be warned.

The strain upon Key and his friend was tremendous — the fort being subjected to attack by both land and water — and Baltimore was surely doomed! All night long they paced the deck, mid " the rocket's red glare " and " bombs bursting in air." What was their thrill of joy, " by the dawn's early light," in looking towards the fort to discover " that our flag was still there "!

And Key took from his pocket a bit of paper and then and there wrote the first stanza of " The Star-Spangled Banner." The writer soon withdrew and it did not take long to complete the poem. It was set to an old English drinking-song, " Anacreon in Heaven "; it was struck off in handbills, caught up from camp to camp, and became a precious memento to the soldier of the War of 1812.

And does it still live? Listen every afternoon at sunset when the United States flag is lowered, from fort or flagship, and you shall hear its strains, symbolic always of " the land of the free, and the home of the brave "! If you would see Francis Scott Key's best monument, visit his tomb at Frederick, Maryland, for the lay ordains that for ever over it " the star-spangled banner in triumph doth wave."

On the hill not far from the " Key Mansion " is Oak Knoll Cemetery, the resting-place of John Howard Payne, the author of " Home, Sweet Home." He was a successful actor and playwright, courted by Irving and other literary men for his intellectual

JOHN HOWARD PAYNE'S "HOME SWEET HOME" EAST HAMPTON, L. I.

gifts; and his finest tragedy " Brutus," Keene and Forest and Booth have all tried to immortalise; but his more studied works are now comparatively forgotten, while just one lovely lyric enshrines him in the popular heart.

Payne was born in New York City, but it was his childhood's home at picturesque East Hampton, Long Island, that gives origin to the poem. It was written abroad for his opera " Clari, the Maid of Milan "; Henry Rowley Bishop added the music, and it was sung first, in 1823, at the Covent Garden Theatre, London. The words and music taken together make the appeal in this homesick poem.

About the time that Payne wrote the words his friends in America were receiving letters from him expressing his longing for home. He once said: —

" The world has literally sung my song until every heart is familiar with its melody, and yet I have been a wanderer since my boyhood."

Far from country and friends, he was finally consul in Tunis, where he died in 1852. Years later, the Hon. William W. Corcoran, the Washington philanthropist, who, as a boy, had seen Payne act, determined to have his remains brought from Africa and interred in his *home*-land. They were met in Washington by a military escort, and accompanied by the President and his staff to the cemetery to the music of " Home, Sweet Home."

Another song appeared, in 1832, that gained re-nown for its writer, Dr. Smith, a Baptist clergyman. This is "My Country, 'tis of thee." It was used for the first time in Boston, at a children's "Fourth of July" festival. Dr. Smith was a classmate at Harvard of Oliver Wendell Holmes, and our remi-niscent poet at a class re-union thus summarises his friend's title to fame: —

> "And there's a nice youngster of excellent pith,
> Yale tried to conceal him by naming him Smith;
> But he chanted a song for the brave and the free,
> Just read on his medal — 'My Country of thee!'"

And there is another song which set to a German melody has been sung — with its passion and pathos — all over the English-speaking world. Who does not know "Ben Bolt"? It was written in 1843, by Thomas Dunn English, a physician of Fort Lee, New Jersey.

N. P. Willis, editor of "The New York Mirror," a paper run on a very small capital, had asked Dr. English to contribute a sea-poem, and he sat down to write; but he drifted away from sea-thoughts into memories of his boyhood: "Sweet Alice" and "the old mill," "the log-cabin" and "the school" in-truded themselves into the poem — and he was near-ing the end when he *remembered* Willis's request. So to fulfil his promise, in the very last line he apostrophises: "Ben Bolt of the salt-sea gale!"

Dr. English never made a penny out of the famous

poem, and he sometimes almost resented its wide popularity as compared with that awarded to his more carefully prepared works.

And just one Southern folk-song we must add to our list. This is " Dixie," composed by Daniel Decatur Emmett, or " Dan " Emmett, as he is usually called. A poor boy, he picked up enough education to be compositor in a printing-office; then he joined the army as a fifer, and later the circus, and in 1843, he organised in New York the " Virginia Minstrels," minstrelsy being at that time a novel form of entertainment, and Dan used to declare that when he blackened his face and donned his kinky white wig, he made the best old negro that ever lived.

Later as a member of the " Bryant Troupe," he was stage performer and wrote songs. He was specially successful in " walk-arounds "— a " walk-around " being a genuine bit of plantation life that always ends a show. On a September day, in 1859, Bryant told Emmett that a new " walk-around " was needed, and that he would give him two days in which to write it. That night he tried with his fiddle — but neither words nor tune would come! His wife encouraged him, promising to be his audience the moment it was finished.

The next day was bleak and dismal in New York. Emmett recalled his life as a circus performer, and how he enjoyed travelling over the " Sunny South "; and how when they were at the North, the members of the troupe would often say, " I wish I was in Dixie!" Then burst a sudden idea — *this* was the line for him! He took his fiddle, and very soon words and tune had sung themselves into a jovial plantation melody.

The next evening " Away down South in Dixie!" was received with great applause, and its author was paid for it five hundred dollars. Soon it was heard from one end of the land to the other, and in 1861, it was flashed over the whole South as the Civil War lyric that led the soldiers to battle.

On the outskirts of Mount Vernon, Ohio, old Dan Emmett spent the last days of his life. In a tiny house, with a little garden-patch, he earned his living principally by raising chickens. A kindly old man, he often might be seen sitting in the sun, reading his Bible. After his death, several interesting manuscripts were found: — one entitled " Emmett's Standard Drummer "; another a grace, in which he thanks the Lord " for this frugal meal and all other meals Thou hast permitted me to enjoy during my past existence."

It has been said that when eighty years of age, he " had a taste of what it is to be famous," and many an ovation was tendered him at the South. So it is hoped that this contented old minstrel was always happy in the thought that over the wide earth, tribute was constantly paid to his " walk-around " warsong —" Dixie."

We have wandered far afield — even from fairy-land to folk-song — and our excuse for linking the genius of a Drake and Halleck with patriotic airs and the song of Dan Emmett is, that all have presented to our literature some of its single, striking inspirations.

XVI

JOHN GREENLEAF WHITTIER (1807-1892)

WHITTIER-LAND nestles in the valley of the Merrimac, from the granite hills, to where " the lower river " seeks the ocean at Newburyport; and on " its broad, smooth current," Haverhill

> " overlooks on either hand
> A rich and many watered land."

Three miles beyond this hill-city, a little back from the highway, stands the primitive Whittier homestead, hardly altered from the olden day. In it is shown the room where, on December seventeenth, 1807, the " Quaker-Poet " first saw the light. The mother's bedroom remains with linen and blankets woven by her own hand.

The great fireplace in the kitchen is almost as large as a modern kitchenette. In this swings " the crane and pendent trammels," and never has New England kitchen been so hallowed by poetic touch. For it was in this " old, rude-furnished room," many years after Whittier had left his early home, that he stretched " The hands of memory forth " and gathered the household; and as the firelight illumined their faces, he threw upon the screen the picture of the family group, and this he presented to the world in " Snow-Bound," a perfect poem of New England winter life.

Let us glance at the picture. Here is the father, " Prompt, decisive man "; the mother rehearsing

> " The story of her early days;"

Aunt Mercy —

> " The sweetest woman ever Fate
> Perverse denied a household mate";

and story-telling Uncle Moses, who though

> ". . . innocent of books,
> Was rich in lore of field and brooks."

And among the other faces is that of the older sister who has learned " The secret of self-sacrifice "; and of the " youngest " and " dearest," who

> ". . . let her heart
> Against the household bosom lean."

The picture is as realistic in word as the Dutch artist could have painted it with his brush — and it has transformed the Haverhill kitchen into a pilgrim's shrine.

Lingering outside the homestead, many poems are recalled. Here was laid the scene of " Telling the Bees "; the bridle-post; the well with its long sweep;

the brook; the stone-wall upon which once sat a
" Barefoot boy, with cheek of tan! " Near by is
the meadow where Maud Muller met the judge; a
short distance up a narrow road stands the cottage
where Lydia Ayer, the heroine of " In School-days,"
lived her brief life of seventeen years. Here are
treasured her school-books, and each is inscribed in
tiny, faded writing: " Lydia Ayer — her book."

Across the road, beyond the Whittier elm, a tablet
marks the site of " the school-house by the road,"
and

> " Around it still the sumachs grow,
> And blackberry-vines are running."

Local tradition has it that John and Lydia always
walked to school together; and we *do* know that
forty years later, John tenderly remembered the
" sweet child-face " of the little maiden who hated
" to go above " him.

The literary elements associated with Whittier's
childhood home, apart from the district-school, were
very few. There were the Bible and " Pilgrim's
Progress," and some other saintly books, and the
Quaker-meeting. But something interesting happened when the lad was fourteen — the kind of
thing that often happens to a youthful genius and
changes the whole current of life — a copy of Burns's
poems fell into his hands. He read and re-read un-

til the " Ayrshire Ploughman," who could weave a poem from a " tiny field mousie," or a " Wee modest crimson-tipped flower," had cast, by the magic of his lyric song, a spell over the rugged farmer lad — for he even sung into his heart the art of transfiguring daily life.

And as the boy worked on, and carried his lessons and scribbled away, a new spirit was in him — and his own song burst forth — and the early twitter was pleasant to hear on the dreary New England coast; and the song grew louder and more insistent, for he kept on singing for sixty years, and sometimes he has even been honoured by being called " The Burns of New England."

And when he was seventeen, another thing happened. One day when he was helping his father mend the fence, the postman as he rode past tossed over the newspaper. Whittier opened it and discovered one of his own poems in print. He stared again and again at the lines, but for joy and surprise could not read a word. The practical father, seeing him idle, told him to put up the paper and go on with his work.

His sister, it appears, had been his first literary agent, and unknown to him, had sent the manuscript to William Lloyd Garrison, editor of " The Newburyport Free Press." We linger over these happenings because they were big with import.

A little later, Mr. Garrison, having received more

of the youthful poet's rhymes, visited the farm **and** urged Mr. Whittier to give his son an education; **but** all he could do was to allow him a few terms at the Haverhill Academy, and the youth had to teach **and** keep accounts, and make slippers for eight cents a pair, to pay his tuition.

Mr. Garrison, " The Lion-hearted Champion **of** Freedom," next interested his young friend in the anti-slavery question that for many years before **the** Civil War agitated the country; and the poet of " brotherly *love* " was born with such a spirit of " brotherly *rights* " that he threw himself, heart and soul, into the conflict.

It was in 1833, that he openly consecrated himself to the cause to which he gave the best years of his life. In these times of turmoil, he drifted into journalism in Boston, Hartford, Philadelphia, and Washington. He became secretary and journalist for the " Anti-Slavery Society," in Philadelphia. His office was sacked and burned, and here and in other cities, he was several times hounded **and** mobbed.

It mattered not to him! His " Voices of Freedom " rang out like trumpet-calls! His finest denunciation was " Ichabod." This was an impressive lament over the fallen greatness of Daniel Webster, for his attempted compromise with the South, in regard to slavery. But thirty years afterwards, Whittier may have repented his impetuous words;

for in his " Lost Occasion," he represents Webster as trying to save the Union without a struggle, and he mourns the too early death of one

> " Whom the rich heavens did so endow
> With eyes of power and Jove's own brow."

Lowell, who was with Whittier in sentiment, could not refrain from referring to him in his " Fable for Critics " as

> " Preaching brotherly love and then driving it in
> To the brain of the rough old Goliath of sin."

But Lowell said, also, another thing of Whittier that

> " Whenever occasion offered, some burning lyric of his flew across the country like the fiery cross to warn and rally ! "

Whittier, however, lost friends and literary influence through his " Voices of Freedom "; and yet he said : —

> " I set a higher value on my name as appended to the Anti-Slavery Declaration of 1833 than on the title-page of my works."

And the martial Quaker worked on with lyre and pen until that day when in the meeting-house he heard the glad bells ring out the news of the passage of the Constitutional Amendment, abolishing slavery, and he sat right down and wrote his " Laus Deo! " beginning : —

> " It is done!
> Clang of bell and roar of gun
> Send the tidings up and down.
> How the belfries rock and reel!
> How the great guns, peal on peal,
> Fling the joy from town to town! "

And now freedom achieved, the blast of the war-trumpeter changed into a calm, sweet song, and by degrees it broadened into fuller, richer tones.

After his father's death, Whittier sold the ancestral farm at Haverhill, and bought a house for his mother and sister at Amesbury, where they might be near the meeting-house. Though Whittier never married, he loved his fireside, and was never further from it than Washington. Once perhaps he might have been elected to Congress but in his diffidence, he withdrew his candidacy.

He was poor until his masterpiece " Snow-Bound " appeared, in 1866, and this — his heart inspiration — brought him large returns. The world read and honoured this charming winter idyl. It was in the same year that Harvard College bestowed upon him an LL.D.

His summer idyl, " The Tent on the Beach," soon

HOME OF JOHN GREENLEAF WHITTIER, AMESBURY, MASS.

followed. This is a story-book, in form like Longfellow's " Tales of a Wayside Inn "; and to enjoy it
fully we must pitch our tent on Salisbury Beach, " beside the waves, where the sea winds blow," and where

> " The mighty deep expands
> From its white line of gleaming sands."

Open Whittier's poems anywhere, one is attracted
by verse or legend or ballad, and it is difficult to sug-
gest how best to read into his works. He always
tells a story easily so that the plot is never strained.
Ever in sympathy with the sons of toil, there are
homely songs of labour, appealing to the lumberman
or fisherman or shoemaker.

How he revels in an autumn scene as in " The
Pumpkin " when

> " On the fields of his harvest the Yankee looks forth
> Where crook-necks are coiling and yellow fruit shines,
>
> .   .   .   .
>
> What moistens the lip and what brightens the eye?
> What calls back the past, like the rich pumpkin-pie? "

Of his Indian legends, the aboriginal story, " The
Bridal of Pennacook "— its scene laid on the banks
of the classic Merrimac — is perhaps the finest.

In his portrayal of colonial life, a most striking
poem is " Skipper Ireson's Ride ": —

" The strangest ride that ever was sped
   Was Ireson's, out of Marblehead!
   Old Floyd Ireson for his hard heart,
Tarred and feathered and carried on a cart
   By the women of Marblehead."

A pleasing contrast is found in " Amy Wentworth,"
or " The Countess," or in the Christian " Swan-Song
of Parson Avery."　The Quaker maiden, Cassandra
Southwick, the witch's daughter, Mabel Martin, and
Barbara Freitchie — with her lesson of defiant patriotism already voiced by generations of New England school-children — are all familiar pictures.
Many regard " The Pipes at Lucknow " as Whittier's lyrical masterpiece.　His religious creed often
finds beautiful expression, specially in that stanza in
" The Eternal Goodness," where he writes : —

" I know not where His islands lift
   Their fronded palms in air;
I only know I cannot drift
   Beyond His love and care."

Whittier's prose does not equal his poetry — consisting mostly of letters, criticisms, and editorials.
His only extensive work was " Margaret Smith's
Journal."　This is a quaint description of her visit
to New England, in 1678.　She embodies this in
letters which she sends to her betrothed in England.
The whole is a realistic account of the old Puritan

age. Whittier was an admirer of the saintly old Quaker, John Woolman, and he was happy in editing his " Journal."

Whittier once said: " I never had any methods. When I felt like it, I wrote. I had neither health nor patience to work over it afterwards." He had his faults; he often wrote too diffusely, unequally, and carelessly, and there are many lines and stanzas that might better have been omitted; but even if he wrote very much, many lines will live always.

He was the " Poet of New England "— its sights and sounds and loves and hopes — but his verse was almost too local to be appreciated abroad. Richardson calls him : —

"The laureate of the ocean beach, the inland lake, the little wood-flower, and the divine sky ";

and Holmes says : —

" Our stern New England hills and vales and streams,
Thy tuneful idyls make them all thine own."

Whittier came of sturdy New England stock but he was never very robust, and his later years were passed quietly in his Amesbury home, and in long visits to friends — and several households to-day recall with pleasure their honoured guest. His neighbours were devoted to him, because as one said: "He talks just like common folks." He never entered a theatre but was a regular attendant at Quaker-meeting, conforming his garb and manner to Quaker simplicity. " A shy, peace-loving man," he called himself.

For literary companionship, he sometimes sought Mrs. Field's parlour gatherings in Boston, and belonged to literary clubs with other New England poets. His old age was enriched by many friendships. Among those with whom he came in touch were Longfellow, Lowell, Emerson, Bryant, Bayard Taylor, Curtis, Mrs. Stowe, Mrs. Spofford, and Garibaldi. To some of these he wrote personal poems, and they, if they were able, returned the compliment.

It was while Whittier was sojourning with friends at Oak Knolls, that he died, on the seventh of September, 1892. His last words — typical of his creed — were: " My love to the world." A great concourse gathered in the sunny orchard back of the Amesbury house to attend the funeral service: even boys were seated on the fence and in the apple-trees. Edmund Clarence Stedman paid a glowing tribute to the Quaker bard. He was laid in the burying-ground on the hillside; and on his tombstone is engraved just his name — and the words from Oliver Wendell Holmes: *" Here Whittier lies."*

There **are** two ways, in which one may become familiar with the personality of this loved poet. *One* is to read his life as written by himself in his various poems, beginning with " The Barefoot Boy," and following on through

> " The grand historic years
> When liberty had need of work and word ";

and even to the calmer, wiser days when as " A man grey grown," we may follow him along his " River Path," where

> A long, slant splendour downward flowed
>
> .   .   .   .   .   .
>
> And borne on piers of mist, allied
> The shadowy with the sunlit side! "

The *other* most charming way is, in Whittieresque spirit, to visit " Whittier-Land." All along the road from Haverhill to Amesbury, and off to where the ocean breaks on Salisbury and the Hampton Beaches, there are bits of landscape immortalised in the poems of " The Wood-Thrush of Essex."

Mr. and Mrs. Pickard — the latter a favourite niece of the poet, who lived with him during the last years of his life — still occupy the Amesbury house. Mr. Pickard is the author not only of " Life and Letters of J. G. Whittier," but of " Whittier-Land," which contains many anecdotes and poems not before made public; and it is indeed delightful to hear Mr. Pickard's gentle and humourous reminiscences from his own lips.

The house is a place in which one cannot fail to *be* reminiscent, for hall and parlour and garden-room are full of associations. Here Whittier received many men and women famed in letters. Here is the mother's picture; the desk upon which " Snow-Bound " was written; an album presented to the poet on his eightieth birthday, containing signatures of all the members of Congress and many other notable men. There are engravings and books and chair and lounge that he enjoyed — even coat and hat and boots — and as we look and listen all seem but one living monument inscribed with Whittier's name.

Whittier was perhaps not a great man, but who would not be satisfied with such a

> " Lifelong record closed without a stain —
> A blameless memory shrined in deathless song."

SELECTED FROM POEM ON " BURNS "

> " Wild heather-bells and Robert Burns!
>   The moorland flower and peasant!
> How, at their mention, memory turns
>   Her pages old and pleasant!

.   .   .   .

> I call to mind the summer day,
>   The early harvest mowing,
> The sky with sun and clouds at play,
>   And flowers with breezes blowing.

.   .   .   .

JOHN GREENLEAF WHITTIER

Bees hummed, birds twittered, overhead
  I heard the squirrels leaping,
The good dog listened while I read,
  And wagged his tail in keeping.

  .   .   .   .   .

I watched him while in sportive mood
  I read ' The Twa Dogs' ' story,
And half believed he understood
  The poet's allegory.

  .   .   .   .   .

I matched with Scotland's heathery hills,
  The sweetbrier and the clover;
With Ayr and Doon, my native rills,
  Their wood-hymns chanting over.

  .   .   .   .   .

With clearer eyes I saw the worth
  Of life among the lowly;
The Bible at his Cotter's hearth
  Had made my own more holy.

  .   .   .   .   .

Give lettered pomp to teeth of Time,
  To ' Bonny Doon ' but tarry;
Blot out the Epic's stately rhyme,
  But spare his Highland Mary! "

— *Whittier.*

THE RIVER PATH

" No bird-song floated down the hill,
  The tangled bank below was still;

  No rustle from the birchen stem,
  No ripple from the water's hem.

137

The dusk of twilight round us grew,
We felt the falling of the dew;

For, from us, ere the day was done,
The wooded hills shut out the sun.

But on the river's farther side
We saw the hill-tops glorified,—

A tender glow, exceeding fair,
A dream of day without its glare.

With us the damp, the chill, the gloom:
'With them the sunset's rosy bloom;

While dark, through willowy vistas seen,
The river rolled in shade between.

From out the darkness where we trod,
We gazed upon those hills of God,

Whose light seemed not of moon or sun,
We spake not, but our thought was one.

We paused, as if from that bright shore
Beckoned our dear ones gone before;

And stilled our beating hearts to hear
The voices lost to mortal ear!

Sudden our pathway turned from night;
The hills swung open to the light;

JOHN GREENLEAF WHITTIER

Through their green gates the sunshine showed,
A long, slant splendour downward flowed.

Down glade and glen, and bank it rolled;
It bridged the shaded stream with gold;

And, borne on piers of mist, allied
The shadowy with the sunlit side!

"So," prayed we, "when our feet draw near,
The river dark, with mortal fear,

"And the night cometh chill with dew,
O Father! let thy light break through!

"So let the hills of doubt divide,
So bridge with faith the sunless tide!

"So let the eyes that fail on earth
On thy eternal hills look forth;

"And in thy beckoning angels know
The dear ones whom we loved below!"

— *Whittier.*

XVII

ONE has well said: —

" Many's the thing liberty has got to do before we have achieved liberty. Some day we'll make that word real — give it universal meaning! "

Our country won its independence through its makers of freedom; but as we have seen, at the very outset of United States History, there were two perfectly distinct ideas of government: *one* believing in a strong central power at Washington — the *other* in rights of the independent States; one the Federalist or Whig party — the other, the Anti-Federalist or Democratic; and while both parties were attempting to adjust the government to sectional differences, discussions about slavery became prominent. This was practised both in the North and South; but more in the latter, for the negro liked not the colder climate, while he seemed to flourish on the Southern plantation. And the question took this form: " Is slavery an evil? If so, should it be allowed in new States being rapidly admitted to the Union? "

And oratory came again to the fore — not so impassioned and picturesque as that belonging to the Revolutionary era — but more intellectual and masterful; and we must glance at the characteristics of these intellectual giants in order to appreciate our American citizenship.

In the stormy times during the first half of the nineteenth century, the two parties — Whigs and Democrats — were merged in three. There were the " Fire-Eaters," or secessionists of the South, who felt that they had sacrificed much in joining the Union. One part of the compact that they had made was that their property was to be preserved, and that their slaves were their property. The leaders were John Randolph, of Roanoke, and John C. Calhoun, of South Carolina.

We speak first of the brilliant, eccentric, and explosive John Randolph, who was sent, in 1800, to Congress from Virginia. Believing fully in State rights, he so inveighed against the growing spirit of consolidation that he became a perfect prophet of disunion. In regard to slavery, with his clear vision he prophesied its fall. He opposed it in theory while he clung to it in practice. With awkward manner, bitter temper, and shrill voice, he was feared by friend and foe — but Congress was always forced to *listen* when John, Randolph spoke!

And Randolph prepared the way for keen, logical John C. Calhoun, the famous South Carolinian senator, the most distinguished advocate of State rights. He considered the Union but an assembly of friendly powers, willing to act together when expedient, but otherwise free to follow their own convictions; and he thought, too, that a State could, if it so pleased, *nullify* a law of Congress. Hence, in 1832, appeared the " Nullification Ordinance " of South Carolina.

Calhoun battled bravely for slavery; for he believed that slaves were property and that attacks on property were in direct violation of the Constitution. His personality was splendid, and he fought Daniel Webster with candour, courage, and loyalty. His own party was absolutely with him; and is it a wonder that through his influence, South Carolina, in 1860, led the other States in secession from the Union?

And over against the secessionists of the South were the abolitionists of the North, making up in zeal what they lacked in numbers. Their text was — that slavery was an awful crime that must be stamped out, even though the Union was dissolved in doing it. Some of them went too fast and too far, knowing only by report the thing that they attacked; but even so, theirs was the entering wedge that achieved a final triumph. Their most potent forces were William Lloyd Garrison, Wendell Phillips, Charles Sumner, and Harriet Beecher Stowe.

William Lloyd Garrison (1805-1879), was the

WILLIAM LLOYD GARRISON

DANIEL WEBSTER

HENRY CLAY

HARRIET BEECHER STOWE

fearless leader. A Newburyport printer, he began life with the honest conviction that slavery threatened civilisation, and he was ready to arouse people to violence in order to exterminate it.

As an incitement to active war, he started " The Liberator " as the official organ of the New England abolitionists, and in it he aroused grave prejudice by the following challenge : —

" I will be as harsh as truth, and as uncompromising as justice, and I will be heard ! "

For thirty-five years he edited " The Liberator," and he declaimed his principles with sonorous voice, though many times hounded and mobbed; but after his cause finally prevailed, he was counted, in the last years of his life, a national hero.

Wendell Phillips (1811-1884), seeing Garrison dragged through the streets of Boston with a rope tied about his waist, at once joined the cause. He made his bow to the public at a meeting in Faneuil Hall, Boston, where abolition was being attacked. He jumped upon the platform, interrupting the speaker, took the meeting into his own hands, turned the tide, and his fame was assured.

He always delighted in captivating warlike audiences; first gaining their sympathy, and then with a courtesy born of gentle-breeding, and with graceful and finished eloquence, leading them on to conclusions from which their judgment often rebelled. So with perfectly trained voice and rich utterances, this silver-tongued orator exhorted the North and antagonised the South; and in his later lecture tours, when the war was over, he spoke on many other subjects, two prominent ones being temperance and woman's rights.

A short time ago, on the one hundredth anniversary of his birth, Wendell Phillips was called " A Knight-errant of Humanity," " because he met the burning questions of his time with dauntless courage and a faith that never wavered."

And now we must set forward yet another abolitionist from Massachusetts, the scholarly senator Charles Sumner (1811-1894), whom the slave-holders in Congress feared and hated. He wrote in twelve compact volumes the history of the anti-slavery movement, proclaiming most aggressively his " New Declaration of Independence "; and he established his oratorical fame by his celebrated address on " The True Grandeur of Nations."

Garrison was the journalist — Whittier the poet — Phillips the orator — and Sumner the historian of the abolitionists; and there remains the novel of the party, which, perhaps more than any other force, precipitated the Civil War. This was " Uncle Tom's Cabin," written by " a little bit of a woman," Mrs. Harriet Beecher Stowe.

She belonged to a noteworthy family; and her

father, Rev. Dr. Lyman Beecher, regarded the abolition movement as " an instance of infatuation permitted by Heaven for purposes of national retribution." As a girl, Mrs. Stowe's home was for a while in Cincinnati, on the borderland of slavery. She had seen the fugitives and heard their stories at firsthand, and she had, also, visited a Kentucky plantation.

When the " Fugitive Slave Law " was passed, in 1850, requiring citizens of free States to return those who escaped to them, she was filled with indignation. At this time her husband was a professor in Bowdoin College, and she determined — with six little children, the youngest not a year old, and with constant difficulty in obtaining household service — to write a novel with a grand purpose! She knew that to make it appealing, it must be brilliant in colouring; and she became the spinner of a realistic tale that went right to the heart of the Northerner, while it excited intense and bitter feeling at the South.

The plot was rambling and carelessly strung together — its syntax was faulty — and it had many literary crudities; but Uncle Tom and little Eva were tremendously alive, and the book was full of emotional interest. It broke down New England prejudice against novel-reading and theatre-going — for even the Puritan read it, and entered the theatre for the first time to see it played.

And "Uncle Tom's Cabin" had pointed its moral; it had larger circulation both here and abroad than any other American book that had been published; it was translated into between thirty and forty languages, inspiring many, even in Eastern lands, with an enlarged spirit of brotherhood. This remains Mrs. Stowe's master-stroke of genius, though she followed it with other valuable books.

In her "Life," recently written by her son and grandson, this story is told:

"When Mr. Seward introduced Mrs. Stowe to President Lincoln, the latter rose, saying: "Why, Mrs. Stowe, right glad to see you!" and then with humourous twinkle in his eye, he added: "So you're the little woman who wrote the book that made this great war!"

We have alluded to the influence of the secession and abolition parties, both of which were willing to destroy the Union, if needful to gain their ends. The third, or conservative party, believed that compromise must be made to secure at any cost liberty and union, and from them this is called "The Compromise Period." The most formidable exponents of the party were Henry Clay, of Virginia, and Daniel Webster, of New Hampshire.

Henry Clay (1777-1852), was a poor boy whose academic education was gained in a log-cabin, but he was very clever and rose rapidly, and was in political life in Washington until he was seventy-three, always representing his adopted State, Kentucky.

With Calhoun, he advocated State rights, but with Webster, he felt that they must imperil the Union. He was a winning orator; his delivery was impressive; and he painted the evils of *dis*-union in such vivid colours that the crisis was long postponed. The thing in which he was most active was in securing, in 1820, the "Missouri Compromise," accomplished after long and hot debates in Congress. This allowed Missouri to come in as a slave State, but forbade slavery henceforth to be carried North of its Southern line.

Senatorial and Cabinet honours came to Clay; and while he stoutly asserted that he "would rather be right than to be President," he was keenly disappointed when the latter high office did *not* come his way.

And at Henry Clay's side, must always stand Daniel Webster (1782-1852). A poor boy, working on a stubborn New Hampshire farm, he early declaimed his political views to the horses and cattle in the fields. With his clothes tied up in a bandanna handkerchief, he walked into Exeter and appeared at Phillips Academy, and begged an education. He won laurels there; and afterwards was so prominent at Dartmouth College, that at eighteen, he was invited to deliver the "Fourth of July" oration, and "Liberty and Union" then as ever was his text.

His style was, at first, rather of the spread-eagle kind that was most fashionable in those days, but a friend laughed at him, and he struggled hard until he transformed it into a simple, sturdy, Saxon diction; and it was not long before he could strike mighty blows with argumentative force. We may not follow him as a successful lawyer and statesman, wherein he showed marvellous insight in discussing either law or fact; but it is his commanding power as an orator that brings him into our literary story.

His reputation was established by an address at Plymouth, on the two-hundredth anniversary of the landing of the Pilgrims. There were two famous orations in connection with the Bunker Hill Monument; noted eulogies on Adams and Jefferson; and realistic portrayals of many other subjects. Highest honours, however, came to him in his renowned speech, in 1830 —" The Reply to Hayne."

At this time, Calhoun was Vice-President, and through his lieutenant, Robert T. Hayne, he presented his argument for severing the Union.

Daniel Webster employed his finest sentences to prove that the Nation was greater than any State, and for four hours he held the attention of the vast audience — and he proved his point. His oration closed with the words: " Liberty and Union, now and forever, one and inseparable! "

He was very fond of this triplicate form of utterance. Another illustration is: " Let our object be our country, our whole country, and nothing but our country "; and yet a stronger one: " I was born an American, I live an American, I die an American." These phrases became watchwords, or better rally-ing-cries, for the Whig party to take up the sword in defence of liberty.

Young Emerson, for one, in his fascination " fol-lowed his great forehead from court-house to Senate chamber, from the caucus to the street!" And speaking of his " great forehead " suggests his strik-ing appearance. People turned to gaze at him in the street, for as one has said, " He looked great!" and Whittier — who for a time gave him hero-wor-ship — describes him as

> " New England's stateliest type of man,
> In port and speech Olympian;
> Whom no one met, at first, but took
> A second awed and wondering look."

As party contests waxed more sharp, Webster still maintained the fight; and then there came to him an ambition to be President, and for this to win the Southern vote; and in his last striking oration de-livered in 1850, there was too much compromise — too much yielding to the " Fugitive Slave Law "— so odious to his adopted State, Massachusetts, that never could tolerate any modern views. As a result, Webster was denounced by the North; and Whittier, in his poem, "Ichabod!" represented his idol as "So fallen! so lost!"

But may not the great statesman have been misjudged? May he not have felt that yet more compromise would preserve his "Liberty and Union" without war? Who can tell? Webster, however, was disappointed and embittered by criticism and political defeat, and his health began to fail. His last words were, "I still live"— and he does live to-day as our most masterful orator.

On the exterior of Saunders's Theatre, the oratorical centre of Harvard College, are seen seven sculptured heads, representing the world's supreme orators. They are Demosthenes, Cicero, St. Chrysostom, Bossuet, Chatham, Burke — and Daniel Webster!

War literature was not without its many inspiring poems and songs, and we may give space to but a single utterance on both sides. Father Ryan, a chaplain in the Southern army, loved the South, and worked for his fellowmen with gentleness and sympathy. He was laureate of the Confederacy; and in his poem, "The Conquered Banner," he voiced the feelings of a heart-broken people. We quote the first and last stanzas:—

"Furl that Banner, for 'tis weary;
 Round its staff 'tis drooping dreary;
 Furl it, fold it,— it is best:

LINCOLN EMANCIPATION STATUE AT WASHINGTON, D. C.

For there's not a man to wave it,
And there's not a sword to save it,
And there's not one left to lave it
In the blood which heroes gave it,
And its foes now scorn and brave it;

Furl it, hide it,—let it rest!
Furl that Banner, softly, slowly!
Treat it gently — it is holy,
For it droops above the dead,
Touch it not — unfold it never;
Let it droop there, furled forever,—
For its people's hopes are fled."

And Mrs. Julia Ward Howe became the laureate of the Union army as her magnetic " Battle Hymn of the Republic" sang itself into being. The story of its writing is familiar: One day returning with her old pastor, Rev. Dr. James Freeman Clarke, from witnessing a parade outside of Washington, they heard the soldiers singing " John Brown's Body," and Dr. Clarke asked her to put more suitable words to the music. She, at first, declined; but in the grey of the following morning, the inspiration came to her, and rising, she jotted down the stanzas from which we select a few lines: —

" In the beauty of the lilies Christ was born across the sea,
With a glory in His bosom that transfigures you and me;
As He died to make men holy, let us die to make men free,
While God is marching on."

And now we need just one more character to unite our scattered parties and to complete our chronicle — and this must be Abraham Lincoln, " The Emancipator." Think of introducing a man with less than a year's schooling into a literary record! But this man had as a boy manifested indomitable will in freeing himself from the fetters of ignorance. He had read over and over a few good books, until from them he had gained the golden art of speaking and writing distinctly and to the point.

Thus he had shaped a style of his own, unsurpassed in strength, sincerity, and directness. His State papers were models of expression, and he won national fame in his debates with Senator Douglas.

A plain blunt man, he was abounding in wit and humour, but often carrying a sad heart, weighed down by the burdens of his fellows — and the greater the occasion, the more his heart was touched, the more were his soul depths revealed — and yet he hardly thought of literary fame; but he has bequeathed us two masterpieces that belong quite as much to literature as to politics.

One was his " Second Inaugural," delivered on March fourth, 1865, " With malice toward none; with charity for all "— it was full of faith and spirituality, and seemed like a benediction — so soon was it followed by the tragedy that closed his life. Perhaps, however, the address that will make him longest remembered is the one delivered at

Gettysburg, on November nineteenth, 1863, on the day when the National Cemetery was consecrated to the long-sought liberty.

Edward Everett, called "the most accomplished gentleman of his time," who was in turn editor, preacher, foreign minister, member of Congress, Secretary of State, Governor of Massachusetts, and President of Harvard College — preceded the speaker of the day. With graceful and dignified mien, he gave one of his smooth and flowing musical addresses which lasted for two hours, and which was greeted by enthusiastic applause.

President Lincoln had been too busy to prepare a speech but en route from Washington he had written with the stub of a pencil on a bit of wrapping-paper — a few notes, and when Mr. Everett took his seat he rose awkwardly, "without grace of look or manner," and in a high, thin voice made his brief address, and seated himself. Perfect silence followed — he knew that he had failed!

After all was over, he congratulated Mr. Everett, and Mr. Everett in his reply said: "I should be glad if I could flatter myself that I came as near the central idea of the occasion in two hours as you did in two minutes!" And to-day President Lincoln's "Gettysburg Address" is called, "The Top and Crown of American Eloquence." It is displayed on one of the walls of Oxford University to show the students how much can be said in less than three hundred words, and for the same reason it is mentioned here that our American youth may acquire from it the habit of concise utterance.

THE GETTYSBURG ADDRESS
November nineteenth, 1863

" Fourscore and seven years ago our fathers brought forth upon this continent a new nation, conceived in liberty, and dedicated to the proposition that all men are created equal. Now we are engaged in a great civil war, testing whether that nation, or any nation so conceived and so dedicated, can long endure. We are met on a great battle-field of that war. We have come to dedicate a portion of that field as a final resting-place for those who here gave their lives that that nation might live. It is altogether fitting and proper that we should do this. But in a larger sense we cannot dedicate, we cannot consecrate, we cannot hallow this ground. The brave men, living and dead, who struggled here, have consecrated it far above our power to add or detract. The world will little note, nor long remember, what we say here, but it can never forget what they did here. It is for us, the living, rather to be dedicated here to the unfinished work which they who fought here have thus far so nobly advanced.

It is rather for us to be here dedicated to the great task remaining before us, that from these honoured dead we take increased devotion to that cause for which they gave the last full measure of devotion; that we here highly resolve that these dead shall not have died in vain; that this nation, under God, shall have a new birth of freedom, and that government of the people, by the people, and for the people, shall not perish from the earth."

— *Lincoln.*

FROM "THE BUILDING OF THE SHIP"

" Thou, too, sail on, O ship of State!
Sail on, O Union, strong and great!
Humanity with all its fears,
With all the hopes of future years,
Is hanging breathless on thy fate!
We know what Master laid thy keel,
What workmen wrought thy ribs of steel,
Who made each mast, and sail, and rope,
What anvils rang, what hammers beat,
In what a forge and what a heat
Were shaped the anchors of thy hope!
Fear not each sudden sound and shock,
'Tis of the wave and not the rock;
'Tis but the flapping of the sail,
And not a rent made by the gale!
In spite of rock and tempest's roar,
In spite of false lights on the shore,
Sail on, nor fear to breast the sea!
Our hearts, our hopes, are all with thee,
Our hearts, our hopes, our prayers, our tears,
Our faith triumphant o'er our fears,
Are all with thee,— are all with thee!"

— *Longfellow.*

XVIII

BANCROFT AND PRESCOTT

GEORGE BANCROFT (1800-1891)

WILLIAM HICKLING PRESCOTT (1796-1859)

CENTURIES have rolled by! do they mean anything to the eager youth of our day, who, absorbed in modern interests, almost forget that there is a past, for they have so little time to pore over its story, and to gaze upon their ancestors from many lands. They may call history dull. Well there are, as Carlyle says, two kinds — one " dry as dust," the other " alive "— and any youth will find it an invaluable stimulus to read himself into a love for " alive " history; for " alive " history is like a panorama, unrolling in miniature scenes of adventure and exploration and war and camp and court and senate.

Do we realise the gratitude which we owe the historian? Think of what he must possess and what he must do. He should first have plenty of leisure to spend in investigation and plenty of money to conduct this investigation by travel — sometimes covering hundreds of miles to verify a single fact. Added to these, are the study of languages, and the purchase of costly maps and pictures and manuscripts. Extreme patience and perseverance are required in unearthing dusty records, and finally all are to be collected and arranged in correct perspective.

And the historian must steer most carefully between Scylla and Charybdis; knowing that if his work is too poetic or imaginative, it will not be counted accurate — while if it is unadorned, it will not be read. All honour to the successful one!

We recall many faithful historians — those who have well exploited our past: the colonial took part in the scenes which he describes, while others looked back at them over the centuries; and there are many to-day in the ranks working earnestly. As our study is not with living authors, we select four of those who wrote in the nineteenth century, and from each we shall try to obtain a memory picture that may prove a sesame to unlock an interest in their spirited work. These are Bancroft and Prescott, Motley and Parkman.

George Bancroft (1800-1891), the son of a Congregational minister at Worcester, Massachusetts, came into the world with the century. An alert, shrewd boy, he graduated at Harvard at sixteen, taking such high rank that at the request of the college, he was sent to Germany to study. Here again he proved an eager student in both history and philosophy, and he specially equipped himself as a linguist.

He enjoyed rather unusual experiences for a young American of his time, for he was received with honour by such distinguished Germans as Goethe, Von Humboldt, Bunsen, and Niebuhr. Besides, he met Byron and other English literary men.

After five years he returned home. Shortly he published a small book of poems; and in the same year, with a friend he established the Round Hill School for boys, at Northampton, Massachusetts. For some time, this was most successful, for boys of prominent families came from all over the land; and in this building may be seen the little study in which Bancroft commenced his stupendous work, "The History of the United States." After a decade, the school lost its popularity and the boys stampeded.

Bancroft, nevertheless, was not discouraged. He presently was appointed collector of the port of Boston, and later Secretary of the Navy; and while he could not pilot a boat, he determined that others should be proficient in sea-tactics, and urged the founding of the Naval Academy at Annapolis. In time, he was sent on diplomatic missions to both England and Germany. But wherever he lived or whatever he did, other duties were never permitted to interfere with his wide and painstaking research into historical studies.

His principal work was "The History of the United States from the Discovery of the Continent to the Establishment of the Constitution in 1789."

This was in several volumes, to which were afterwards added two more, " The History of the Formation of the Constitution." The first volume was published in 1850 — the last in 1874 — and they were extensively read as they came out. Through all, the writer adhered to a rigid rule to secure perfect accuracy. The work is clear, concise, and excellent — and indispensable in a well-equipped reference library.

Bancroft believed so fully in the dignity of history that his actors are often statuesque rather than soulful. He perhaps digressed too much; and he was such an intense upholder of everything American that he is sometimes more patriotic than critical.

But Bancroft's narrative is masterful, and more than as teacher, poet, essayist, traveller, philologist, or diplomat — will he be held in remembrance as the historian of our United States. Perchance because he toiled so zealously and to such a good old age, he is sometimes designated " A prose Homer," or again " A modern Herodotus."

He was twice married, and lived for years in Twenty-first Street, New York; but he is more associated with his Washington house, near the Congressional Library. He was so fond of politics that naturally life at the Capital was absorbing, and as he lived ninety-one years, he came into touch with successive generations of statesmen.

Here it was that his library grew into vast proportions — from floor to ceiling, on the window-seats, overflowing into other rooms — for he literally burrowed in books, sparing neither time nor money in the selection of his twelve thousand volumes, and in procuring authentic copies of State documents.

His summer residence was at Newport, Rhode Island. Here he set his rose-garden to bloom with as much energy as he bestowed upon his library in winter — for books and flowers were his loves.

There are two kinds of history: One may be compared to a map with its exact dimensions, distances, and angles. Such a history is Bancroft's — reliable, definite, and exact; the other is found in the histories of William Hickling Prescott (1796-1859), in which we forget the boundaries, for he painted his scenes in such gorgeous colouring that Daniel Webster exclaimed, after reading his first work: " A new meteor has suddenly blazed forth in full splendour."

And as we turn to Prescott's shaded life, we realise in what striking contrast it stands to his writings. His brave, literary ancestry is shown in two crossed swords that hang on the walls of the Massachusetts Historical Society: one belonged to his grandfather, Gen. Prescott, who fought on the American side at Bunker Hill — the other to his maternal grandfather, a British officer in an earlier war.

The homestead was at Pepperell, Massachusetts,

FRANCIS PARKMAN JOHN LOTHROP MOTLEY

GEORGE BANCROFT WILLIAM H. PRESCOTT

but Prescott's birthplace was Salem, where his father was a prominent lawyer. He liked to read and to tell a story; but he was not fond of applying himself, and after he had successfully passed his examinations at Harvard, he wrote home that he felt twenty pounds lighter. A graceful, interesting youth, with wealth and sparkling social qualities, he seemed to have everything to make life attractive when suddenly his whole future was changed by a simple crust of bread. This crust thrown across the table in a students' frolic at Harvard hit Prescott in the eye and entirely destroyed its vision.

He struggled manfully with the situation, and attempted to go on with his studies, and then was sent to the Azores and to Europe for his health; but brave living in a darkened room, and the advice of the best physicians were of no avail — the other eye sympathised more and more until its light almost went out — and Prescott faced the question what should he *do* with his future.

He might spend it in leisure, always tagged with " I am blind," and thus gain the sympathy of the world; but with unflinching purpose he decided that loss of eyesight should not ruin his career. He could not be a lawyer as he had planned, but he might become a scholar and write books, and like Milton, he " cared not how late he came into life, only that he came fit."

An indifferent pupil as a boy, he now studied

grammar and rhetoric and French and German and Spanish and Latin classics, and he found in London a noctograph, or blind-man's writing-machine, which helped him greatly. His plan for a working-day was seven hours, in which he might use his eyes five minutes at a time for perhaps thirty-five minutes; for the rest, his secretary read to him so that, as he said, his *ears* should assist his *eyes*.

He learned to concentrate his mind upon a single theme and to assimilate facts to an extraordinary degree, so that he finally could dictate as many as fifty or sixty pages a day, and sometimes he would for days carry many pages in his mind. Often he would be weary, but he prodded himself on, until he had spent ten years in preparation for a literary life.

Spain — always alluring to our romancers — attracted him as it did Irving, for his internal vision gloried in the rich colouring, and yet he specially disliked searching into old records; but readers read to him, and copyists copied for him in large script so that he might make his own corrections; and while walking and driving, he mentally arranged his scenes and fought his battles.

In 1837, his " History of Ferdinand and Isabella " was published, and at once was most successful both here and abroad, and coming out just before Christmas, it became the fashionable holiday gift. Encouraged by its reception, he sent fifteen hundred dollars to Madrid, for manuscript copies of Spanish State papers, and in 1843, his " Conquest of Mexico " appeared. This was the subject on which Irving had intended to write but which he gracefully surrendered to Prescott; and Prescott revelled in the early and magnificent civilisation of Mexico, and somehow he made this history of Cortez's achievement read just like a tale of chivalry.

This was followed, in 1847, by " The Conquest of Peru," in which we have the daring exploits of a handful of adventurers under Pizarro, their intrepid leader, capturing the land of the Incas, and again enriching Spain with gold and jewels. How Prescott loved the gorgeous pageantry! for truly " the glint of armour is in it, the crimson and gold and floating banners and the movement of advancing hosts." His last book, " The History of Philip II," he did not live to complete.

It was in his home in Beacon Street, Boston, in his darkened library, reached by a concealed stairway, that he toiled assiduously, year after year, with his noctograph, reader, and copyist. His patient, persevering effort was rewarded by admiring friends on both sides of the ocean. Oxford gave him a degree; Macaulay, and Thackeray and Gladstone greatly honoured him; and his books were translated into five foreign languages — and yet Prescott was sensible of his limitations. Once he said: " I have as good bairns as fall to lot of most men; a wife whom a quarter of century of love has made my better half — but the sweet fountain of intellectual vision of which I drunk in boyhood is sealed to me for ever."

And yet he said again: " There is no happiness so great as that of a permanent and lovely interest in some intellectual labour." Truly he must have realised Jean Ingelow's words: " Work is Heaven's Hest."

The noblest monument of Prescott is his sunshiny disposition. Bancroft said of him: —

" He was greater than his writings."

XIX

JOHN LOTHROP MOTLEY (1814-1877)

FRANCIS PARKMAN (1823-1893)

JOHN LOTHROP MOTLEY was born in Dorchester, Massachusetts, and died near Dorchester, England. His genial biographer, Oliver Wendell Holmes, gives a happy picture of his childhood days in the Walnut Street home, in Boston.

Here the great attic and garden were given over to the sports of this "Embryo Dramatist" of a nation's life, and his two playfellows, Wendell Phillips, "The Silver-tongued Orator" to be, and Gold Appleton, the future wit and essayist, of whom Holmes has well said that "he has spilled more good things on the wasteful air in conversation than would carry a diner-out through half a dozen London seasons."

With cloaks and doublets and plumed hats, these youthful knights or bandits enacted all kinds of impromptu dramas. One day, for example, the younger brother was found upon the floor wrapped in a shawl, and kept quiet by sweetmeats, while figuring as the "Dead Cæsar," while over the prostrate figure one of the literary trio was declaring Mark Antony's oration!

Young Motley was always reading or studying, and at the age of eleven, he surprised his family with two chapters of a novel — but it was never completed. When he went to boarding-school, he wrote home for books and newspapers —" Nothing to eat, nothing to drink, *but books!*" For a time he studied under Bancroft, at the Round Hill School, and at seventeen, graduated from Harvard — an impulsive youth, of striking personal beauty, but too haughty to be popular. He was already a fine conversationalist and devoted to society.

Then he went abroad and at Göttingen and Berlin, he established with his fellow-student, Bismarck, a life-long intimacy. The beauty of his eyes and the ease with which he acquired German were what first attracted the great diplomat. On his return, he married the sister of Park Benjamin — editor, poet, and lecturer — read law, wrote two unsuccessful novels, and could not decide what next.

Finally, some historical sketches delighting his friends, they urged him to continue them, and at last he concluded to become a historian. He looked about for a field not already pre-empted, and the story of plucky Holland appealed to him, and how this small determined nation had won her freedom, against tremendous odds, from aggressive Spain.

He made three divisions of this text: First, " The Rise of the Dutch Republic "; Second, " The History of the United Netherlands "; Third, " The History of the Thirty Years' War." He did not live to finish the third, but was working on " John of Barneveld, Advocate," when he died.

The Netherlands, at that time, formed a subject comparatively sealed to the outside world, and Motley went abroad to study, and followed his quest from country to country; and owing to the courtesy of the Queen of Holland, and the liberality of many governments, archives buried for centuries were freely thrown open, and he spent years in just poring over them.

He found a key to State secrets, and read " the bribings and the windings " of old despots, who had previously appeared only on State occasions; and he said one day: " I remain among my fellow-worms, feeding on their musty mulberry leaves, out of which we are afterward to spin our silk." The deeper he went, the more fascinated he grew, until he called himself a perfect stranger in the modern world — and felt that if he might only appear in the sixteenth century, he would find himself on terms of intimacy with the leading men of that age; and it was not until he was fully in touch with his subject that he began to write.

And how quaintly he describes that sturdy little land —

" That rides at anchor and is moored,
    In which they do not live but go aboard ";

and in what eloquent language he paints her desperate struggle for civil and religious liberty.   There
are vignettes of bigoted Philip Second, inconstant
Queen Elizabeth, and William " the Liberator,"
whose motto even in those tumultuous days was:
" Always tranquil amid the waves "— and who,
though a most genial man, became William, " the
Silent," because with rare sagacity, he knew when
not to speak!

The volumes are full of dramatic scenes in this age
when intrigue and assassination were shadowed
everywhere.   There is the tale of Margaret of
Parma and the Beggars; the depicting of stern, cruel
battles; the defence of beautiful Leyden with its
orchards and gardens and pigeons, and its he-
roie rescue by " The Beggars of the Sea."   Motley
does not close his narrative, till Holland has
achieved absolute independence.   Truly, he swept
" The black past like Van Tromp with his
broom "!

Freedom and art grew together in Holland, and
in visiting this picturesque land we see how the
Dutch painters of its " Golden Age " have perpetuated her victory on the walls of her galleries; and in
reading Motley's word-pictures painted, too, with
minute detail, we find that he, also, has perpetuated

the story of liberty and made the Dutch museum as interesting as the galleries.

Motley was himself such a lover of freedom that perhaps his principal fault as a historian was, that he could not write dispassionately; but his books read just like fiction and they were accorded everywhere the warmest reception. He belonged to the " Saturday Club," with Emerson and Hawthorne and Lowell and Whipple and Whittier and Agassiz and Irving and Prescott and Bancroft and Holmes; and in 1857, when he was leaving for England, the members came together to bid him farewell, and the last lines of the " Parting Health " written by Holmes were : —

" The true Knight of Learning, the world holds him dear,
  Love bless him, joy crown him, God speed his career!"

Motley several times received the honour awarded to many of our literary men of being appointed minister to foreign courts. He was at St. Petersburg and London, and during the whole of the Civil War, in Vienna. He had the courtly manners and conversational gifts that would be his passport anywhere, but for some reason, he was not always successful as a diplomat. He may have been indiscreet, and certainly political intrigues were formed against him.

He was disappointed, but always consoled by his social and scholarly triumphs, the marked courtesies shown him at great functions, and the admiration expressed by Froude and Macaulay and other men of letters, for his works. He lived much abroad, specially during the later years of his life, and he died in England, and with his wife is buried in Kensal Green Cemetery. Bryant, who highly regarded him, wrote a sonnet from which we quote this line:—

"Sleep, Motley, with the great of ancient days!"

What different subjects attract different historians! One devotes his life to the enthusiastic study of his own land; another glories in mighty Spain; while a third applauds heroic Holland, in wresting herself from the grasp and aggressions of this same mighty Spain; and Francis Parkman looks off upon a country of forests and Indians and adventure, of French and English encounter, and resolves to centre his labours upon such themes. He was drawn to them even as a boy; for although his home was in Boston, as he was not strong he was sent when very young to sojourn at his grandfather's home at Medway, then on the edge of a vast forest. Here he learned but little from books; for walking to school through the woods, he spent most of his time in making the acquaintance of birds and squirrels and reptiles and insects, and in conjuring all kinds of savage escapades. Even as a sophomore in college, his purpose was fixed to be a historian, and he selected the subject on which he would ever afterwards write, and he never wavered.

His general topic was " France and England in North America," and it ranged from the period of early French settlement in the New World and the alliance with the Indians, to the victories of the English over these French and Indian allies.   There are eight volumes.   As a preparation, Motley spent his college vacations in tramps in Adirondack and Canadian forests; he was sent to Europe for his health, and in Rome lodged in a monastery, to discover the character of the Jesuit priests and their mission.   He searched thoroughly everywhere, as we have seen, for whatever might be introduced in his writings.

Then, in 1846, with a friend he travelled West over the Rocky Mountains to study the Indian at first-hand.   He met many tribes and visited nearly every spot which he later described.   Always armed and on the watch, he camped for months with the Sioux, joining their feast or war-hunt or ceremonial, or defiling with the wild cavalcade through the gorges.   Thus he gained insight into the character of the olden day savage, with his bow and arrow and paint and embroidery and war-plumes and fluttering trophies.   No wonder that to Parkman is given the palm of a masterly treatment of the " Red Man."

But exposure weakened a constitution that was never strong; wigwam, smoke, and sunlight so injured his eyes that he was threatened with total

blindness; and when he left the Western land, his
health was impaired for life.   For long, he was not
allowed to work at all, and finally only permitted to
use his eyes every other minute, for two or three
hours daily.   In 1849, by means of dictation, he was
able to publish his " Oregon Trail "— the history
of his own trip — and a thrilling résumé of out-door
experiences.

And Parkman rose above every obstacle.   He
visited the European libraries several times to collect
copies of valuable manuscripts.   He learned to employ a " literary gridiron," a frame of parallel wires,
laid on the paper to guide his hand.   Like Prescott,
he worked slowly and laboriously; but like Prescott,
his pages grew to chapters, and his chapters grew
in time to eight completed volumes — a library of
captivating diversion to the youth of to-day.

Parkman is not stately like Prescott, nor eloquent
like Motley; but his work is graphic and philosophical, and while illumined with the romance of early
adventure, it is inspired with the spirit of modern
action.

Parkman toiled diligently until he was seventy
years old — almost his whole life.   His admirers
call him " the youngest of our quartette — our finest
historian."   Who may decide?

John Fiske, in one of his eloquent lectures, once
alluded to " Pontiac and His Companions " as " one
of the most brilliant and fascinating books that had

been written by any historian since the days of Herodotus." The words were hardly out of his mouth
when he caught sight of Parkman in the audience,
and he said: —

"I never shall forget the sudden start he gave, the
heightened colour on his noble face, and its curious look of
surprise and pleasure, an expression as honest and simple
as one might see in a school-boy suddenly singled out for
praise."

In his quiet home, in Chestnut Street, Boston,
Parkman lived much in his library, surrounded by
books, Indian relics, Barye statuettes, and pictures of
his favourite cats. His children, after the death of
their mother, had gone to live with their aunt, and
he enjoyed their frequent visits, and later those of
his wonderful grandchildren. Always suffering,
he showed astonishing self-mastery; he so liked to
have his sister read a good story aloud, and often
used family jokes and nonsense to conceal his real
pain.

His summer home, at Jamaica Plains, was an
ideally beautiful one. He was as fond of roses as
Bancroft. He cultivated flowers and wrote a book
about them, maintaining that gardening had saved
his life. He was devoted to rowing, and here on
the border of the lake where he used to moor his
boat, a memorial has been raised in his honour,
adorned with the " Spirit of the Woods "—and Dr.

Holmes added another memorial in the following stanzas: —

" He told the red man's story; far and wide
    He searched the unwritten records of his race;
He sat a listener at the Sachem's side,
    He tracked the hunter through his wild-wood chase.

" High o'er his head the soaring eagle screamed;
    The wolf's long howl rang nightly through the vale;
Tramped the lone bear; the panther's eye-balls gleamed;
    The bison's gallop thundered on the gale.

" Soon o'er the horizon rose the cloud of strife —
    Two proud, strong nations battling for the prize —
Which swarming host should mould a nation's life,
    Which royal banner flaunt the Western skies.

" Long raged the conflict; on the crimson sod
    Native and alien joined their hosts in vain —
The lilies withered where the lion trod,
    Till peace lay panting on the ravaged plain."

XX

PURITANISM that had made New England famous as a literary centre held sway there until about a hundred years ago; but its views were such that it did little towards bringing about a broader culture, even though Franklin was doing much for Philadelphia, and New York was enjoying her " Knickerbocker Group." But in the nineteenth century, there came to New England a marked spiritual and intellectual awakening — a " Golden Age " of literature which centred in Concord and Boston. This was the result of many influences.

As the United States claimed independence, new social and political views were agitated. There was the abolitionist movement; newspapers multiplied; the Kantean philosophy was imported from Germany, and books on free thought from England. Then William Ellery Channing, a devout and eloquent preacher in Boston, led the Unitarian movement, in a belief that insisted on more liberal religious thought.

By the Puritan, literature and a love for beauty had been frowned upon, because they had drawn the attention from matters of greater religious moment

— and now these very things were considered helpful to religious life; for as Emerson says in his " Rhodora " : —

". . . . if eyes were made for seeing,
Then Beauty is its own excuse for being,"

and culture of all kinds became fashionable.

And now, too, Transcendentalism comes to the front — a vague theory that in its day had such powerful followers that we may not pass it by, though what it ever accomplished remains a problem!

And first the word " transcendental "; its direct meaning is " a speculating on matters which transcend the range of human intellect, even until these become the motives that govern our lives." It is a gospel alike of free-thinking and individualism — all to be strengthened by communion with Nature. It included enthusiastic study of many " isms ": among them, idealism, liberalism, individualism, Unitarianism — and as to patriotism, it made the strongest kind of protest against slavery. Lowell said that in it, " Everybody had a chance to attend to everybody else's business."

Communities were established where everything was *common* — but *common sense!* Some would not eat meat and preached a " potato gospel "; others gave up flour; while yet others were confident that there would be an instant millennium as soon as hooks

SCHOOL OF PHILOSOPHY, CONCORD, MASS.

and eyes should be substituted for buttons! There were discussions and conversations, led by Calvinists, Unitarians, abolitionists, and cranks! "The Dial" was the organ of the club, and its first editor was the eccentric prophetess, Margaret Fuller.

She was a clever woman who had studied Latin at six, read Shakespeare at eight, and at twenty-two had covered the range of modern literature. A brilliant conversationalist, her words were said to irradiate any subject. Emerson called her: "The pivotal mind in modern literature."

She had firm faith in demonology, always imagining that she was being moved by some mysterious, fateful power. Although an ardent student of Goethe, she heartily interested herself for a time in the Transcendental movement. For two years, she struggled to make "The Dial" a success, and then renounced to Emerson its editorship.

Under Horace Greeley, she next went to New York as a critic on "The Tribune." Then she journeyed abroad and met Carlyle in England. Her next prominent move was made in Italy, where, like Mrs. Browning, she threw herself with burning zeal into the struggle for "Italy free!" Here she secretly married D'Ossoli, a friend of Mazzini's. In 1850, she was returning to America with her husband and child, bringing a manuscript which she had written on the Italian Revolution, and the family was shipwrecked off Fire Island.

The leading apostle of Transcendentalism was Amos Bronson Alcott of Concord — a man so saturated with theories that he never could descend to assist his household in their heroic efforts for daily bread. Upon a side hill near his home a chapel was built where his " School of Philosophy " was established. Louisa Alcott wrote: —

" The town swarms with budding philosophers and they roost on our steps like hens waiting for corn."

But in the chapel gathered philosophers from all the world over to take part in weighty arguments, and to listen to Dr. Alcott's sublime " Conversations." The school continued from 1878 until 1888 — its closing service being a memorial to Dr. Alcott who had died a short time before. Others interested were Dr. Channing, Dr. Parker, Dr. Ripley, James Freeman Clarke, Emerson, and Elizabeth Peabody. Some were visionary — some were practical — but all were united in enthusiasm for " plain living and high thinking."

Another expression of modern thought was manifested in the " Brook Farm Social Settlement," at West Roxbury. This was founded by about twenty eager intellects under the leadership of Dr. Ripley, a Unitarian clergyman, who later was an editor. The number of members increased to nearly two hundred. Among the chosen spirits were Hawthorne, and the graceful essayist and magazine-writer, George William Curtis. The text of the community was: "To live on the faculties of the soul." There were to be at the same time plenty of work and plenty of leisure. But many of the members knew nothing about agriculture, and after ten hours of daily labour, they were not alert to " soul thought."

After several years, the principal building which had cost ten thousand dollars was burned, and Brook Farm went to pieces for financial reasons. However, out of all the influences that were at work, a vital note *was* struck for intellectual and spiritual freedom, and it became insistent in the lives of the authors about whom we are now to speak.

XXI

RALPH WALDO EMERSON was the most famous of the Transcendentalists, and in his day, America's greatest philosopher; and he came naturally by his learning, for he had an ancestry of seven or eight generations of preachers. The father, a scholarly man, was settled over a Boston parish when Ralph was born, and although the child was sent almost at once to a dame's school, his father deplored that, at three, he could not read very well! The little fellow was extremely gentle, and we may imagine that he was inculcated with high moral standards.

N. P. Willis, the poet, however, who used to see him playing on the street has the audacity to call him: "One of those pale little moral-sublimes, with turned-over shirt-collar, who were recognised by Boston school-boys as having fathers that are Unitarians!"

Ralph was but eight when his father died, and he always remembered with pride the stately funeral, at which the "Ancient and Honourable Artillery" escorted the body of their late chaplain to the grave; and the child had other memories, too, and these were of poverty and self-denial — of sharing his

brother's overcoat so that in winter he could go to
school only on alternate days; or how sometimes
when the children were hungry, the mother entertained them with traditions of their heroic ancestors.

She was a woman of highest ideals, this mother;
the church honoured her and helped her a little, but
even so the way was difficult. And there was, also,
Spartan-like Aunt Mary, who always held with the
mother that the boys were born to be educated; and
she urged them on with such inspiring phrases as
these: " Scorn trifles "—" Always do what you are
afraid to do! "

When Ralph was eleven, Dr. Ezra Ripley, pastor
over the church at Concord, took his step-son's
widow and children to live with him there in the
storied " Old Manse." It was in this home that
Ralph's grandfather, the militant preacher, had
lived; and it was Ralph who wrote later the poem
read at the anniversary of the fight. This poem is
really almost as famous as the fight; for it contains
the following immortal lines which are emblazoned
on the " Minute-man ": —

" By the rude bridge that arched the flood,
    Their flag to April's breeze unfurled,
'Here once the embattled farmers stood,
    And fired the shot heard round the world! "

The Emerson family remained but a few years
in Concord, and on their return to Boston, Mrs.

Emerson took boarders, and Dr. Ripley sent her a cow which Ralph drove to pasture through what is now a fashionable part of the city; and finally the boys *did* enter college, through the Boston Latin School, and Ralph did many things to pay his expenses. He carried the President's official messages; waited on table at commons; declaimed on occasion; wrote themes for other fellows; and tutored in vacation. Once he actually sent his mother five dollars to buy a shawl, but it went to pay the butcher's bill.

He graduated at eighteen, and with what courage he would have walked forth could he have foreseen that to-day "Emerson Hall," in Harvard, attests to the honour in which his life-work is held. Until his graduation, he had always been "Ralph"; now he announced that he would prefer to be called "Waldo." He aided his brother in one young ladies' school in Boston, and then was usher in another. Some of the girls were older than he, and they *did* like to make him blush; but they dared not take any real liberties with his youth, for he had such a scholarly mien and carried himself with such dignity.

Later his brother went to Göttingen, and Waldo entered the Divinity School, at Cambridge. He quite naturally slipped into the ancestral profession in those days when over forty per cent. of the Harvard graduates studied for the ministry. The classical scholar, Edward Everett, was not only his master in Greek, but had much to do in shaping his life thought. In due time, Emerson was " approbated " to preach, and he was at first the assistant and then pastor of a leading Unitarian church in Boston. He also, in 1829, married a wife, a Miss Tucker, who proved one of his truest inspirations. She, however, died soon afterwards, leaving her husband an annuity of twelve hundred dollars.

It was during these years that Emerson's views on individuality began to assert themselves — views influenced by the free thought that had been imported in German and English books. He adopted the motto: " Be bold, be free, be true, be right, else you will be enslaved cowards." The rites of his church hampered him, for more and more he believed in spirit not in form. " Religion is obsolete," he claimed, " when lives do not proceed from it." Finally he resigned both pastorate and ministry, and his health giving way, he sailed, in 1832, on a brig for Europe, then a month distant from our land.

It was to be a scholarly pilgrimage; he was desirous to meet in the flesh Wordsworth whose Nature teachings had interested him, and Carlyle, " the gun of guns " for depth, and he had the pleasure of seeing not only these but many other authors. He found Carlyle buried among his Scottish moors, and their chance for acquaintance was a white day in both lives. Carlyle called Emerson " one of the most lovable creatures " he " had ever looked upon ";

and Emerson was one of the first to hail Carlyle, and he made his works known here almost before they were abroad.

On Emerson's return, he determined to devote his whole future to literature, and he made his home in Concord, which is situated in a level country like Warwickshire; it has a winding river like the Avon, and besides it was near the stage route to Boston. Emerson said of it that it had " no seaport, no cotton, no shoe trade, no water-power, neither gold, lead, coal, oil, or marble." But he would do with it what Agassiz was doing with the Harvard Museum, make it a shrine that all Europeans must visit. And " The Sage of Concord " succeeded in converting the town into a literary Mecca; for was it not the cherished home of Hawthorne and Thoreau and the Alcotts and Channing and Sanborn, and others associated with our literature?

In 1836, Emerson was married again — this time to Lydia Jackson of Plymouth; and the wedding-journey was the chaise-ride from Plymouth up to Concord. He purchased a farm, but did not realise until later what a bargain he had made in blue-birds, bobolinks and thrushes — in sunrises and sunsets. The large square house was " stocked with books and papers and as many friends as possible." Its host's welcoming motto was: " Any one that knocks at my door shall have my attention." An old-fashioned flower-garden shortly displayed itself, for Emerson

RALPH WALDO EMERSON   NATHANIEL HAWTHORNE

found, after he married, that though he planted corn ever so often, it was sure to come up tulips."

A man of simple, sturdy habits, he believed in manual labour. " My own right hand my cup-bearer shall be," he asserted, and he could do almost anything except handle tools; with these he was so awkward that little Waldo, one day as he watched him digging, exclaimed: " Papa, I am afraid you will dig your leg! "

And Emerson walked very pleasantly with the towns-people, interesting many in his views about " plain living and high thinking." He was de-lighted with his pupil Thoreau, who was for two years an inmate in his home, and who was so ingenious that he made himself most useful in both house and garden. Then there was the dreamy, profound Dr. Alcott, who lived over the way, and Hawthorne whom he often encountered in the woodsy path. And a special attraction was added in the clear-eyed girls and manly boys of the town, and he called the latter " masters of the play-ground and the street."

He tried to help them as he walked among them, with sentiments of right thinking, brave speech, and cheerful work. He was uneasy at the number of books that were appearing to divert them from the standard authors that he had loved. He begged them to be moderate in all things; to beware of the words " intense " and " exquisite "; and in writing to avoid italics.

" Lecture Lyceums " were now being organised in different parts of New England, and Emerson not only wrote but made the platform his " free pulpit," and young people greatly liked to hear him lecture. The youthful Higginson and Lowell, for example, very often could not understand what he was talking about — but they went again and again —" not to hear what Emerson said but to hear Emerson." " Were we enthusiasts? " Lowell says. " I hope and believe we were, and am thankful to the man who made us worth something for once in our lives."

The corner-stone to Emerson's fame was the oration, " The American Scholar," which he delivered in 1837, before the " Phi Beta Kappa Society," at Harvard. He had been deemed a preacher of mysticism, and was glad of this opportunity to express his practical ideas. In the oration, he urged the young men of Puritan New England to individualism, self-reliance, sincerity, and courage, and above all to cultivate soul freedom: " We will walk on our own feet; we will work with our own hands; we will speak our own minds." Daring words these! and an eager crowd listened breathlessly to this new voice.

Holmes styled the oration " our intellectual Declaration of Independence," and said that the young men went out from it as if a prophet had been declaiming: " Thus saith the Lord." Carlyle, after reading it, wrote to Emerson: "You are a new era, my man, in your huge country." And from this time until nearly the end of his life, Emerson delivered lectures all over the United States and Europe; but never a one was so logical as this that took Cambridge by storm and caused great unrest.

Another stepping-stone to Emerson's fame was his "Essay on Nature," which was a text for his future philosophy. It was written in the "Old Manse," at Concord, not long before he established his home there, and was published in book form, in 1839. It is full of descriptive passages and his aim in this is to set forth his idealistic philosophy, proving that the beauty of the universe belongs to every individual who will lay claim to it, and that through communion with Nature, we may feel in us the presence of the God of Nature, and free ourselves from the tyranny of materialisation.

Though Emerson had not the heart-love of a Burns or a Bryant, he was really very fond of Nature. He studied in the dreamy woods, where he heard wandering voices in the air and whispers in the breeze. Another delight was to get into the little boat moored in the river just back of his house, and with one stroke of the paddle pass from the world into the serene realm of sunset and moonlight.

Emerson jotted down everything in his journal which he always carried, naming it his "savings-bank." Apart from a memorial to Margaret Fuller, his writings were mostly essays, and these were largely from the striking passages in his lectures, and sometimes he would spend years in stringing together selections from one of them. His constant habit, in composing either prose or poetry, was to think out each sentence or line without regard to what was to follow — so his writings are rather collections of proverbs than smooth, harmonious pages. But what other man has created such living epigrams for a nation!

Plato was always his master; and like his master, he strove to think deep and high. Sometimes he would wander so far away that he found it difficult to explain his own philosophy. At least once when he was asked to make clear a somewhat obscure passage, he was forced — like Robert Browning under the same circumstances — to confess that he did not know what he meant, saying: "I suppose that I felt that way when I wrote it."

His essays appeared in series, 1841-1878 — and readers do not agree as to which are best; but among the most helpful are "Compensation," "Friendship," "Self-reliance," "Books," "Society and Solitude," and "Considerations by the Way." His prose in his day overshadowed his poetry, and we do not know now which will abide the longer. The poetry, also, was full of high theories and Nature was prominent. There are many good lines and some holding ones.

Emerson had his ideal, and he knew that he fell short of it. Many think that his " Humble-Bee " is his most exquisite poem: —

> " Burly, dozing humble-bee!
>
> .   .   .   .   .
>
> Zigzag steerer, desert cheerer,
>
> .   .   .   .
>
> Yellow-breeched philosopher."

He shows patriotism in " The Volunteers "; his Nature sympathy in " The Woodnotes "; his religious outlook in " The Problem "; and his grief for his boy Waldo, who died at five, in " Threnody." And there are in his two volumes of poetry many rare gems of hopeful, uplifting thought. Indeed, he has sometimes been called " Optimist of Optimists."

Emerson is to-day read by the few, for the Anglo-Saxon mind seeks definiteness and his new reasoning is not fully interpreted. His work is a curious combination of common sense and mysticism. His views of the whence and the wherefore seem like those of the Orientals, nebulous and problematical. He is frequently styled " The Buddha of the West "— and he was likewise " A soaring nature ballasted with sense."

His son, Dr. Emerson, seldom presumed to ask a very serious question. He says: " I ventured to ask my father what he thought about immortality — and this was the answer: ' I think we may be sure that whatever may come after death, no one will be disappointed.' "

In 1847, Emerson visited Europe for the second time in a literary tour, and his lecture, " Representative Men," was a marked success, and this furnished material for a volume, in 1850.   He spent four days with Carlyle, and he describes his talk as " like a river, full and never ceasing."   Among others that he met were De Quincey, Macaulay, Thackeray, Tennyson, and George Eliot.   The latter rejoiced that in Emerson she beheld a man! He saw Paris in the throes of the Revolution of '48· He must have been held in high repute in England, for on his return, he was nominated to the Rectorship of Glasgow University, receiving five hundred votes against Lord Beaconsfield's seven hundred.

Coming back to America, he settled down again in his Concord home, and as the years rolled on, his character grew more and more tranquil.   He was interested in the schools and reading-room and belonged to the fire-brigade.   He advised the farmers and traders on philosophical subjects, and always observed the old-time road custom of salutation to passers-by.

Emerson had no skill in debate, but from principle attended political meetings.   He was in spirit an abolitionist but he ranked brotherhood above patriotism.   Concord, with both war and literary associations, had many " high days," and Emerson was constantly asked to speak at such celebrations.

One of the special town interests was a " Circle of Twenty-five," that met on Monday evenings, in his library; and here as one has said: " Emerson sought to bind all the wide-flying embroidery of discussion into a web of clear, good sense." " The Circle " still exists; and some of the older ones yet remember the day when it numbered among its members sublime Dr. Alcott, Ellery Channing, Thoreau, and Hawthorne who sat apart and and rarely spoke.

In 1872, Emerson's house caught fire and was nearly destroyed, and the family barely escaped with scant clothing; and now his admiring towns-people begged him to take his devoted daughter Ellen and go abroad until all should be restored; and they went, and this time sailed up the Nile. Concord prepared an ovation to greet the home-coming of its " Sage." The bells rang as the station was reached; men, women and children thronged to welcome him; he was taken into his perfectly renewed house, under a triumphal arch. " I am not wood or stone," he exclaimed, but he could say only a few words.

And now as Emerson grew older, his powers of memory began to fail. John Burroughs — our beloved poet-naturalist, in reminiscing of his own early days writes: —

" I was an ardent disciple of Emerson and I wrote subconsciously in Emersonian style. . .. The musk of

Emerson was on the garments of all of us young men who were writing at that time, and even now I sometimes get a whiff of it in my writings."

Burroughs met Emerson near the close of his life and said: "He could not speak to us for his mind was breaking down and he was losing his memory of men and faces. He sat there silent, with a wonderful look in his deep, far-seeing astral eyes."

Whittier took me up to introduce me. He did not remember me. Whittier said: "Thee knows him!" but when I started to ask Emerson about Thoreau, he seemed to understand, for he beckoned to a common friend to come and tell me about him.

Finally, on April twenty-seventh, 1882, "The Concord Sage," sank peacefully to rest, and he was buried near Hawthorne, in Sleepy Hollow Cemetery; and ever the pines which soothed him keep watch over his unhewn granite boulder on the hillside.

After his death, his son, Dr. Emerson, one of the citizens of whom Concord proudly boasts, gave Mr. Cabot the facts and incidents of his father's life, which he himself wrote for neighbours and near friends; and we have drawn our incidents from these memoirs and from a visit to the home of the great thinker. The library is just as he left it; his chair is in place and his pen and inkstand on the table;

HOME OF RALPH WALDO EMERSON, CONCORD, MASS.

Michael Angelo's "Three Fates" over the mantel; and on the shelves gift-books inscribed with the names of noted authors.

The whole house, mounted in its old mahogany furniture, with art treasures and pictures, is delightfully reminiscent. There are busts of Plato and Goethe, and certainly two pictures of special significance — one brought to Emerson from Europe by Margaret Fuller, and while she was shipwrecked it floated ashore, and was marked with his name. Another, Guido's "Aurora," was sent by Carlyle as a wedding present to Mrs. Emerson, and on the back we read in the donor's writing: —

"It is my wife's memorial to your wife. Two houses divided by wide seas are to understand always that they are united nevertheless. Will the lady of Concord hang up the Italian sun-chariot somewhere in her drawing-room, and looking at it, think sometimes of a household here which has good cause never to forget her?"

—*T. Carlyle.*

And after rambling over the house, one must not fail to look out upon the same pines and chestnuts, the old-fashioned garden, and the woods and river, whence came many inspirations.

At the Emerson "Centenary," in Concord, in 1903, William Lorenzo Eaton, superintendent of public schools, made an address before the pupils, in which he said: —

" Hitch your waggon to yonder star, and with him travel into unexplored depths of space; watch the birds in their flight and where they rest, and name them without a gun. . . .

" In the long winter evenings when mayhap the snow is swirling around your house, and shuts you from the outer world, take down your volume of Emerson, and in ' a tumultuous privacy of storm ' read and think, and think and read, until something coming to you out of that great spirit shall have moulded your lives to nobler thoughts and deeds."

SELECTIONS FROM EMERSON

" O tenderly the haughty day
Fills his blue urn with fire."
— *Concord Ode.*

" Hast thou named all the birds without a gun?
Loved the wood-rose and left it on its stalk?

.   .   .   .

O be my friend, and teach me to be thine."
— *Forbearance.*

" Life is too short to waste
In critic peep or cynic bark,
Quarrel or reprimand,
'Twill soon be dark."
— *Tact.*

" I thought the sparrow's note from heaven
Singing at dawn on the alder bough;
I brought him home, in his nest, at even;
He sings the song, but it pleases not now;

For I did not bring home the river and sky;
He sang to my ear — *they* sang to my eye."

      — *Each and All.*

" 'Twas one of the charméd days
 When the genius of God doth flow,
The wind may alter twenty ways,
 A tempest cannot blow;
It may blow north, it still is warm;
 Or south, it still is clear;
Or east, it smells like a clover farm;
 Or west, no thunder fear."

      — *Woodnotes.*

" The Mountain and the Squirrel
Had a quarrel,
And the former called the latter 'Little Prig!'
Bun replied,
'You are doubtless very big,
But all sorts of things and weather
Must be taken in together
To make up a year,
And a sphere;
And I think it no disgrace
To occupy my place;
If I'm not so large as you,
You are not so small as I,
And not half so spry;
I'll not deny you make
A very pretty squirrel track.
Talents differ; all is well and wisely put;
If I cannot carry forests on my back,
Neither can you crack a nut.' "

      — *Emerson.*

XXII

HENRY DAVID THOREAU (1817-1862)

ONE of the Concord group held fast to the town all through life, even spending his travel days in the woods, and on near-by streams. This was Henry David Thoreau, who was born here in 1817. The father of French descent was a small, deaf, unobtrusive man, who made lead-pencils, while the mother, daughter of a New England clergyman, was very dressy and very talkative.

Thoreau's delightful biographer, Frank Sanborn, tells of her such a characteristic story that we must insert it right here: One day when Mrs. Thoreau was seventy years old, she called upon Miss Mary Emerson, the austere aunt of " The Sage," who was then eighty-four. She wore a bonnet adorned with bright ribbons of goodly length. During the call Miss Emerson kept her eyes closed, and when her guest rose to leave, she said: " Perhaps you noticed, Mrs. Thoreau, that I kept my eyes closed during your call; I did so because I did not wish to look on the ribbons you are wearing, so unsuitable for a child of God and a person of your age! "

Such were the parents; while the boy Henry, from earliest childhood, displayed a stubborn will which made it difficult to direct him in " the way he should go." He was, however, fitted at the Concord Academy to enter Harvard, where he graduated in 1837. As a profession, he tried school-teaching but not with marked ability, but he lectured year after year in the " Concord Lyceum " course. He also worked at the lead-pencil craft; but when he had succeeded in producing the best kind of pencil, he refused to make another, for with other Transcendentalists, he held to the belief of never doing the same thing twice.

He was very skilful with tools, and had a good knowledge of mathematics, so he became both carpenter and surveyor; and did his work so well that the neighbours liked to employ him. His idea of thoroughness was — in driving a nail home — " to clench it so faithfully that you can wake up in the night and think of your work with satisfaction! " Although Thoreau was always poor, earning a livelihood never troubled him much — he wished just money enough to live.

His wealth was in the woods and on the streams, and he sought " a wide margin of leisure," in which to enjoy it. Sometimes he would spend weeks earning money to last for a certain period, and then he would stop and enter into his Nature study, until his funds were exhausted. He delighted in the sermons of his lay preacher, Emerson, for if any one ever believed in a gospel of individualism, it was Thoreau, and Emerson helped him in many ways.

He would often meet him on his walks, carrying under his arm a music-book to press plants, and in his pocket drawing-pencils, microscope, jack-knife, and twine.

From the day he graduated, to the end of his short life, Thoreau kept a journal, which was chiefly descriptive of his out-of-door observations. With his brother he studied the motion of fishes and the flight of birds, until the two were able to fashion a boat and rig it. This they loaded with potatoes and melons and started on a trip — a trip probably as important to Thoreau as that on the Nile to Sir Samuel Baker; for in 1849, he published a book about it, entitled " A Week on the Concord and Merrimac."

This has many picturesque descriptions, and includes reminiscences of Indian and pioneer life and of the Puritanical observance of the Sabbath. But alas! for the edition of a thousand volumes — over seven hundred were unsold, and Thoreau brought them home and laughingly told of the unexpected addition to his library. The book, however, is more valued to-day.

His " Walden," published several years later, gave him more immediate fame. This was the recountal of a two years' sojourn in the woods. This woodland belonged to Emerson; here it was that the philosopher often lingered with his muse who guided his facile pen through his " Woodnotes." In the cen-

THE THOREAU CAIRN AND THOREAU COVE, LAKE WALDEN

tre, in its setting of pines and oaks, nestles a clear little pond with a pebbly beach, and over it hovers an Indian legend whence it derives its name; for it is said that one day in the ages agone, the Indians were holding a wicked pow-wow on the hill just beyond, and there was so much swearing that the hill collapsed, and all the naughty tongues were swallowed up. But one good squaw — Walden — was saved, and Walden Woods and Walden Pond perpetuate her virtues.

Thoreau did not come as a hermit as many have asserted, but he wished to live deliberately and economically, and he had work to do that he could better accomplish alone with Nature. His friends aided him in raising a hut that was curtainless and lockless, and that held the simplest furniture. Here he consorted with his guests, many of them coming from curiosity, others like Emerson, Alcott and Curtis, to discuss weighty subjects.

Thoreau's expenses here amounted to twenty-seven cents a day. He called himself a " self-appointed inspector of snow-storms and rain-storms," and to the tenants of the forest and water, he became a kind of St. Francis. " He learned to sit so immovable upon a rock that the bird, reptile or fish that had retired, would return. Snakes coiled about his legs; fishes swam into his hand; foxes fled to him for protection from the hunter; and birds would hop upon his shoulder, even while he dug his little bean-patch."

He was like the man of whom " Quaint Old Thomas Fuller " writes : —

" Either he had told the bees things, or the bees had told him! "

Open " Walden " anywhere and you will find an interesting page. This one, for example: —

" Let us spend our day as deliberately as Nature, and not be thrown off the track by every nut-shell and mosquito-wing that falls on the rail. Let us rise early and fast or *break*-fast gently and without perturbation; let company come and let company go; let the bells ring and the children cry. Let us not be upset and overwhelmed in that terrible rapid and whirlpool called a dinner. Weather this danger and you are safe, for the rest of the way is down-hill."

And here is another extract in which he talks of the pickerel of Walden Pond as if they were fabulous fishes: —

" They are so foreign to the woods, foreign as Arabia to our Concord life. They possess a quite dazzling and transcendental beauty which separates them by a wide interval from the cadaverous cod and haddock, whose fame is impaled in our streets. They are not green like the pines, nor grey like the stones, nor blue like the sky; but they have, to my eyes, if possible, yet rarer colours, like flowers and precious stones. . . . They are Walden all over and all through; are themselves small Waldens, in the animal kingdom, Waldenses. It is surprising that they are caught here — that in this deep and capacious spring far beneath the rattling teams and chaises and tinkling sleighs that travel the Walden road this great gold and emerald fish swims. I never chanced to see its kind in any market; it would be the cynosure of all eyes there."

Thoreau stayed at the pond for two years, coquetting with Nature, alert to every sight and sound, and " Walden " for its clear and exact details has passed into a classic. It is not so introspective but more crisp and fuller of life than his " Week on the Concord and Merrimac." His " Church of Sunday-Walkers to Walden Pond " was most active in his time; and the pilgrimage still keeps on, and on the road one may meet travellers from all parts of the world, and each one adds a memorial stone to the cairn that stands on the site of the old hut.

The two books named were all that Thoreau published; but after his death, selections were made from his journal, so that now his works include nine or ten volumes. His " Maine Woods," " Cape Cod," and " A Yankee in Canada," are used as guide-books. There are many more Nature-lovers now than in his day, and in this enthusiasm which Thoreau so really aroused, his books hold their own niche in American literature.

Thoreau was not in any sense a misanthrope as one may find in visiting his Concord home. He was devoted to young people, and with his flute and bright anecdotes, he liked to make merry, and was easily the centre of any gathering. On the other hand, he revelled in solitude, and it must be granted that he *did* live a life of eccentricities and negations. He never ate much or drank wine, or used a trap or gun; he never went to church and never married; he had a contempt for elegant society, always avoiding inns, dwelling instead in the house of the farmer or fisherman, and yet his ancestry and belongings were those of refinement.

He would never pay his taxes, and spent certainly one night in prison, because — as he said — he would not give money to the collector to support slavery. His description of this night is amusing. He says: —

"I was put in jail just as I was going to the shoemaker to get a shoe which was mended. . . . I lay in bed and it seemed as if I had never heard the town-clock strike before nor the evening sounds of the village; for we slept with the windows open which were inside the grating. It was to see my native village in the light of the Middle Ages, and our Concord River was changed into a Rhine stream, and visions of knights and castles passed before me. When I was let out the next morning, I proceeded to finish my errand, and having put on my mended shoe, joined a huckleberry party, who were impatient to put themselves under my conduct!"

With all Thoreau's peculiarities, he was on the whole a vigorous and brave-hearted American. His life was a short one, for undue exposure ended in consumption and he died at forty-five, and was buried near Emerson in Sleepy Hollow Cemetery. A line of a prayer that he wrote may be suggestive of his religious feeling:—

"Whatever we leave to God, God blesses."

In the rooms of the "Antiquarian Society," in Concord, are preserved many articles which he used at Walden: the bed, rocking-chair and table; a dresser filled with dishes matched and unmatched, among them a Lowenstoft bowl; a desk, containing with other things his Bible, and copy of "Paradise Lost," a picture of John Brown, inscribed with "Farewell, God bless you," and his grandfather's Chinese spectacles.

But one gets very close to Thoreau, in the privilege of meeting his biographer, Frank Sanborn, who for two years dined with him almost daily, joining him on his walks and river voyages. Mr. Sanborn is one of the famous Concord coterie, who, apart from his literary biographies and his influence in establishing the "Concord School of Philosophy," is noted for the reckless zeal with which he threw himself into the anti-slavery crusade — even to the shielding of John Brown, and it is a rare pleasure to hear him converse familiarly on many subjects. 'He is Concord's twentieth century scholar.

And there is yet one other of whom we would

speak — through whose influence Thoreau's spirit will ever be kept alive — and this is our gentle " Naturalist-Philosopher," John Burroughs. He resembles Thoreau in his Nature-love and Nature-touch and Nature-vision, but he is not so eccentric. Dr. Mabie says: —

" Thoreau would have devoted more time to a wood-chuck than to Carlyle, Arnold, or Whitman, while Burroughs emphasises his indebtedness to the authors. His is a broader outlook, and we are thankful to-day to have a sunny, inspiring guide to " fresh fields " and " pastures new."

Truly with Robert Louis Stevenson we feel that

" To live close to Nature is to keep your soul alive."

XXIII

"He was makin' himsel' a' the time, but he dinna ken may be what he was about till years had passed." So said Shortreid of Sir Walter Scott, "Wizard of the North "— and so say we of our Nathaniel Hawthorne, "Wizard of New England."

Bold ancestors had our "Wizard": one of Revolutionary fame; another, a stern old judge, known for bitter denouncement of witches. His father, a sea-captain, lived in a small gambrel-roofed house which may still be seen in Salem, and here on July Fourth, 1804, Nathaniel was born, and he was only four years old when his father died in South America.

The beautiful mother, overcome with grief, literally withdrew herself from society for forty years, even taking her meals apart from her children, and as they caught her sad spirit, their childhood fell away from them. Nathaniel inherited from his mother a shyness and love of solitude that were only partially conquered long afterwards when he went abroad. Even as a boy, strange fancies haunted him and he invented odd stories.

His boyhood was varied by a sojourn of a year or

two with an uncle who owned a large tract of primeval forest, on the banks of Sebago Lake, Maine. Here —" free as a bird in the air "— he skated and swam and fished and devoured books, but this way of existence only increased his longing to be alone; and without conscious effort, the sensitive, earnest youth, was lured on by his muse into paths of weird, haunted lore. She interested him alike in studying the character of the sternest New England Puritan; in Shakespeare's dramas, and Bunyan's allegory; and she made Spenser's "Fairie Queene" so fascinating that with his first money he bought a copy and stored his mind with many fanciful visions. But it was long before these took definite form in his soul, and in the meantime, we glance at the practical years that intervened.

In 1821, Hawthorne entered Bowdoin College, and the very handsome, athletic youth, with his " tremulous sapphire eyes," won the admiration of his classmates. They nicknamed him " Oberon! " and an old gipsy, meeting him one day, asked: " Are you man or angel? " Longfellow, Franklin Pierce, and Horatio Bridge were members of the class, and all became life-long friends. Pierce and Bridge were always encouraging Hawthorne, and prophesying his future success.

He graduated in 1825, and went home to Salem and lived there for years, just like his mother, as a recluse, perhaps only venturing out after dark to walk on the lone sea-shore. But he was continually writing, and often burning what he wrote, for as he later said: "I waited a long time for the world to know me." But his grasp grew firmer, and short stories appeared in the serials by an anonymous author. In 1837, they were gathered into a slender volume called "Twice-Told Tales," because they had already been printed. The book was welcomed by the reading world; and Longfellow who now had won fame for his poems was among the first to honour Hawthorne, and even critical Poe foretold his future greatness.

About this time Bancroft, the historian, was collector at the port of Boston, and through his influence, Hawthorne was made weigher and gauger there, and we catch glimpses of our gentle dreamer, weighing coal and overhauling ships. But presently politics changed: he lost his position but had earned one thousand dollars which he was enabled to put into the Brook Farm enterprise.

The Brook Farm episode which comes next is associated with the romantic period of Hawthorne's career when he was in love — and like many another lover and many another literary man, he was led astray by the "isms" of his day. He lived for a year at Brook Farm, assisting much in the hard work, and very little in the conversations. Margaret Fuller then edited "The Dial" and flashed out in all her brilliancy; and Hawthorne milked a cow, and expounded on the fractious character of Margaret Fuller's transcendental heifer!

This gifted woman must have impressed him, for years later in his " Blithedale Romance "— which contains artistic and humorous accounts of Brook Farm happenings — he introduces " Zenobia," his most dramatic female character, and many think that it is a reproduction of the ardent prophetess. But she was not his true love — *that* was the delightful Sophia Peabody whom he married in 1842, and never did wife more gladden and enrich the life of husband. They took up their abode in the " Old Manse," at Concord, associated with ancestral Emersons and Ripleys.

Hawthorne describes it in his " Mosses " as a house that a priest had built, and other priests had lived in, and it was " awful to reflect how many sermons must have been written there "; but he added a hope that " wisdom would descend " upon him — and it *did* as we shall see. He took for his study the room in which Emerson had written " Nature," and for three years filled it with gleaming visions of fancy and allegory — and what were some of the " Mosses " that were rooted here? Among them are the unresting " Old Apple-Dealer," " Rappaccini's Daughter," " Birds and Bird Voices," and numerous " Sketches from Memory." Perhaps the most assertive " Moss " is " The Town-Pump," " that all day long at the busiest corner poured forth

OLD MANSE, CONCORD, MASS.

alike a stream of eloquence and a stream of water."
It held stoutly to the fact that it was " Town Treasurer," " Overseer of the Poor," " Head of the Fire
Department," and " Cup-Bearer to the Parched Pop-
ulation," always discharging its duties " in a cool,
steady, upright, downright " way.

But charming beyond all was the " Old Manse "
itself which Hawthorne literally wrote into renown;
the " Mosses " grew year by year, until there were
enough to gather into a book. Many visited the
house, and Mrs. Hawthorne was a gracious hostess
— and allowed her husband to maintain his usual
aloofness. The river was just back of the sloping
meadow. Thoreau had sold Hawthorne a boat and
taught him to paddle, so it was easy to escape —
specially if he saw Dr. Alcott approaching to advocate Transcendentalism, which Hawthorne detested.
Emerson sometimes broke in upon his musings, and
when Franklin Pierce came, the whole town was invited to meet him.

Mrs. Julia Ward Howe writes playfully of her
first visit. Mrs. Hawthorne received her most
charmingly, promising that she should know her
husband. Presently a figure descended the stairs.
" My Husband," cried Mrs. Hawthorne, " here
are Dr. and Mrs. Howe! " What they did see, was
a broad hat, pulled down over a hidden face, and a
figure that quickly vanished through an opposite door,
and Mrs. Hawthorne made some excuse about an

appointment which called her husband to go up the river with Thoreau. And Mrs. Howe adds naïvely: "So the first time I *saw* Hawthorne — I did *not* see him!" Many like pleasing reminiscences — from the attic "Saints' Room" to the peaceful river — are recalled as we are permitted to enter this old romantic "Manse."

But in Hawthorne's day, literature was too poorly paid to support a family; and in 1845, through the kindness of friends, he was appointed surveyor at the custom-house, in Salem — a town that from earliest boyhood had made upon him a curious impression. Here he was interviewed by all manner of folk on all manner of subjects, and he noted down scenes and characters for future use. Custom-house doings would have seemed prosaic to most men, but unceasingly "a romance was growling" in Hawthorne's brain; and when after four years, he lost his office, owing to political changes, he took from the drawer a half-finished manuscript. His wife was rejoiced — she had saved money for household expenses, and he should *write!*

Now he spent a winter upon his first long work, "The Scarlet Letter" — a tale of sin and penalty — the theme taken from a letter embroidered upon a mantle. He brooded over it and shaped the moral, and so felt its pathos that he grew thinner and thinner, and "a knot of sorrow appeared in his forehead." He became so oblivious to his surroundings that his wife one day found in her basket a piece of work cut up into bits. Indeed, he had a habit of whittling off his table and the arms of his chair as he wrote.

When the story was finished, Hawthorne read it to his wife, until she was overcome and pressed her hands to her ears — for she could listen no longer. So he knew that it must have force, and he sent it to his optimistic friend, James T. Fields, the publisher, who sat up all night to read it through, and then, in 1880, it belonged to the public. It tells of only four lives, but it presents so really the manners and morals of an earlier period, that it will ever be an artistic and powerful masterpiece of Puritan literature.

To-day, in Salem, we may visit the tall, grim house haunted with secrets, where lived Hester Prynne and little Pearl. The introductory chapter to " The Scarlet Letter," which is exceedingly humourous, relieves the sombre tale which did offend for a while the good people of Salem, who thought that they recognised in it sketches of old officials; indeed they neither knew nor wished to know the morbid author who spent his days in writing stories and his nights in burning them. But now Salem speaks the name of Hawthorne with reverence; and with the aid of Rudyard Kipling, the town is attempting to raise fifty thousand dollars for his monument.

The financial gains from " The Scarlet Letter "

were so great that Mrs. Hawthorne wrote to a friend as follows: "Will you ask father to go to Earle's and order for Mr. Hawthorne a suit of clothes; the coat to be of broadcloth of six or seven dollars a yard; the pantaloons of Kerseymere or broadcloth to correspond; and the rest of satin — all to be black."

And now, not long afterwards, there came yet another family move — this time to what Hawthorne called "The ugliest little farmhouse in the Lenox woods." His friends, however, thought it the cosiest kind of home. Among his writings here was the "Wonder-Book for Children." He loved children and entered into their every caprice — and his daughter says "there never was such a playmate"— and he was constantly telling stories. Years before, his "Grandfather's Chair" had introduced them to historical New England, even from the landing of the *Mayflower;* and now the "Wonder-Book" and "Tanglewood Tales" laid open such marvellous legends of old romance which go right to the heart of a child; and in their mythical and moral setting — these books are among the loveliest of young people's classics.

Perhaps one of these most typical stories is the "Snow Image," which tells of the statue fashioned by two children. Then Jack Frost and the West Wind endowed it with life, and it became a little snow-sister, and a source of every-day happiness. But the practical father disenchanted the children, and destroyed their ideal — leaving only the moral!

While in the Lenox woods, Hawthorne wrote his " House of the Seven Gables "— which portrays the fulfilment of a curse upon the distant descendants of a wrong-doer. In this house in Salem, dwelt stern, Puritanical Hepzibah Pyncheon and her brother Clifford, and Phœbe is the ray of sunshine that brings custom to the cent-shop. In the book, again four Puritan characters are drawn with the realism of a tiny Dutch picture, and while planning it, Hawthorne wrote one day: —

" My house of the seven gables is so to speak finished; only I am hammering away a little on the roof and doing up a few jobs that were left incomplete."

The plot was less gloomy than that of " The Scarlet Letter," and like that was quickly successful.

And now, in 1852, Hawthorne returned to Concord, and bought one of Dr. Alcott's old homes. He christened it " The Wayside," for he said that he was pausing " by the wayside of life." But he was hardly settled, before his college friend, Franklin Pierce, now President of the United States, appointed him consul to Liverpool; and in 1853, he went with his family abroad, and was gone for seven years. During the first four, in the consulate, he became familiar with English life; then resigning his position, he travelled on the Continent, and lingered sufficiently long in Rome and Florence to gather materials for his " Marble Faun." Italy fascinated him, and Rome drew itself into his heart " as even little Concord or sleepy old Salem never did." It was curious but it seemed strangely homelike. In the Palazzo Barberini, the favourite meeting-place of Americans, he came in touch with foreigners and countrymen. He dined with T. B. Read, met Gibson and Story, walked with Motley, found in Mrs. Jameson a sensible old lady, took tea with Frederica Bremer, " the funniest little old lady," and later on in Florence greatly enjoyed the Brownings.

Among works of art, he found special beauty in Praxiteles's " Marble Faun," with which he somehow associated all kinds of fun and pathos; and he saw a young man that to his mind resembled it, and from the two, he evolved the title of his romance. And he determined to bring in Torro del Simio, with its legend of light ever burning at the " Virgin's Shrine," and another romance began to shape itself, and he commenced to work it out in Rome, and continued it in the Florentine villa where he later sojourned. That had a moss-grown, tradition-haunted tower, just the thing to clap into the project, and once more four characters stand out— but against a Roman background.

These are Kenyon, the sculptor, Donatello, " the Faun," Miriam the artist, and Hilda, the Puritan maid, who copied masterpieces and tended the Virgin's lamp in the tower. The romance conceived in Italy was ended in England. "The Marble Faun" is shadowy and mysterious. Possibly its fame rests rather on its being such an excellent guide-book for Rome rather than on the thread of story running through it.

After seven years' absence, we find Hawthorne at "The Wayside," and here he spent the last four years of his life. On his arrival, Emerson tendered him a reception, and all were surprised at the ease and grace of manner acquired by social intercourse in Europe. He enlarged the house, adding among other conveniences a tower to which he might readily retreat. He planted trees, arranged woodland walks, and was much disappointed that he could not make the place resemble an English park. His favourite resort was the hillside back of the house, where for hours he would pace back and forth, listening to the music of the pines, and thinking thoughts; then he would hurry up to the turret-room and note them down, or sometimes climb up many steps to write in his rural bower. Here he converted his "English Notes" into "Our Old Home," one of his most interesting works, descriptive of his consular life.

Here, too, he outlined and began to write his "Dolliver Romance," which he had promised "The Atlantic Monthly." He did not live to complete it. He "let fall the pen and left the tale half-told."

He enjoyed the gatherings of " The Circle," held as we have said on Monday evenings, at Emerson's. His evenings at home were always delightful. The family assembled about the astral lamp — Mrs. Hawthorne with her work — and the young people eager-eyed — while the father read aloud. He made the world of Nature and of life beautiful to them. Rose once said: " The presence of my father filled my heart "; and Julian told of the home when he became his father's intimate biographer.

One thing, however, sorely distressed the great romancer, and this was the national storm that gathered, and in 1861, burst into Civil War. Then almost abruptly his health gave way; he took short trips with his son to Boston and Washington or to some near-by seaside resort, but he did not grow better; and finally he was persuaded to go on another journey with his old friend, Ex-President Pierce, and he died suddenly, at Plymouth, New Hampshire, on May eighteenth, 1864.

Upon his coffin was placed his " tale half-told," and a wreath of apple-blossoms from the " Manse." In the procession that followed him to his burial were Emerson, Longfellow, Lowell, Agassiz, Whipple, Dr. Alcott, and Fields, and his best-loved Channing and Pierce; and James Freeman Clarke said over his remains the last sad service, and he was laid

THE WAYSIDE: HOME OF NATHANIEL HAWTHORNE, CONCORD, MASS.

to rest in Sleepy Hollow Cemetery, near " the hill-top hearsed with pines."

Hawthorne was a man of deep and reverent religious faith. He loved his Bible, and wished that it were published in small volumes that he might carry it in his pocket. Possessed of unusual magnetism, he was so reserved that he was understood by few — literally a *gentle*-man. Emerson discovered in him a strongly feminine element. He was devoted to his family, his intimate friends, flowers and pets, and was seldom at ease in a social function for he lived in a magical region all his own. Emerson, in his tribute, says: " He rode so well his horse of the night," and Stedman begins his poem on Hawthorne with the following lines: —

" Two natures in him strove
Like day with night, his sunshine and his gloom."

With unique creative art, he pictured to the world as no other has done the New England Puritan conscience — he revealed souls rather than faces — and he gave it a symbolic setting; and Moncure Conway says that " unlike many others, Hawthorne wrote himself out."

To-day, Mrs. Lothrop, the widow of the publisher, owns " The Wayside." We know her better as " Margaret Sidney," the author, who, with lively imagination and rare story-telling gift, has brought into being " The Five Little Peppers." It is such a pleasure to hear her tell how these little " Peppers," in thought, came to stay with her and follow her everywhere — until at last she could not help setting down some of their doings. She sent the manuscript to " Wide Awake "; the children called for more; and as the " Peppers " grew up, their most original words and deeds filled eleven volumes of stories.

Mrs. Lothrop, with tact and exquisite taste, has preserved Hawthorne's home as nearly as possible as it was in his day. There is the same dining-room where " the sunshine comes in warmly and brightly thro' the better half of a winter's day "; Hawthorne's bedroom; the table upon which he and his wife revised manuscripts; the tower-study with its remarkable pictorial illustrations, and the standing-desk where he wrote; and back of the house the pine-clad slope which Mrs. Hawthorne named his " Mount of Vision." The " School of Philosophy " is near, with closed doors.

Here it was, at " The Wayside," that Mrs. Lothrop planned a Hawthorne " Centenary "; and on July fourth, fifth and sixth, 1904, many eminent men and women gathered in this building to honour the memory of Nathaniel Hawthorne. Here on the hillside Beatrice Hawthorne, granddaughter of " The Wizard of New England," unveiled a bronze tablet, set in a rough boulder, on which is inscribed: —

NATHANIEL HAWTHORNE (1804–1864)

"This tablet placed
At the centennial exercises
July 4, 1904
Commemorates
Nathaniel Hawthorne
He trod daily this path to the hill
To formulate
As he paced to and fro
Upon its summit
His marvellous romances."

And was there ever such another town as Concord! For apart from those of whom we have spoken, it cherishes memories of Webster and Kossuth and Agassiz and Lafayette and Harriet Hosmer; yes — and of many more who came either "to drink in wisdom" at its "School of Philosophy," or to bask in the presence of its sages. Then Concord has its battle-ground and monuments and inscribed tablets; its literary homes; its library, with one alcove given to its own authors; and its Sleepy Hollow Cemetery —"voiceless yet eloquent with great names."

XXIV

IN a great square house in Portland, " City by the Sea," on February twenty-seventh, 1807, Henry W. Longfellow was born. It was a quiet, well-ordered home, with a winsome mother, devoted to art, music, and poetry — the father, a leading lawyer and member of Congress. From the former, the boy inherited a love for those things that made him as a man, the most popular poet in America; from the latter, genuine courtesy, and clear, practical habits of thought and action. And there was for him, also, another source of wealth: the perpetual fascination of the rock-girt bay, with sunrise and moonlight playing over it — the sleet and storm and fog-bell — the beacon-light, and the sunny isles — all these very early inspired him with

> " The beauty and the mystery of ships,
> And the magic of the sea."

Henry was a *most* youthful prodigy. He attended a dame's school at three; was half through his Latin grammar at seven; was delighted with Irving's " Sketch-Book " at 'twelve; and at thirteen, slipped his first poem, " The Battle of Lovell's

Pond," into the letter-box of " The Portland Gazette." Two or three times he peeked into the window to see the printers at work upon the paper; and his joy was equal to that of Whittier's, on a similar occasion, when he saw his verses in print. Long years later, he said: " I don't think any other literary success in my life has made me quite so happy."

At fourteen, Longfellow entered Hawthorne's class at Bowdoin College; and his studious and genial nature made him friends among both professors and students. He had already determined to be eminent in *something*, and it was during his four years here that he more and more eagerly aspired to a literary career. The prudent father looked coldly on such a project, for literature would never give his son support. So the latter finally decided on law for his " real existence," while literature should be his " ideal one."

However, good fortune waited on him, for it appears that Madame Bowdoin had left one thousand dollars in her will, to establish in the college a chair of modern languages. The faculty appreciated Longfellow's scholarly way and the ease with which he mastered a foreign tongue, and they knew his great desire. So young as he was, he was offered the professorship, if he would first go abroad and qualify for it, and he sailed away and was gone three years. He worked very hard and returned a master in French, Spanish, Italian, and German; and in

1829, when but twenty-two years old, entered upon his college duties. He prepared his own text-books, kept well abreast of his pupils, and filled them with enthusiasm for their work.

In 1831, he married "a beauteous being," Miss Mary Potter. Two years later, he published "Outre-Mer," a collection of sketches, describing his life abroad. They resemble Irving's, though written in a lighter, more graceful vein. And Longfellow's reputation was so assured at Bowdoin, that after six years of service, he was called to a greater honour — no less than to succeed George Ticknor, in the chair of modern languages at Harvard — and again he went abroad to equip himself — this time in Germany, Scandinavia, Denmark, and Holland. A great sorrow came to him while in Rotterdam, and this was the death of his "beauteous being."

But he spent three years in very earnest preparation, and so was enabled, in 1836, to assume his professorship at Cambridge. Modern languages, with the wealth of modern literature which they unlock, was a comparatively new subject to the students, who before had been content with ancient classics; and Longfellow was rapidly popular as a lecturer, because he brought to them such rich treasures in art and song and tradition. He really created a new atmosphere of modern culture, and now he had time to write.

In 1839, "Hyperion" came out, so entitled be-

HENRY WADSWORTH
LONGFELLOW

JAMES RUSSELL LOWELL

OLIVER WENDELL HOLMES

JOHN GREENLEAF WHITTIER

cause it moved *on high,* among the clouds and stars. This is the story of Paul Fleming, a young, poetic pilgrim, who buries himself in books in order to get in touch with German life, and at the same time, falls in love with Mary Ashburton. It is couched in choicest language, holds bits of philosophy, history, and Alpine scenery — and it is so full of legends of castled Rhenish towers that it may serve as a guide-book. The final tribute is made to Goethe, who had just died. It is needless to add that Paul Fleming is Longfellow himself, and Mary Ashburton, the Frances Appleton whom he met abroad and later married.

With " Hyperion," we dismiss Longfellow's prose works which were but three; the others being " Outre-Mer," of which we have already spoken, and " Kavanagh," a story of New England life.

But his poems gave him wider fame, and they are so various that it is hard to know upon which to pause. In 1839, appeared his " Voices of the Night "; among them " The Reaper and the Flowers," " The Footsteps of Angels," and " The Psalm of Life." For the last, written on the back of an old invitation, he had been promised, on its first publication, five dollars; he never received a cent, but perhaps later on he realised what it did for the world!

" The Voices " was followed by a collection called " Ballads and Other Poems." In this were two ballads that in strength, simplicity, rapid movement, and picturesqueness, rivalled those of the mediæval day. In the first, " The Skeleton in Armour," the skeleton tells how he as " a Viking bold " had won the daughter of a Norwegian king; and how, his suit being denied, he had borne away his prize " through the wild hurricane." " The Wreck of the Hesperus," picturing a disaster off the Gloucester coast, came to the poet at midnight, in stanzas; and the two fully established his ability as a story-teller in verse. In the same collection, we trace upward the youthful yearnings of " Excelsior." Here, too, is " The Village Blacksmith " which he called his *second* " Psalm of Life," and it took a very human pen to give such a subject poetic setting.

In 1842, he made a short trip abroad for his health, visited Belgium, and climbing up into the belfry of Bruges, found a suggestion for a poem. The boisterous return voyage lasted fifteen days, and during sleepless nights, he meditated over seven anti-slavery poems, which in the mornings were written out. They were full of earnest feeling, but not passionate like Whittier's.

Shortly after, he married Miss Appleton, the sister of Motley's friend, and soon another volume of poems was announced, its opening one being " The Belfry of Bruges." In this volume is the bit of optimism, " The Arrow and the Song," which he wrote one morning before church, with the speed of an arrow. In this, too, we listen to " The Old Clock on the Stairs," which still holds its own at Elm Knoll, near Pittsfield; and here, in 1912, it ticked out to Miss Alice Longfellow the same refrain: —

" Forever — never!
Never — forever! "

that it gave to her father, in 1845, when on his wedding-tour, he and his bride paused in that mansion of " Free-hearted Hospitality."

Like his swallow-flights of song, his longer poems were greeted, and none more heartily than " Evangeline "— the flower of American idyls. The story is founded on a tradition previously proposed to Hawthorne; and Longfellow liked it and begged him, if he had decided not to use it for a story, to give it to him for a legendary poem. Hawthorne willingly consented, and later highly praised Longfellow's version.

The story is of two Acadian lovers, who, in the War of 1755, were parted on their marriage morn; and we follow the saintly maiden, Evangeline, in her weary quest for her lost Gabriel. It tells of unrest, hope deferred, and a death-bed meeting; but it is woven in flowing hexameter lines and we catch pleasing glimpses of Acadia, the moonlight forest, picturesque trappers, the river bank and ocean shore; and we hear the exquisite song of the mocking-bird, wildest of singers. Indeed, Longfellow cast over the region such a halo of romance that it is known as " Evangeline's Land "— and " on the shores of the Basin of Minas " maidens still " by the evening fire repeat Evangeline's story." Years later, when Longfellow was graciously received by Queen Victoria, the servants stood in the hall to see him as he passed, because they had heard Prince Albert read " Evangeline " to the royal children.

It was not long after " Evangeline " made its appearance before Longfellow announced yet " another stone rolled off the hilltop." This was the collection called " By the Seaside and by the Fireside "; and in this we read " The Building of the Ship," one of our finest national poems, closing with its magnificent apostrophe to the Union; and then, in 1854, he resigned his Cambridge professorship to Lowell, for he wished to devote the rest of his life to society and his " ideal world of poetry."

In about a year, we are introduced to the Indian epic, " Hiawatha." Longfellow had meditated much upon this aboriginal race; Cooper had given it a romantic setting; Parkman, a historical one; and he desired to treat it poetically; and " Hiawatha,' in ringing metre, is a unique addition to our native literature. It forms a series of legends of the uncut forests, war, and hunting-scenes, figures strange and beautiful, and savage beasts that play their part.

We may hear the whir of the partridge and most

alluring of bird-notes. We watch the youthful Hiawatha as he learns of " every bird its language ";
we follow him on his quest to the wigwam where

> " Sat the ancient arrow-maker
> In the land of the Dakotas,
> Making arrow-heads of jasper."

We find him wooing the lovely daughter, Minnehaha, and then they depart, leaving

> ". . . the old man standing lonely
> At the doorway of his wigwam,"

and hear the Falls of Minnehaha

> " Calling to them from the distance,
> Crying to them from afar off,
> ' Fare thee well, O Minnehaha!' "

and we trace through dreadful famine and Minnehaha's death, the slender thread of the story, following the noble Hiawatha as he journeys onward to

> " The land of the Hereafter."

And next Longfellow— the poet of the Indian —
becomes in " The Courtship of Miles Standish," the
poet of the Puritan. Now we are in old Plymouth,
with its graves on the hill, its meeting-house, Puritan
homes, and busy spinning-wheels. Here are the bluff

Captain, a better fighter than lover, loyal John Alden, and the damsel Priscilla : —

> " Beautiful with her beauty,
>   And rich with the wealth of her being."

And one must read the poem to appreciate the quizzing, pivotal question : —

> " Why don't you speak for yourself, John? "

In " The Tales of a Wayside Inn," the scene is laid in a hostelry, at Sudbury, Massachusetts,—

> " Built in the old colonial day
>   When men lived in a grander way
>   With ampler hospitality."

Here, in imagination, there assembled, from time to time, about the blazing hearth, a coterie of merry guests, among them Ole Bull, Professor Tredwell, Luigi Monti, and the poet himself; and each told a story —" well or ill "— after the manner of the " Decameron," or " Canterbury Tales "; and for these " Tales " Longfellow drew upon his knowledge of old legends. Here in one we may wake to " the midnight message of Paul Revere "— in another, the melodious chant in " King Robert of Sicily."

Few poets dare attempt such lengthy poems as " Evangeline," " Hiawatha," " The Courtship of Miles Standish," and " The Tales of a Wayside

Inn "— but each fills an honoured niche in American literature; and Longfellow **has** also **w**ritten many sonnets.

We next open to some of his poems of place that came from his great " Library of Poetry and Song," the treasure-house that he translated from the Old World to the New. As a romancer, he loved to wander far, and to return laden with word-pictures to gladden those at home. There **are** many

> " Old legends of the monkish pages,
> Traditions of the saint and sages,
> Tales that have the rime of ages,
> And chronicles of eld,"

and it is a confusion of riches, from which to select.

We grow drowsy over the English " Curfew " as it tolls forth : —

> " Cover the embers,
>   And put out the light;
> Toil comes with the morning
>   And rest with the night.
>
> .   .   .   .   .
>
> Song sinks into silence,
>   The story is told,
> The windows are darkened,
>   The hearth-stone is cold.
>
> Darker and darker
>   The black shadows fall;
> Sleep and oblivion
>   Reign over all."

Again, in Bruges, we hear the bells: —

> "Low at times and loud at times,
> And changing like a poet's rhymes,
> Rang the beautiful wild chimes
> From the Belfry in the market
> Of the ancient town of Bruges."

At Wartburg, he recalls the tale of Walter Von der Vogelweid, the Minnesinger, and his bequest to the birds. We may not tell "Where repose the poet's bones,"—

> "But around the vast cathedral,
> By sweet echoes multiplied,
> Still the birds repeat the legend,
> And the name of Vogelweid."

At Nuremberg,—

> "Quaint old town of toil and traffic,
> Quaint old town of art and song,"

he "sang in thought his careless lay," and gathered from memories of Albrecht Dürer, "the Evangelist of Art," and Hans Sach, the "cobbler-bard,"—

> "The nobility of labour,— the long pedigree of toil."

Longfellow says somewhere in speaking of his travel: —

"In fancy I can hear again
   The Alpine torrent roar,
The mule bells on the hills of Spain,
   The Sea at Elsinore.

I see the convent's gleaming walls
   Rise from its grove of pine,
And towers of old Cathedral tall,
   And castles by the Rhine."

So in his poems he voiced various aspirations, both native and foreign; but as we study into his life, we find his spirit more and more dominated by his " Christus." It was a theme upon which he pondered many years, for it was in 1841, that he wrote in his diary: " This evening it has come into my mind to undertake a long and elaborate poem by the name of ' Christ,' " and thirty-two years later, in 1863, the poem was finished. It is a trilogy — embodying the apostolic, the mediæval, and the Puritan conception of the Christ. The mediæval, " The Golden Legend," came out first, in 1851. This enters very intimately into the temper of the monk in the age when the land was " white with convent-walls "; when

"Men climb the consecrated stair
   With weary feet and bleeding hearts;
And leave the world and its delights,
   Its passions, struggles and despair,
For contemplation and for prayer
   In cloister cells of cenobites."

This was followed, in 1868, by the " New England Tragedies," in which from a study of old colonial authors, he illustrated his theme with the persecution of Quakers and witches. We remember how Leonardo da Vinci, in his " Last Supper," painted the head of Christ last — so Longfellow left his " Christus " for his final conception, though it came first in order. " The Christus " was published in 1863; and at the conclusion of all, he writes: —

> " My work is finished; I am strong
> In faith and hope and charity;
> For I have written the things I see,
> The things that have been and shall be,
> Conscious of right, nor fearing wrong;
> Because I am in love with love . . .
> . . . And love is life."

Was it after reading " The Christus " that one has beautifully named Longfellow " The St. John of our American Apostles "?

During all these years, Longfellow dwelt in the old " Cragle House," with his wife, and his children: —

> ¯" Grave Alice and laughing Allegra,
> And Edith with golden hair."

The library kept by his daughter as in the olden day is lined with pictures and antique book-cases. Upon the standing-desk, in the window where he used to write, is his statuette of Goethe. Upon the round

CRAIGIE HOUSE: HOME OF HENRY W. LONGFELLOW, CAMBRIDGE, MASS.

table, in the centre, are the inkstands of Coleridge and Tom Moore and his own quill-pen.

There, too, is his deep armchair where he so often mused before he wrote; and another chair, made from the wood of " The Spreading Chestnut Tree." This was presented to him on his seventy-second birthday by the Cambridge children. The library is rich in happy reminiscences. Here often came the poet's lifelong friends — among them Felton, Whittier, Lowell, Hawthorne, Agassiz, Holmes, and Bayard Taylor.

Specially in later life, the " rosy-cheeked patriarch " grew to be a familiar figure in Cambridge; and he tried to be kind to relic-hunters and even to autograph-seekers. One day an Englishman introduced himself with this remark: " In other countries, you know, we go to see ruins and the like; but you have no ruins in your country, and I thought — I thought — I'd call and see you! " Once he had a request, asking him to copy his poem, " Break, break, break," for the writer; again a stranger called to inquire if Shakespeare lived in the neighbourhood, and he replied that he knew " no such person."

But he enjoyed, also, a far pleasanter kind of popularity, as when Professor Kneeland, returning from Iceland, bore back the following message: " Tell Longfellow that we love him, that Iceland knows him by heart! " And a workman in the streets of London stopped him to ask " to shake hands with the man who made the ' Psalm of Life ' "; and an Englishman once wrote of him as " The bard whose sweet songs have more than aught else bound two worlds together "; and George William Curtis tells us that Longfellow is so popular because he expresses his sentiment in such a simple, melodious manner.

In July, 1861, Longfellow's wife was burned to death before the eyes of her family; and in his sudden distress at the shock, he sought refuge in making a translation of " Dante."   He studied it line by line, and has preserved both form and spirit of the " Divine Comedy."

In 1868, once more he went to Europe, with his daughter; visited Tennyson in the Isle of Wight; received degrees from Oxford and Cambridge; and passed the winter in Rome.   England lavished attention upon our poet, and his bust stands to-day in Westminster Abbey.

His lines, written in the after-glow of his life, increased in depth and fullness, and this is evinced in his " Morituri Salutamus," which he read on the fiftieth anniversary of his graduation from Bowdoin College, before the remaining members of his class, and Professor Packard, the one surviving instructor. It opens as follows: —

> " ' O Cæsar, we who are about to die
> Salute you!' was the gladiator's cry

In the arena, standing face to face
With death and with the Roman populace,"

and on March twenty-fourth, 1882, the bells of Cambridge tolled out, in seventy-five strokes, the death-knell of Henry Wadsworth Longfellow.

At his public funeral service, his brother, Rev. Samuel Longfellow, read the accompanying lines from " Hiawatha ": —

"He is dead, the sweet musician!
He the sweetest of all singers!
He has gone from us forever,
He has moved a little nearer
To the Master of all music,
To the Master of all singing!"

and his remains were laid in Mt. Auburn Cemetery, and there went up a cry of personal loss both at home and abroad; above all, from the children, who were so dear to him. They claimed him as their *own* — for they loved his wonderful songs and marvellous tales. They could understand his meaning. Schools all over the land reverently draped their halls in memory, and some yet observe Longfellow's birthday, February twenty-seventh.

And the common people mourned; for to them he had taught optimism and aspiration. This we may realise as we bring to mind some of his helpful tenets : —

"But to act that each to-morrow
Finds us farther than to-day."

"Know how sublime a thing it is,
To suffer and be strong."

"Lives of great men all remind us,
We can make our lives sublime,
And departing, leave behind us,
Footprints on the sands of time."

"The heights by great men reached and kept,
Were not attained by sudden flight;
But they, while their companions slept,
Were toiling upward in the night."

Longfellow had his critics — and who has not? Poe thought his poems didactic rather than beautiful; others, that they were too diffuse or imitative, and using too much freedom with dates and facts of history. But his was truly, as Stedman says, "The gospel of good-will set to music." He had a song to sing to humanity, and he sang it!

His fellow-authors grieved for him and talked about him to one another. Lowell writes: —

"His nature was consecrated ground, into which no unclean spirit could ever enter";

and Professor Norton: —

"The sweetness, the gentleness, the grace, the purity, the humanity of his verse were as the image of his own soul."

And Stedman says further: —

HENRY WADSWORTH LONGFELLOW

"I see him, a silver-haired minstrel, touching melodious keys, playing and singing in the twilight within sound of the note of the sea. There he lingers late, the curfew-bell has tolled and the darkness closes round, till at last that tender voice is silent, and he softly moves into his rest."

And Richardson adds one final word: —

"His song shall last until another shall sing the same song better."

SONNET ON CHAUCER

"An old man in a lodge within a park;
 The chamber walls depicted all around
With portraitures of huntsman, hawk, and hound,
 And the hurt deer. He listeneth to the lark,
Whose song comes with the sunshine through the dark
 Of painted glass in leaden lattice bound;
He listeneth and he laugheth at the sound,
 Then writeth in a book like any clerk,
He is the Poet of the Dawn, who wrote
 The Canterbury Tales, and his old age
 Made beautiful with song; and as I read
I hear the crowing cock, I hear the note
 Of lark and linnet, and from every page
 Rise odours of ploughed field or flowery mead."
— *Longfellow.*

THE ARROW AND THE SONG

"I shot an arrow into the air,
 It fell to earth, I knew not where;
 For, so swiftly it flew, the sight
 Could not follow it in its flight.

I breathed a song into the air,
It fell to earth, I knew not where;
For who has sight so keen and strong,
That it can follow the flight of song?

Long, long afterward, in an oak
I found the arrow, still unbroke;
And the song, from beginning to end,
I found again in the heart of a friend."
                                    — *Longfellow.*

SERENADE — FROM " THE SPANISH STUDENT "

" Stars of the summer night!
    Far in yon azure deeps,
  Hide, hide your golden light!
    She sleeps!
  My lady sleeps!
    Sleeps!

  Moon of the summer night!
    Far down yon western steeps,
  Sink, sink in silver light!
    She sleeps!
  My lady sleeps!
    Sleeps!

  Dream of the summer night!
    Where yonder woodbine creeps,
  Fold, fold thy pinions light!
    She sleeps!
  My lady sleeps!
    Sleeps!

HENRY WADSWORTH LONGFELLOW

Wind of the summer night!
   Tell her, her lover keeps
Watch! while in slumbers light
   She sleeps!
My lady sleeps!
   Sleeps! "

                — *Longfellow.*

XXV

James Russell Lowell (1819-1891)

THERE stands to-day, in Cambridge, an ancestral colonial mansion called " Elmwood," because the roadway to its entrance was originally arched by noble elms. Here, on February twenty-second, 1819, James Russell Lowell was born; here he always lived; and here he died on August twelfth, 1891. He belonged to a distinguished family. An uncle introduced cotton-spinning into a neighbouring town, and the busy, populous city is christened Lowell, in his honour. Another relative made a will at the Temple of Luxor, in Egypt, in which he left an educational endowment, that brought into being Lowell Institute in Boston; and James Russell — poet, critic, professor, lecturer, editor, essayist, diplomat and speaker on occasion — bravely upheld the family name. He was the son of a " learned, saintly, and discreet Unitarian minister of Boston." His versatile, poetic mother of Scotch descent, early taught her children to love the ballads of the " North Countrie," and to her, " the patron of his youthful muse," he dedicated his first effusion.

The lad, after the fashion of the day, attended a dame's school, and he later reminisced over it as follows : —

JAMES RUSSELL LOWELL (1819–1891)

> " Propped on the marsh, a dwelling now I see
> The humble school-house of my A, B, C,
> Where well-drilled urchins, each behind his tire,
> Waited in ranks the wicked command to fire;
> Then all together, when the signal came,
> Discharged their *a-b abs* against the dame."

James was a quiet lad, devoted to reading, and in due time, following the family tradition, he entered Harvard. Here he read everything he liked, instead of ordained text-books; and for this he was rusticated to Concord, where he studied under Dr. Ripley, and he enjoyed meeting there a galaxy of authors much better than the definite work arranged for him in college. His fellow-students, at Cambridge, who had read his verses, thought him inspired with divine fire, and they flattered him by appointing him class-poet; and his father, hearing this, sadly exclaimed: " Oh, dear, James promised me that he would quit writing poetry and go to work!" One poem was a satire on Transcendentalism, to which, after his marriage, he became a devotee.

In 1838, upon receiving his degree, he made a nominal study of law, but it proved distasteful, so he turned his life-thought to literature. But for some years how to earn a living was a problem. He published a slender volume of his verses, and called it " A Year's Work." These he later denounced as

> " The firstlings of my muse,
> Poor windfalls of unripe experience."

Then with Poe and Hawthorne, he attempted to establish a magazine, but only three numbers were issued, and he also gave a lecture in Concord for which he received five dollars. Besides, in 1844, he married a wife. This was a Miss White, a woman of great loveliness, but of decided views, both transcendental and anti-slavery. She lived only nine years, but this was quite long enough to convert her young husband from a cold, imitative, literary style, to such a heart-love for brotherhood and patriotism that in his new vision of " The Present Crisis," he exclaimed : —

" Truth forever on the scaffold, wrong forever on the throne;
   Yet that scaffold sways the future, and behind the dim un-
      known,
   Standeth God within the shadow, keeping watch above
      His own."

And now life and fuller work and real success, broadened out before Lowell. His second volume contained some of his most charming fancies. Among them " Rhoecus," the Greek legend of the wood-nymph and the bee; and " A Legend of Brittany," considered by Poe the best American poem. It is made in flowery lines, but the tale, somehow, lacks distinctness.

Lowell called " 1848 " his " annus mirabilis," and it was indeed the wonderful year of his life, for in it appeared all three of his masterpieces: " The Vision

of Sir Launfal," " The Fable for Critics," and the
first series of " The Biglow Papers."

Sir Launfal's vision embodies the search for the
Holy Grail, that legend so dear to romancers. (It
was a sudden inspiration, for it was completed in
forty-eight hours, during which he hardly ate or
slept; and the portrayal of the noble lesson of sympathy and suffering was most sincere and reverent.
It would be difficult to decide which passage is most
popular — the one beginning : —

> " And what is so rare as a day in June?
> Then, if ever, come perfect days;
> Then Heaven tries the earth if it be in tune,
> And over it softly her warm ear lays:
> Whether we look, or whether we listen,
> We hear life murmur, or see it glisten:"

or that other, conveying its tender lesson : —

> " Not what we give, but what we share,
> For the gift without the giver is bare.
> Who gives himself with his alms feeds three,
> Himself, his hungering neighbour, and Me."

(Lowell turns most easily from spiritual sentiment
to frolicsome mood, as we discover on opening his
" Fable for Critics." This audacious, playful sur-
vey of contemporary authors was first made for
his own amusement, and then he allowed it to appear

anonymously,) and, as one has said, he " flecked himself with his own whip " as follows: —

> " There is Lowell, who's striving Parnassus to climb
> With a whole bale of *isms* tied together with rhyme,
> He might get on alone, spite of brambles and boulders,
> But he can't with that bundle he has on his shoulders,
> The top of the hill he will ne'er come nigh reaching
> Till he learns the distinction 'twixt singing and preaching."

The poem, composed by one of the youngest of the
guild of letters, is at once a masterpiece of humour,
satire, and prophecy.

"The Biglow Papers," which Whittier said
" could only be written in Yankee New England, by
a New England Yankee," were in two series. In
both, Hosea Biglow, a shrewd-witted, down-East
Yankee, attempts in the broadest dialect to rouse his
fellow-citizens to military fervour. Birdofredum
Sawin, and the preacher, Homer Wilbur, insert their
original ideas.

In the first series, these views relate to the Mexican
War, in connection with our claim on Texas. They
are a satire on Daniel Webster and his party, for
yielding to the demands of the South. The opening
paper contains the lines: —

> " Massachusetts, God forgive her,
>   She's a-kneelin' with the rest,
>   She, thet ough' to ha' clung forever
>   In her grand old eagle-nest."

These sentiments did not stop the war; but they voiced the feeling of the people and well illustrate the wisdom, beauty and humour, which Lowell delighted to express in dialect form.) And among the episodes introduced to relieve the tension, are some lyric strains; as, for example, when Hawthorne asked Lowell to try his hand at Yankee love-making, and Lowell, in response, wrote " The Courtin'," which is introduced between the first and second series of " The Biglow Papers." (The delicious bit of " courtin' " took place on a " night all white and still," when

> " Zekle crep' up quite unbeknown
>   An' peeked in thru the winder,
>   An' there sot Huldy all alone,
>   'Ith no one nigh to hender.")

The second part of the " Papers " was not printed in book form until twenty years after the first; and in this, Hosea Biglow's humour is more grim than before, as he aims his satiric weapons against both slavery and the Civil War. Among other things, he insists that the quarrel is a family one and criticises England for daring to interfere with what a free, high-minded people hold sacred. The most caustic satire is Brother Jonathan's protest to John Bull, in which he asserts: —

> " It don't seem hardly right, John,
>   When both my hands was full,

> To stump me to a fight, John —
> Your cousin, too, John Bull!
>
> .   .   .   .   .   .
>
> We know we've got a cause, John,
> Thet's honest, just, an' true;
> We thought 'twould win applause, John,
> Ef nowhere else, from you."

Hosea Biglow is as unique in literature as Leather Stocking, and his words, in their swinging rhyme, are a splendid thrust at scorn for cowardice, and show deep insight into truth.   They are full of proverbial hits, and, more than anything else in our literature, immortalise the Yankee character and dialect. They naturally caused great excitement both North and South.   Lowell once said: " I am sorry that I began by making Hosea such a detestable speller." We are sorry, too, for if it were only easier to understand the dialect, we might better realise what a brilliant addition " The Biglow Papers " made to the serio-comic literature of the world.

In 1857, Lowell took his family abroad, and his little son, Walter, died in Rome.   On the home voyage, they met Thackeray, and with the English master, Lowell formed one of the pleasant friendships of his life, for they had much in common.

But after his return, another sorrow came to him; his inspiring wife died, leaving him with one little daughter, and it was well for him that new duties soon claimed his interest; for on Longfellow's resignation in 1855, Lowell was called upon to succeed him in the chair of modern languages and polite literature at Cambridge, and he was given two preparatory years abroad.

In 1857, he married again, and also entered upon his professional career, and no man was ever better fitted to lecture on the whole range of literature; usually stimulating, sometimes indolent, he was most popular with the students. His lectures on Chaucer, Spenser, Shakespeare, Dryden, Pope, and others, were the result of profound investigation — and on " Dante " he spent twenty years, before he gave it to his class. It is pleasant to think of both Longfellow and Lowell, who lived near together, holding " sweet converse," and linked for so many years with Harvard, for Lowell retained his professorship until 1877.

Ever since his failure in early life, Lowell had meditated on again trying a serial venture; and in 1857, he started " The Atlantic Monthly," in which he decidedly advanced the standard of magazine writing. In this, his second series of " Biglow Papers " came out, one by one; also, in 1865, his stirring " Harvard Commemoration Ode," written in honour of those who fell in the battles of the Civil War, and read at the festival to welcome the surviving students and graduates on their return.

Lowell remained as the head of " The Atlantic " for four years, and in 1863, joined Charles Eliot

Norton as an editor of " The North American Review." To both of these magazines, he contributed not only poems but essays on many subjects, which revealed him as a man of the very broadest culture, with remarkable gift of expression. Such were his " Fireside Travels," " Among my Books," and " From my Study Windows."

His lectures and essays grew out of each other; some were arranged for political questions, while others were suggested by his English dramatists. These essays, very varied in kind, make up the body of his prose writings. Sometimes they show want of perspective, and lack in continuity and sustained thought; but many of them are most attractive, and interest even those not usually fond of reading. They are full of suggestions to seek further. They enliven the fancy, too, as in the following quotation from " At Sea ": —

" I sometimes sit and pity Noah, but even he had this advantage over all succeeding navigators, that, whenever he landed, he was sure to get no ill news from home. He should be canonized as the patron saint of newspaper correspondents, being the only man who ever had the very last authentic news from everywhere! "

Lowell's " Essays " furnish a far stronger intellectual stimulus than the gossipy articles to catch the fancy which are offered us to-day by the alert, modern journalist.

ELMWOOD: HOME OF JAMES RUSSELL LOWELL, CAMBRIDGE, MASS.

In poetry, his patriotic verses stand first, for with Whittier, he stood shoulder to shoulder in a fight for American ideals. With the " Harvard Commemoration Ode," three others are ranked; one delivered in 1873, on the centenary of the year in which Washington took command of the forces under the now historic Cambridge " elm "; another, in 1875, on the centenary of the fight at Concord Bridge; and in 1876, a centennial " Fourth of July " ode. These are " the cap-sheaves " of the author's achievement.

And if patriotism was a " ruling passion," Nature was surely another — Nature that always roused him with child-like joy; a charmed feeling animates his lyrics on the trees and birds and flowers of Elmwood — the delicate crispness and alert grace of his birch-trees, " the go-betweens of rustic lovers." The bobolink he immortalises as Shelley does the skylark; watch and listen, as

> " Half-hid in tip-top apple-blooms he swings,
>   Or climbs against the breeze with quiverin' wings,
> Or given way to 't in a mock despair,
>   Runs down, a brook o' laughter thru the air."

Dearest of all is the dandelion — the

> " Common flower that grows beside the way
> Fringing the dusty road with harmless gold "—

and in very ecstasy he exclaims: —

" My childhood's earliest thoughts are linked with thee;
  The sight of thee calls back the robin's song,
Who from the dark old tree
  Beside the door sang clearly all day long,
And I serene in childish piety,
  Listened as if I heard an angel song
  With news from Heaven, which he could bring
Fresh every day to my contented ears,
  When birds and flowers and I were happy peers."

His poems are perfectly finished and among them are many gems. Perhaps the best collection was " Heartsease and Rue," published in 1888, opening with the memorial to Agassiz— one of the world's noted elegies.

In 1877, Lowell was appointed Minister to Spain as a fitting tribute to his brilliant social and intellectual qualities; and later, he was transferred to England. He was, as we have already seen, an intense American; and in an address at Birmingham, on " Democracy," he did not hesitate to enforce his principles as strongly as years earlier, in the protest of Brother Jonathan to John Bull.

But he was, also, a man of unusual tact and dignity; a speaker of rare felicity — he was constantly called upon for public addresses and after-dinner talks. The Queen deeply honoured him, and the people always welcomed him as " His Excellency, the Ambassador of American Literature, to the Court of Shakespeare." And how proud America was of her " Representative *Man* of Letters "!

And when he had grandly completed his mission, he returned to Elmwood, to its

> " Sequestered nooks,
> And all the sweet serenity of books."

He met his " garden acquaintances," received the catbirds' welcome, and with his familiars, the blue-birds, shared among the elms and willows his books and his pipe. He was, in a way, a recluse, but he never failed to make time for his " friendships built firm 'gainst flood and wind"; and he held close intercourse with Wendell Phillips and Garrison and Agassiz and Whittier and Longfellow and Motley and Parkman and his special familiar Holmes.

His library is preserved as he left it, with family portraits and chair and desk and even his clay-pipe, and the crowded cases filled with well-thumbed volumes. High beneath the roof of Elmwood was his study, where he slept as a boy, and where he also did much writing; and in this room one window looks right over on to Mt. Auburn, not far distant. His second wife had died in England, and here at Elmwood, or at his daughter's home, in Southboro, he passed his last years, in poetic seclusion, still writing, sometimes lecturing.

He died at Elmwood, in 1891. Among his pall-bearers were his cherished friends, Holmes, Howells, Curtis, and President Eliot, and he was buried in Mt.

Auburn, not far from Longfellow, and almost in sight of his study-window. He was mourned everywhere in America, and memorial services were held in Westminster Abbey, which gave token of the abiding impress he had made on the heart of England.

While Lowell had irrepressible humour, he does not appeal to so many young people as Longfellow. He is, perhaps, too profound; and he has a curious habit of shifting from the serious to the burlesque, and back again to the serious, that often puzzles the reader; and he *did* possess some impulsive oddities of temper. He was, however, as one has said: " The best of company *in* the best of company." He believed in his own opinions, and loved to talk while his admiring friends would sit about him and listen —and his letters to these friends are indeed delightful.

Surely we have found him a versatile man — this " poet, critic, professor, lecturer, editor, essayist, diplomat, and speaker on occasion "; and this versatility may be well exemplified by adding some of his proverbial sayings, which, like those of Emerson, are fresh and vigorous to-day: —

" He's been true to *one* party, an' thet is himself."

" New times demand new measures and new men."

" A ginooine statesman must be on his guard
Ef he must hev beliefs not to b'leeve them tu hard."

JAMES RUSSELL LOWELL (1819-1891)

"In general those who have nothing to say contrive to spend the longest time in doing it."

"Nothing takes longer in saying than anything else."

"Be a man among men, not a humbug among humbugs."

"They are slaves who dare not be
  In the right with two or three."

"Greatly begin! though thou have time
  But for a line, be that sublime,—
  Not failure, but low aim, is crime."

ALADDIN

When I was a beggarly boy,
  And lived in a cellar damp,
I had not a friend nor a toy,
  But I had Aladdin's lamp;
When I could not sleep for cold,
  I had fire enough in my brain,
And builded with roofs of gold
  My beautiful castles in Spain!

Since then I have toiled day and night,
  I have money and power good store,
But I'd give all my lamps of silver bright
  For the one that is mine no more;
Take, Fortune, whatever you choose,
  You gave, and may snatch again;
I have nothing 't would pain me to lose,
  For I own no more castles in Spain!

— *Lowell.*

THE FIRST SNOW-FALL

"The snow had begun in the gloaming,
   And busily all the night
Had been heaping field and highway
   With a silence deep and white.

Every pine and fir and hemlock
   Wore ermine too dear for an earl,
And the poorest twig on the elm-tree
   Was ridged inch-deep with pearl,

From sheds new-roofed with Carrara
   Came Chanticleer's muffled crow,
The stiff rails were softened to swan's-down,
   And still fluttered down the snow.

I stood and watched by the window
   The noiseless work of the sky,
And the sudden flurries of snow-birds,
   Like brown leaves whirling by.

I thought of a mound in sweet Auburn
   Where a little headstone stood;
How the flakes were folding it gently,
   As did robins the babes in the wood.

Up spoke our own little Mabel,
   Saying, 'Father, who makes it snow?'
And I told of the good All-father
   Who cares for us here below.

Again I looked at the snow-fall,
   And thought of the leaden sky
That arched o'er our first great sorrow,
   When that mound was heaped so high.

I remembered the gradual patience
  That fell from that cloud like snow,
Flake by flake, healing and hiding
  The scar of our deep-plunged woe.

And again to the child I whispered,
  'The snow that husheth all,
Darling, the merciful Father
  Alone can make it fall!'

Then, with eyes that saw not, I kissed her;
  And she, kissing back, could not know
That *my* kiss was given to her sister,
  Folded close under deepening snow."

— Lowell.

XXVI

OLIVER WENDELL HOLMES (1809-1894)

EMERSON, the seer — Whittier, the patriotic bard — Hawthorne, the romancer — Lowell, the critic — and Longfellow, laureate of the human heart — were leaders of the most gifted group of men of letters that has appeared in this country. About the middle of the nineteenth century, they immortalised Concord, made Boston, for a second time, " The Literary Hub," and did very much towards creating a literature that educated the people to a taste for the *best*. They were men of great variety of attainment — and how the libraries of the land expanded as they wrote! Just one more member and the group is complete. He must be a humourist to make the rest laugh — and an optimist, to teach them to pay proper tribute, one to the other — and Oliver Wendell Holmes steps forth as the survivor of the grand old coterie.

He was born on August twenty-ninth, 1809, in a great gambrel-roofed house in Cambridge, Massachusetts — a house haunted by four or five generations of gentlemen and gentlewomen. Among his ancestors was Anne Bradstreet, " The Tenth Muse "; and as he had very strong views about the necessity of selecting good forbears, it is well that his own were so honourable.

His was a scholarly home, and the boys " bumped about the bookshelves in the library "; and long years after, Oliver told the world that he liked books because he was " born among them." The father, who wrote " The Annals of America," was, for forty years, settled over a Congregational church in Cambridge, and finally deposed for refusing to accept Unitarian tenets; and the old house, too, was deposed, for just a stone-slab marks to-day the site where " Oliver Wendell Holmes was born."

He prepared, at Phillips Academy, Andover, for entrance to Harvard College, and carried with him a fondness for rhyming. He graduated in the " Class of '29," in which every member turned out famous for something. In it were the noted author and Unitarian clergyman, James Freeman Clarke; and Samuel J. Smith, who, as the writer of " America," would be known — so Holmes believed — long after other poets of the day were in oblivion. But what gave the class wider notoriety, were the forty or more anniversary poems, which Holmes, as laureate, dedicated to it.

The year after graduating, he was one day shocked to read that it was proposed to break up the frigate *Constitution,* which was universally known as " Old Ironsides," because in the War of 1812 it had won such a splendid victory over the British *Guer-*

riere — and, like the *Maine* of later history, it
was an object of national pride. With hot indignation, Holmes quickly wrote his " Old Ironsides," beginning : —

> " Ay, tear her tattered ensign down!
>   Long has it waved on high,
> And many an eye has danced to see
>   That banner in the sky;
> Beneath it rang the battle shout,
>   And burst the cannon's roar; —
> The meteor of the ocean air
>   Shall sweep the clouds no more."

He hurried with his manuscript to the office of " The
Boston Advertiser," and it was at once accepted and
copied all over the land; and it so roused public feeling that the frigate was saved, and Holmes's impromptu outburst became a standard lyric.

Holmes first took up law but very soon renounced
it for medicine. This he studied in Boston; then for
two and a half years most enthusiastically in Europe;
and in 1836 — a well-equipped young doctor — he
took his degree of M.D. He hung out his shingle
in somewhat frolicsome mood, wishing he dared print
on it: " Small fevers gratefully received "; and this
same merry humour and his skill in rhyming somehow
told, at the outset, against his reputation as a physician, and yet this cheeriness made him always a
welcome guest in the sick-room.

His first volume contains " The Last Leaf "— which popular poem, perhaps more than any other, manifests his rare mingling of mirth and pathos. It was suggested by meeting in the street a venerable relic of Revolutionary days — with cocked hat, knee-breeches, buckled shoes, and sturdy cane. Poe loved the poem and sent its author a copy in his own writing; Abraham Lincoln often repeated it; and Holmes read it on occasion, with a meaning which only he could impart. Written in his youth, the words seem prophetic when we think of him as the last survivor of the grand New England group.

In 1839, Holmes became professor of anatomy and physiology in Dartmouth College; and as teacher and lecturer, he proved much more successful than as practising physician. Certain lessons that he had learned from experience, he earnestly taught to his pupils. He begged them, if they wanted success in any one calling, never to let the world know that they were interested in any other; in other words, not to attempt at the same time to make rhymes and prescriptions.

The Miss Jackson whom he now married was the daughter of an Associate-Justice of Massachusetts and she proved an ideal wife. After his marriage, he resigned his professorship and resumed practice in Boston. Then, in 1847, he was appointed professor of anatomy in the Harvard Medical School, holding this chair for thirty-five years. As an instructor, he was remarkably successful, and given to experiments of all kinds. His pupils asserted that he knew as much of the body as the mind, and, by apt and comic illustration, he made the driest matter interesting. He did much scientific writing in connection with his lectures; indeed, most of the prose literary work belonging to these earlier years was on medical topics.

Like Emerson and Lowell, he needed more money than his profession yielded; so he, too, travelled about as a Lyceum lecturer — his " lecture-peddling," he dubbed it. Perhaps the best of these lectures were on the English poets — and he frequently appended an original poem. He had not Emerson's personality and beautiful tones — his voice being not strong but clear and sympathetic. One has described the " plain little dapper man "— his short hair brushed down like a boy's — his countenance glowing with fervour — while with kindly and abundant wit, he moved his audience, looking up at the end of each sentence to be sure they caught the point! Who could *miss* it?

Yet not as a lecturer, but as the author of " The Autocrat of the Breakfast Table "— regarded in its day one of the wisest and wittiest of prose books — will Dr. Holmes be longest known. The suggestion of his subject came to him in " his uncombed literary boyhood," when he wrote two papers and sent them to a magazine; and now twenty years later, he christens " The Atlantic Monthly," and promises Lowell to write for it, because only on that condition will it be brought into existence. And after this casual break of twenty years, he commences his first essay in these words: " I was going to say when I was interrupted "— Thus his " Autocrat " begins.

It is, in form, very like the English " Spectator." Here an autocrat presides over a group of characters that gather, morning after morning, about a boarding-house table. His conversation — chiefly in monologue — on a diversity of practical subjects — is addressed to those about him; among them, are the landlady, an old gentleman, an ancient maiden, a divinity student, and a sweet schoolmistress who seldom presumes to make a remark — all of whom are evidently created to give a turn to his theme, from time to time. Occasionally an illustrative, rambling rhyme or poem is introduced.

Among these is " The Chambered Nautilus "— that most graceful and artistic of Holmes's creations. The thought originated while examining a section of the spiral home of this ingenious builder. He noted the enlarging compartments, in which, as it grew, it dwelt in turn, and thus he wrote this piece of symbolism : —

> " Year after year behold the silent toil
>   That spread his lustrous coil;
>   Still, as the spiral grew,
> He left the past year's dwelling for the next,
> Stole with soft step its shining archway through,
>   Built up its idle door,

Stretched in his last-found home, and knew the old no
  more.

   .   .   .   .

Build thee more stately mansions, O my soul,
  As the swift seasons roll!
  Leave thy low-vaulted past!
Let each new temple, nobler than the last,
Shut thee from heaven with a dome more vast,
  Till thou at length art free,
Leaving thine outgrown shell by life's unresting sea! "

And Dr. Holmes was grateful for the heavenly message from the little silent architect, and more than by
bronze or by marble, he wished to be remembered by
his " Chambered Nautilus."⟩

And other poems, also, were woven into the chapters of " The Autocrat "— among them, " Parson
Turell's Legacy "; and the essays grew until at last
there was a bookful, and in the final paragraph — to
maintain a slender thread of sentiment that moves
throughout — the Autocrat carries off the schoolmistress, that together they may walk " the long pathway of peace."

Years later, " The Professor at the Breakfast
Table " followed, and after another lapse, " The
Poet at the Breakfast Table "; and when Dr.
Holmes was eighty-one, he brought out " Over the
Teacups "; but these monologues belonging to the
evening could not be so exhilarating as those of the
bright, early morning.

Dr. Holmes calls genius " the ability to light one's own fire "; and this he surely did in his " Autocrat " which at once was famous, and helped to give " The Atlantic " a brave start. He was always watching the symptoms of the times; and in these and other essays for current literature, he discussed topics of every-day, and often from a physician's standpoint.

The astonishing success of " The Autocrat " encouraged him to write three novels: " Elsie Venner," " The Guardian Angel," and " The Mortal Antipathy "— all designed to show differing psychological theories. Elsie Venner may fascinate some with her serpent charm, and the sunshiny old bachelor in " The Guardian Angel " is pleasing to meet; but Dr. Holmes does not tell a tale readily and his novels do not evince his highest talent — but he was most particular about the finish of these as of his other works.

His biographies of Motley and Emerson are full of sympathetic appreciation. Motley was always his close friend, and he wrote out of the very fulness of his love. He admired Emerson, and in speaking of him, narrated many characteristic anecdotes; but he could not quite unravel the philosophy of the mammoth thinker, as he shows in the following question:

> " Where in the realm of thought, whose air is song,
>   Does he, the Buddha of the West, belong?
> He seems a wingéd Franklin sweetly wise,
>   Born to unlock the secrets of the skies."

In Morse's " Life and Letters of Dr. Holmes," we may read many of his vivacious letters to Motley, Lowell, Whittier, Agassiz, and others; — and more, in Mrs. Field's " Reminiscences." He was, in a sense, his own Boswell, talking frankly of his personalities to his friends and the world. He sometimes even confesses his petty vanities, for he loved praise and advocated it, and he speaks of himself as —

> " Singing or sad by fits and starts,
> One actor in a dozen parts."

And we love him the better for the human touches; but still we wish that he might have been attended by yet another Boswell, who would have preserved to posterity more of his sparkling conversations.

And we get, too, a many-sided view of this humourist, scientist, teacher, autocrat, essayist, biographer, and letter-writer — when we glance into his three volumes of poetical works which might all have been called " Songs in Many Keys "— for they treat of things so varied.

In "War Time," he was conservative but patriotic, as in " God Save the Flag ! " and the " Army Hymn," of which we select the fourth stanza : —

> " God of all Nations! Sovereign Lord!
> In thy dread name we draw the sword,
> We lift the starry flag on high
> That fills with light our stormy sky."

To instance his clever pen, we name the universal favourite —" The Deacon's Masterpiece "— that " wonderful one-hoss shay," that, after running a hundred years, went to pieces all at once : —

> " All at once, and nothing first,—
> Just as bubbles do when they burst."

And as " the poet of occasion," Holmes is without a peer. Mrs. Field calls him : " King of the Dinner-Table "; Mr. Stedman: " Our most typical University Poet "; another, " The Harvard Mirth-Maker "; and yet one more : " Sweet Minstrel of the Joyous Present." Boston, his " Three-Hilled City," was always inviting him to celebrate *something,* and he was quickly ready for feast or commemoration.

> " I'm a florist in verse, and what would people say,
> If I came to a banquet without my bouquet? "

once exclaimed this unrivalled songster. Such poetic effusions do not always live — but they receive enough instant applause as compensation.

And this master of the gentle craft had many gifted friends. He was a lover of men — for as one has said: " He always made you think you were the best fellow in the world, and he the next best."

He was a brilliant member of the " Saturday Club," that for years brought together in Boston the brightest scholars of the land, and often at its monthly dinners entertained distinguished guests from abroad. Here one found Emerson, Longfellow, Lowell, Hawthorne and Whittier; and often Dr. Holmes, the prince of conversationalists, presided with courtesy and unexampled witticism, and he was one of those, who, when he was in the room, the whole room was conscious of his presence —." Our Yankee Tsar "— as Aldrich styled him.

Dr. Holmes had warm admiration for Professor Agassiz and nicknamed him " Liebig's Extract of the Wisdom of Ages." Of James Freeman Clarke he writes : —

> " With sacred zeal to save, to lead,—
> Long live our dear St. James."

In greeting his faithful friend Lowell, on his return from abroad, he wonders : —

> " By what enchantments, what alluring arts,
> Our truthful James led captive British hearts."

Whittier calls Holmes " our rarest optimist "— and on his eightieth birthday, inscribes to him a sonnet containing the two graceful lines : —

> " Long be it ere the table shall be set
> For the last breakfast of the Autocrat."—

and Holmes, not to be outdone by Whittier, wrote of the latter —:

"Let him live to a hundred; we want him on earth,

. . . . . " . . "

He never will die if he lingers below
Till we've paid him in love half the balance we owe!"

So the members of this New England group believed firmly in one another, paid loving tribute to one another, and held together till death. Very touching are the memorial lines from Holmes to Lowell: —

"*Thou* shouldst have sung the swan-song for the choir"—

In reference to the warm friendships embodied in his poems, we quote this story from Mrs. Field's "Reminiscences": —

"One evening the Doctor came in after the Phi Beta Kappa dinner at Cambridge, and said: 'I can't stop — I just came to read you some verses I gave at the dinner to-day. I wouldn't have brought them, but Hoar says they are the best I have ever done.' Then in the fading sunset light reflected from the river, he read with great tenderness — 'Bill and Joe.'"

Mrs. Field adds: "These are pleasant on the printed page, but divested of the affection with which he read them." Later in life, Dr. Holmes said in reference to similar poems: "The writing of such verses has been a passionate joy."

And now to return to the facts of Dr. Holmes's

life. In the Civil War, his son, Captain Holmes, was wounded at the battle at Ball's Bluff, and after seeking him, he wrote: "My Hunt after the Captain." The son lived "to fight another day" at Bull Run, and also to become the honoured Chief-Justice of Massachusetts.

On Dr. Holmes's seventieth birthday, the publishers of "The Atlantic Monthly" tendered him a great public breakfast to which were summoned many representative men. For this he wrote, "The Iron Gate," a cheerful picture of old age. Truly, as Burroughs said of him: "May is in his heart, and early autumn in his brain."

On resigning his professorship at Harvard, in 1882, the students presented him with a loving-cup inscribed with his own lines: —

"Love Bless Thee, Joy Crown Thee, God Speed Thy Career."

Dr. Holmes had always disliked change of any kind, and except for his lectures, he had travelled very little, for "Better a hash at home than a roast with strangers," had been his motto. So his friends were surprised when, in 1886, fifty years after his first trip, Dr. Holmes took his daughter and went abroad. As "The Autocrat," he was lionised everywhere, and his biographer says that it was only by extreme care that he extricated himself alive from the hospitalities of his British friends. Edinburgh,

Cambridge, and Oxford conferred degrees upon him; and as he appeared on the platform at Oxford, the students shrieked: " Did he come in the One-Hoss Shay? " Upon his return to America he wrote, " One Hundred Days in Europe."

The Autocrat spent his summers at Beverly Farms; and here, on his vine-covered verandah, overlooking the ocean, he passed " many days of glowing hours." His winter home was in Boston, which was to him the veritable " Hub of the Universe "— while to his admirers, his library was " the hub " of Boston. His latest residence was on Beacon Street, near the homes of Mr. Howells and other old-time friends. How many to-day recall his cordial welcome as they visited him in his luxurious library, with the changing view upon Back Bay. Upon the wall hung a treasured Copley, the portrait of his ancestor, " Dorothy Q." In his dainty poem addressed to her, he acquaints us with her thus: —

" Grandmother's mother: her age, I guess,
Thirteen summers, or something less;
Girlish bust, but womanly air;
Smooth, square forehead with uprolled hair;
Lips that lover has never kissed;
Taper fingers and slender wrist;
Hanging sleeves of stiff brocade;
So they painted the little maid.

On her hand a parrot green
Sits unmoving and broods serene."

And in his library, in the sunset of life, he enjoyed looking out of the big bay-window, over the expanse of water, watching the tide and craft and sea-gulls; and just beyond, Cambridge where he was born, Harvard College with which he had been so long allied, and Mt. Auburn Cemetery where his remains would rest. His final volume of poems, published in 1888, was entitled " Before the Curfew." Its text seemingly is: " The curfew tells me — cover up the fire."

All the years he had been devoted to " The Boys of '29," even when " The poor old raft was going to pieces and it was hard to get any together ";— and finally, in 1889, he wrote his parting tribute. So run the first three stanzas: —

> " The Play is over. While the light
>   Yet lingers in the darkening hall,
> I come to say a last Good-night
>   Before the final *Exeunt all.*
>
> We gathered once, a joyous throng;
>   The jovial toasts went gayly round;
> With jest, and laugh, and shout, and song,
>   We made the floors and walls resound.
>
> We come with feeble steps and slow,
>   A little band of four or five,
> Left from the wrecks of long ago,
>   Still pleased to find ourselves alive.

.   .   .   .

So ends 'The Boys,'— a lifelong play
  We, too, must hear the Prompter's call
To fairer scenes and brighter day:
  Farewell! I let the curtain fall."

It is pathetic to note that, in the next year, at the only subsequent meeting of the class, but three were present, and there was no poem.

After the death of his wife, the genial "Autocrat" had been guarded very carefully by his son and daughter-in-law. The end came quietly on August seventh, 1894. His funeral took place from King's Chapel, Cambridge, where he had worshipped for many years, and he sleeps in Mt. Auburn, not far from Longfellow and Lowell — and with his death, the famous epoch closes. For many friends he had written memorials;— and among those prepared for himself was the following from London "Punch":—

"'The Last Leaf,' can it be true
We have turned it, and on you,
  Friend of all?

. . . . . .

Of sweet singers the most sane,
Of keen wits the most humane.

. . . . . .

With a manly breadth of soul,
And a fancy quaint and droll,
  Ripe and mellow.

. . . . . .

Years your spirit could not tame,
And they will not dim your fame;

England joys
In your songs, all strength and ease,
And the dreams you made to please
  Grey-haired boys."

BILL AND JOE.

"Come, dear old comrade, you and I
Will steal an hour from days gone by,
The shining days when life was new,
And all was bright with morning dew,
The lusty days of long ago,
When you were Bill and I was Joe.

Your name may flaunt a titled trail
Proud as a cockerel's rainbow tail,
And mine as brief appendix wear
As Tam O'Shanter's luckless mare;
To-day, old friend, remember still
That I am Joe and you are Bill.

You've won the great world's envied prize,
And grand you look in people's eyes,
With HON. and LL.D.
In big brave letters, fair to see,—
Your fist, old fellow! off they go! —
How are you, Bill?   How are you, Joe?

You've worn the judge's ermined robe;
You've taught your name to half the globe;
You've sung mankind a deathless strain;
You've made the dead past live again:
The world may call you what it will,
But you and I are Joe and Bill.

The chaffing young folks stare and say
'See those old buffers, bent and grey,—
They talk like fellows in their teens!
Mad, poor old boys!   That's what it means,'—
And shake their heads; they little know
The throbbing hearts of Bill and Joe! —

How Bill forgets his hour of pride,
While Joe sits smiling at his side;
How Joe, in spite of time's disguise,
Finds the old schoolmate in his eyes,—
Those calm, stern eyes that melt and fill
As Joe looks fondly up at Bill.

Ah, pensive scholar, what is fame?
A fitful tongue of leaping flame;
A giddy whirlwind's fickle gust,
That lifts a pinch of mortal dust;
A few swift years, and who can show
Which dust was Bill and which was Joe?

The weary idol takes his stand,
Holds out his bruised and aching hand,
While gaping thousands come and go,—
How vain it seems, this empty show!
Till all at once his pulses thrill;—
'Tis poor old Joe's 'God bless you, Bill!'

And shall we breathe in happier spheres
The names that pleased our mortal ears,
In some sweet lull of harp and song
For earth-born spirits none too long,
Just whispering of the world below
Where this was Bill and that was Joe?

No matter; while our home is here
No sounding name is half so dear;
When fades at length our lingering day,
Who cares what pompous tombstones say?
Read on the hearts that love us still,
Hic jacet Joe.   *Hic jacet* Bill."

—*Holmes.*

XXVII

EDGAR ALLAN POE (1809-1849)

EDGAR ALLAN POE, the most famous Southern
author, and one of the renowned literary artists of
the world, stands apart — a solitary, statuesque figure
in American literature.   Born in the same year with
Oliver Wendell Holmes, the character of the morose
and sensitive genius was in striking contrast to that
of the gentle, lovable humourist.

His grandfather, a Revolutionary patriot, founded
the family in Maryland; and Poe's dashing young
father, while studying law in Baltimore in 1805,
alienated himself from his parents, by marrying a
pretty English actress, and adopting his wife's profession; and it was on January nineteenth, 1809,
while these strolling players were fulfilling an engage-
ment in Boston, that Edgar was born; a little later,
both parents died in the same month, leaving three
small children to the tender mercies of the world.
It seems a remarkable fact that all three were
adopted by wealthy people.

Mr. Allan, a tobacco merchant of Richmond, Virginia, was attracted by the precocious little Edgar,
and from a home of poverty, he was transferred to
one of real Southern luxury.   Mrs. Allan petted and

caressed him, while his foster-father indulged him in every wish. At six years old, the gifted child, with his bright eyes and dark curls and dressed like a prince, would stand upon a table, and, in sweetest tone, declaim to guests, or pledge them "right roguishly" in a glass of wine.

When he was seven, he was taken abroad and placed in an English school, and later in Richmond was carefully prepared to enter college. With musical ear and wonderful memory, he learned to recite with surprising effect some of the finest passages from the English poets. Literature and history, French and Latin, always charmed him. He was excellent in debate, led in athletics, and made a remarkable swimming record, and the boys cultivated him because he always had plenty of pocket-money.

The University of Virginia had been recently established by the patriotic efforts of Thomas Jefferson, and was numbering as its students distinguished young men from all parts of the Southland; and here, at seventeen years of age, Poe was admitted — accomplished, capricious, imperious, and handsome — and living in the confidence that he was to inherit a fortune. He won creditable honours as a scholar; he covered his walls with his sketches; wrote rhyming squibs to entertain his class; and presently gave way to temptation in drinking and gambling, and after he had lost hundreds of dollars, Mr. Allan removed him

EDGAR ALLAN POE

SIDNEY LANIER

PAUL H. HAYNE

REV. JOHN B TABB

from the University and placed him in his counting-house.

The gay youth with fascinating eyes, winning smile, pleasing voice, and aristocratic manners, enjoyed the polished society of Richmond. He cared not for men, but began now to form those ideal loves for women that dominated his life. It mattered not what their age; the mother of one of his friends was probably the inspiration of his poem " Lenore."

For a time all went well; soon, however, he fell again into temptation; gambling-debts increased, and Mr. Allan refused to pay them, reprimanding him severely — and at last the high-spirited youth who would brook no restraint broke loose from his environment. Mr. Allan had married again and would have nothing to do with his wayward protégé, and when he died a few years later did not even mention him in his will.

Poe probably drifted away to the home of his aunt, Mrs. Clemm, in Baltimore. He also entered the army under an assumed name, for like his idol, Lord Byron, he determined to assist in some struggle for freedom. He was summoned back to Richmond by Mrs. Allan's illness, and she was dead when he arrived, but a temporary reconciliation took place with his foster-father.

It was now time to decide upon a profession and Edgar resolved to enter the army, and Mr. Allan obtained for him admission to West Point. Again, for a little all went well; then he began to show contempt for military duties — any routine annoyed him. He wrote Mr. Allan, begging him to recall him, and Mr. Allan refusing, he arranged himself to be expelled by shirking parole and absenting himself from roll-call. He was, as one has said, "perhaps the most gifted, but least creditable cadet that ever entered that celebrated school-of-arms."

Before leaving, he arranged with the cadets to subscribe to a volume of his poems which he promised to dedicate to them, and as soon as he was free, determined to support himself by writing, for authorship was the only thing in his life that he ever treated seriously. Very soon, " Tamerlane and Other Poems " was published, dedicated " To the U. S. Corps of Cadets," which the cadets, by the way, thought " rubbish," because they did not contain the promised squibs — and apart from West Point, the book made no impression in the world.

From 1832-1849, we face the struggling years of Poe's life, in which he made his wonderful literary record. His aunt, Mrs. Clemm, the one friend always faithful to him, was too poor to support him, and for a long time after leaving West Point, he suffered for both food and clothing. One day he learned that " The Saturday Visitor " of Baltimore had offered a hundred dollar prize for the best story. He wrote " A MS. Found in a Bottle," and sent it in, and was the fortunate winner. John Pendleton Kennedy, the statesman-author and one of the judges, was interested in this book, so " highly imaginative and a little given to the terrific," and sought out its young author, whom he found living in an attic in poverty; he offered him full access to the comforts of his home, and a horse to ride when he needed exercise. Best of all, he became Poe's literary sponsor, securing him a position on the editorial staff of " The Southern Literary Messenger " of Richmond, with an annual salary of five hundred and twenty dollars. And now with an assured living, Poe married his " starry-eyed " little cousin, Virginia Clemm, who had always fascinated him and who was now just fourteen, and his devotion to his child-wife is one of the noblest things in his character. And success came to him; he was asked for all the short stories he could write; and as they appeared, they won many readers by their striking vigour and novelty and their weird, imaginative power.

Poe was an artist in rhetorical form, and in his editorial work proved a keen critic of current literature. He was really the first to emphasise this form of writing. Book after book was sent him for review, and he naturally exposed many pretentious humbugs, who claimed to be men of letters. But he was too much of a free lance, allowing personal feelings to influence his mood, and so he made enemies. He took savage delight in slashing criticisms of his famous contemporaries; for one, he attacked Longfellow, while

Longfellow read and admired Poe. As for Gris-wold, the compiler of " Poets and Poetry of Amer-ica," he lashed his work so severely that Gris-wold revenged himself; for when, after Poe's death, he compiled his works, he appended to them such a distorted, malicious biography, that although many of his statements have been contradicted by later re-viewers, it is difficult even yet to be sure of the true facts about Poe.

But whatever mistakes Poe made, he worked with rapidity on tales, critiques, and poems; and the maga-zine grew in importance, lengthening its list of sub-scribers. He had a happy home with loving wife and mother-in-law, and was much honoured in Rich-mond society, and the world enjoyed and compli-mented his works.

Suddenly he let fortune slip again; perhaps his petty, quarrelsome temper was the cause — perhaps too much conviviality — but in 1837, we find him homeless and struggling for means of subsistence. He removed to Philadelphia, where he sometimes worked as a sort of hack-writer, again as editor, and here, in a luxurious Southern home he produced his most original work, " Tales of the Grotesque and Arabesque." Poe always made it easy to break his engagements, and in 1844, he left Philadelphia for New York, where he remained for the last five years of his short life. Here, too, for his brilliant reputa-tion, he was received into the select literary coterie.

With artists and men of letters he was a frequent guest, at the gatherings at the home of Miss Anna C. Lynch, in Waverley Place, and sometimes he brought his wife. N. P. Willis, the sentimental poet and graceful prose-writer, befriended him and finally associated him with himself on " The Evening Mirror "; he was, also, at one time editor of " The Broadway Journal," and occasionally, took the lecture platform.

Yet we may not linger over his successes, for another conflict is just before him — for now his health was shattered by bad habits and overwork, and his wife was dying of consumption. Feeling the need of country air, they removed in 1847, to a tiny cottage of four rooms, in Fordham. It still stands there, opposite Poe Park, and on its exterior is a big, black raven, and a tablet marked, " Here Poe lived."

Mrs. Clemm was the presiding genius, and never was mother-in-law rewarded by sweeter tribute than that which Poe dedicated to her as " Mother." She deserved it for she gave her life to her two children: marketing, cooking, searching the waste-basket for manuscripts which she tried to sell, buying clothes and gloves and cravats for her " Eddie " as she always called Poe; but the family grew poorer and poorer, and sometimes when there was no money, Poe, after seeking for work, would walk all the way home from New York, proudly, too, with head erect.

He watched by the bedside of his child-wife as she wasted away, and in the bleak winter, in their destitution, he tried to keep her warm, covering her with his great coat and the family cat.

Bunner has perpetuated the dreary Fordham home in a poem from which we quote: —

> " Here lived the soul enchanted
>   By melody of song;
> Here dwelt the spirit haunted
>   By a demoniac throng;
>
> Here sang the lips elated;
> Here grief and death were sated;
> Here loved and here unmated
>   Was he, so frail, so strong."

After the death of his wife, Poe more than ever yielded to despair and opiates. Vain and passionate, he believed in himself, and felt himself the victim of circumstances rather than wrong-doing. He had like a spoiled child, always begging for more; and drifted from one friend and one purpose to another yet he once said: " My life has been whim — impulse — passion — a longing for solitude — a scorn of all things present, in an earnest desire for the future."

His idolised Virginia was the inspiration of his " Annabel Lee "; and of " Eulalie "— the only poem that he wrote in 1847 — its wandering lines beginning: —

> " I dwelt alone
> In a world of moan,
> And my soul was a stagnant tide,
> Till the fair and gentle Eulalie became
> My blushing bride—"

We may touch but lightly on the facts of Poe's own death, which occurred on October seventh, 1849. Perhaps he was preparing to marry again and perhaps he had just been refused. In passing through Baltimore, he was found unconscious in the street, and carried to the Marine Hospital where he died. His funeral was attended by only eight persons. One was a veiled old woman who was often seen later, mourning at his grave.

This grave was unmarked for twenty-five years, and then when the facts of Poe's life were more and more lost in recognition of his supernatural tales and emotional poems, the teachers of the Baltimore schools had a memorial slab placed over it, and on November seventeenth, 1875, in the presence of a large assembly — in which were Walt Whitman and other poets — it was consecrated to Poe — " so frail, so strong."

Our special concern, however, is with Poe's works, which form striking contrast to his vacillating career. Hawthorne and Poe stand together as our first brilliant tellers of the short story. Hawthorne dwelt on conscience and moral beauty — Poe on weird, passionate conceits. In his tales there is usually a grand, central figure, which, by the way, often resembles his own personality. The people that move in some of the plots are often in most unearthly guise — so that nothing stands out distinctly. Again there is a secret combining of the strange and terrible, which is skilfully unravelled. Some call Poe our finest writer of detective stories — surely he was our earliest.

Not what he thought with his natural mind, but gloomy forms that came to him when under the influence of opium, may have inspired him as they did Coleridge. There are so many masterpieces that we may not mention all. Among those most read are " Ligeia," " William Wilson," " The Pit and the Pendulum," and " Hans Pfaall," whose hero journeys with his cat, in a balloon, to the moon. " Murders in the Rue Morgue," translated into French, made France rate Poe most highly.

" The Fall of the House of Usher " is typical of his style. Here air and landscape are in harmony with the gloom and horror of the scene: " the wild light, the blood-red moon, the fierce breath of the whirlwind, the mighty walls rushing asunder, the long, tumultuous shouting like the voice of a thousand waters — the deep and dark tarn closing suddenly and silently over the fragments of the ' House of Usher ' "— with such productions, Poe, conjuror-like, enchanted his readers.

Courtesy of Edward Hagaman Hall

POE'S COTTAGE AT FORDHAM, NEW YORK CITY

EDGAR ALLAN POE (1809-1849)

Let us turn to his unique poetry. Incapable of sustained effort in verse as well as in prose, he did not believe in a long poem. The few brief ones, known to everybody, are unlike those of any other poet of his time. His minstrel harp was his pride. To him poetry was " the rhythmical creation of beauty." He caught his colouring from the South, from Europe, and the Orient, and he embodies in his verses ethereal and exquisite strains. Refrain and repetend and onomatopœia are among his rare powers — the latter best shown in " The Bells."

While Holmes and others of his group paid tribute to men, Poe perfectly deified women. Among those that most influenced him were Mrs. Browning, through her poems; Mrs. Whitman, the poetess, and the literary Mrs. Osgood; and to the last two he ever turned for sympathy.

His beautiful but incomprehensible " Israfel " was his favourite among his works. This was suggested by a line from the Koran, describing " the angel Israfel, whose heart-strings are a lute, and who has the sweetest voice of all God's creatures." It seems as if in the last stanza, more than any other, Poe soared to his highest expression : —

> " If I could dwell
>   Where Israfel
>   Hath dwelt, and he where I,
>   He might not sing so wildly well

A mortal melody,
While a bolder note than this might swell
From my lyre within the sky."

And there is " The Raven," popular at home and abroad. The self-possessed fowl, " Once upon a midnight dreary," started him by its " tapping, gently tapping," entered his chamber, perched upon a bust of Pallas, and in reply to all his questioning, uttered the solemn dirge " Never — Nevermore ! "

When Poe had completed the poem, he read it to a friend, and then asked him what he thought of it, and the answer was: " I think it uncommonly fine." " Fine ! " cried Poe, " is that all you can say of it? It is the greatest poem ever written, sir ! " Poe liked to recite it, and in his melodious voice, he gave it indescribable charm, and one could never forget his plaintive " Nevermore ! "

" The Raven " was written, in 1845, in New York, and he received for it ten dollars, but — more than any other poem — it brought him immediate fame. It was copied far and wide and much used as a school recitation. The poets read and pondered it, and Lowell, in his " Fable for Critics " says : —

" There comes Poe with his Raven, like Barnaby Rudge,
Three-fifths of him genius, and two-fifths sheer fudge."

" The Raven "—though somewhat hard to interpret — will always have an abiding place in our literature.

Abroad it was considered Poe's supreme effort; indeed, his tales and poems are more honoured in Europe than those of many of our authors. Tennyson ranked him " the greatest American genius "; and Victor Hugo, " The Prince of American Literature." And to-day everywhere one thinks more of his writings and less of his sad life.

On account of his poetic and Platonic affection for women, the fair sex has done much to increase his fame. A Woman's Club, in Baltimore, is about to erect a heroic statue to Poe. It is to be a seated figure, representing him in an inspired attitude, and to be carved by the noted sculptor, Ezekiel.

Owing to controversy, regarding his life and writings, it was not until 1910 that the New York " Hall of Fame " opened its doors to Poe. In the Metropolitan Museum, there is a memorial tablet, inscribed: —

" He was great in his genius, unhappy in his life, wretched in death, and in his fame he is immortal."

What shall be our verdict?

ANNABEL LEE.

It was many and many a year ago
   In a kingdom by the sea,
That a maiden there lived whom you may know
   By the name of Annabel Lee;
And this maiden she lived with no other thougnt
   Than to love and be loved by me.

I was a child and she was a child,
    In this kingdom by the sea,
But we loved with a love that was more than love,
    I and my Annabel Lee;
With a love that the wingéd seraphs of heaven
    Coveted her and me.

And this was the reason that, long ago,
    In this kingdom by the sea,
A wind blew out of a cloud, chilling
    My beautiful Annabel Lee;
So that her highborn kinsmen came
    And bore her away from me,
To shut her up in a sepulchre
    In this kingdom by the sea.

.   .   .   .

But our love it was stronger by far than the love
    Of those who were older than we,
    Of many far wiser than we;
And neither the angels in heaven above,
    Nor the demons down under the sea,
Can ever dissever my soul from the soul
    Of the beautiful Annabel Lee:

For the moon never beams, without bringing me dreams
    Of the beautiful Annabel Lee;
And the stars never rise, but I feel the bright eyes
    Of the beautiful Annabel Lee;
And so, all the night-tide, I lie down by the side
Of my darling — my darling — my life and my bride,
    In her sepulchre there by the sea,
    In her tomb by the sounding sea.

                                        —*Poe.*

EDGAR ALLAN POE (1809–1849)

FROM "THE BELLS"

I

" Hear the sledges with the bells,
    Silver bells!
What a world of merriment their melody foretells!
  How they tinkle, tinkle, tinkle,
    In the icy air of night!
  While the stars, that oversprinkle
  All the heavens, seem to twinkle
    With a crystalline delight;
  Keeping time, time, time,
  In a sort of Runic rhyme,
To the tintinnabulation that so musically wells
  From the bells, bells, bells, bells,
    Bells, bells, bells —
  From the jingling and the tinkling of the bells.

II

  Hear the mellow wedding bells,
    Golden bells!
What a world of happiness their harmony foretells!
  Through the balmy air of night
  How they ring out their delight!
    From the molten-golden notes,
      And all in tune,
    What a liquid ditty floats
To the turtle-dove that listens, while she gloats
    On the moon!
  Oh, from out the sounding cells,
What a gush of euphony voluminously wells!
    How it swells!
    How it dwells

On the Future! how it tells
Of the rapture that impels
To the swinging and the ringing
Of the bells, bells, bells,
Of the bells, bells, bells, bells,
Bells, bells, bells —
To the rhyming and the chiming of the bells!

—Poe.

XXVIII

OTHER SOUTHERN WRITERS

POE'S name is, thus far, the greatest in Southern literature, and in the colouring of his tales and the music of his verse, he shows many touches of the Southland. His life, however, seems to relate itself more to the North — but as we have said, he stands apart from any group. Before considering other individual lives, we look briefly at the conditions that existed in the South before the Civil War.

There was no public school system; the wealthy employed tutors, or sent their children abroad to be educated. There were no great publishing-houses; no literary centres as Philadelphia, New York, Boston, or Concord. Puritanism and Transcendentalism were almost unknown. The hum of the mill and the factory was not often heard and there was little commercialism. The hospitable plantation mansion was presided over by the cordial but aristocratic gentleman. Its spirit imitated that of English rural life, and the study of English manners and English literature was most popular.

The pride of the South lay in her long line of orators and statesmen, and the famous documents and addresses that she had given to the Union in its

formative period. Virginia laid stress upon being
" The Mother of Presidents." So law and oratory
and politics belonged to Southern traditions, rather
than American literature, which was somewhat ignored, being considered trashy. One subject, however, was of such vital import that it was constantly
discussed, and this was the institution of slavery. It
came increasingly to the fore; the Northerners declaimed against it so fiercely that the Southerners
must needs wonder what they would better do with it;
and we have spoken in a previous chapter of the oratory to which this gave rise.

But there were a few writers of note on other subjects; among them, John Pendleton Kennedy (1795-
1870), a brilliant statesman and one of our earliest
novelists, who, in his books, happily reproduced an
era that has gone. In his " Horse-shoe Robinson,"
he enlarges on the traditions of South Carolina and
Revolutionary days; while his " Swallow Barn "
photographs the customs of a Virginia plantation, at
the end of the eighteenth century. " The aristocratic old edifice sets like a brooding-hen, on the
Southern bank of the James River "— and in typical
Southern style. Kennedy describes as follows the
master's dress as he rides to the court-house: —

" He is then apt to make his appearance in a coat of blue
broadcloth, astonishingly glossy, and with an unusual amount
of plaited ruffles strutting through the folds of a Marseilles

waistcoat. A worshipful finish is given to this costume by a large straw hat, lined with green silk. There is a magisterial fulness in his garments which betokens conditions in the world, and a heavy bunch of seals, suspended by a chain of gold, jingles as he moves, pronouncing him a man of superfluities."

Another writer of this period was William Gilmore Simms (1806-1870), the alert Charleston author, who aspired to lay the foundation of a distinct Southern literature. He made his home the centre of a group of ambitious young men of letters, and he begged them to work and hold together until the world should acknowledge their achievements. It is well that he could not then foresee the blight that the Civil War would cast over their brave efforts.

Simms was an indefatigable writer of thirty novels and seventeen volumes of poetry, besides plays, historical essays, and political pamphlets. His novels which are all that live to-day are very diverse. He made good historical backgrounds; his scenery was picturesque; but his style was pompous, and his finish rough and careless. Feuds and intrigues and massacres and block-house fights took part in the quick action of his plots. He so often introduced the Indian that he is styled " The Cooper of the South." His best tale, " The Yemassee," written in 1835, furnishes a striking picture of the Southern wilderness, in which is an uprising of real, wide-awake Indians.

Among his other works, are " The Partisan," " Donna Florida," and " The Damsel of Darien." Whenever he had finished a book, he was obliged to take a sea-voyage from Charleston to New York in order to arrange with a publisher. The war ruined his prospects, and destroyed his lovely country home, " Woodlands," where for years generous hospitality had been dispensed. Boys yet eagerly read Simms's adventures, which bring anew an interesting era of nearly a century ago; and he must be regarded the pioneer and patron of early Southern literature. Two of the members of the literary group in Charleston — of which he was the genius — were Timrod and Hayne.

Henry Timrod (1829-1867), was one of the most finely endowed of Southern poets. As an editor in Columbia, his printing-office was demolished in Sherman's " March to the Sea "; but it is as the lyrist of love and war and Nature that he displays his clearness and simplicity of utterance. Among his ringing war lyrics are " The Call to Arms " and " Carolina "; and their strain is as direct and lofty an expression of Southern sentiment as some of Whittier's are of Northern. His finest ode was written for the decoration of the soldiers' graves in Magnolia Cemetery. His spontaneous Nature passion, he has shown in several poems of singular beauty. Here is a stanza to Spring : —

" In the deep heart of every forest tree
  The blood is all aglee,
  And there's a look about the leafless bowers
  As if they dreamed of flowers."

Timrod's life was brief, and the two years left him
after the war was over, were but a struggle with
hopeless illness and dire poverty.

Paul Hamilton Hayne (1830-1886), is ranked
" The Laureate of the South." With a beautiful
home, embracing a fine library — every social advantage that aristocratic Charleston could offer — and an
ample fortune — he found it easy to devote his talents
to literature. He was selected as the first editor of
" Russell's Magazine," which, launched in Simms's
library, was intended to equal in popularity " The
Edinburgh Review." Hayne was also the author of
many forms of verse — all of them correct in metre
and profusely figurative. Indeed, in every way, a
bright career seemed opening out before him. Then
the war came, and he served in the field until too ill
either to march or to fight, and at its close, his health
was shattered and his fortune lost. To gain support
and vigour, he fashioned in the Pine Barrens of
Northern Georgia a rude hut, like that of Thoreau,
at Walden Pond. He planted flowers and fruits,
and " Copse Hill " was the gathering-place for his
admiring friends.

With a courageous soul, he turned his thoughts

to Nature, working to the end, on legends and lyrics, for which he found inspiration right about his forest home — in violet or lily, or pine-cone, or lake or storm. The song of the mocking-bird allured him as that of the lark did Shelley — for he tells how its

> ". . . love notes fill the enchanted land;
> Through leaf-wrought bars they storm the stars,
> These love-songs of the mocking-birds!"

Again: —

> "When the winds are whist,
> He follows his mate to their sunset tryst,
> Where the wedded myrtles and jasmine twine,
> Oh! the swell of his music is half divine!"

We have already referred to another poet, Father Ryan, who as chaplain in the Confederate army voiced his attachment to the South. His "Sword of Robert Lee" is a stirring battle-cry, while "The Conquered Banner" is an "eloquent lament" over defeat. Indeed, Ryan has been called "The Laureate of the Lost Cause." Some of his poems, however, are deeply religious; and there was, also, Father Tabb, who served in the Confederate army, was taken prisoner, and placed in Point Lookout. Later, he was ordained a priest of the Roman Church and became a teacher in St. Charles College, Maryland.

During his last years he was blind, and his stanzas of rarely more than eight lines are becoming generally known and winning favour. In these, he gives artistic expression to a single thought, either grave or gay. As one has said: " These little lyrics flew like song-birds from his seclusion "; and they are well worth memorising, as for example: —

> " The waves forever move;
>   The hills forever rest;
>   Yet each the heavens approve,
>   And love alike hath blessed.—
>   A Martha's household care,
>   A Mary's cloistered prayer."

Another one " Solitude ": —

> "Like as a brook that all night long
>   Sings, as at noon, a babble song
>   To sleep's unheeding ear,
>   The poet to himself must sing,
>   When none but God is listening
>   The lullaby to hear."

And how sweetly he proclaims his simple Creed in his poem, " The Christ ": —

> " Thou hast on earth a Trinity,—
>   Thyself, my fellow-man, and me;
>   When one with him, then one with Thee;
>   Nor, save together, Thine are we."

Of this band of Southland poets, Sidney Lanier (1842-1881), ranks next to Poe in his ideals and poetic impulse; but his life-story has in it the same pathos that belongs to the lives of Timrod and Hayne — the desolation of Civil War, and the later almost despairing conflict with feebleness and lack of means. He was born in Macon, Georgia, on February third, 1842, and claimed a musical ancestry, even as far back as Queen Elizabeth. So it was natural that even before he could read well, he could improvise upon the flute, guitar, piano and organ — and he might have included the violin, had not his father discovered that its music affected him strangely.

He graduated at Oglethorpe College, and feeling called to a literary career, he was hoping for a year abroad at a German university. But he was suddenly awakened from his dreams by the opening guns of the Civil War. Responding to the appeals of impassioned orators as the war fever swept over the Southern States, he joined the Confederate army. Three times he was offered promotion, but preferred to remain with a younger brother who enlisted with him. Finally, he was captured and imprisoned in Point Lookout; but he carried with him his beloved flute concealed in his sleeve, and with it he enlivened many tedious hours for the other prisoners, during the five months he was held here. On his release, he made way on foot to his home in Macon. He was an excellent critic and in his novel, " Tiger

Lilies," he later gave his war impressions; and he never recovered from the hard conditions that he had faced.

After the war, he was at one time a clerk, at another he studied law with his father, for he said that he had to win bread for his family while a thousand songs were ringing in his heart. When he could no longer endure such an existence, " taking his flute and pen for sword and staff," he went to live in Baltimore, for there he could listen to orchestras and browse on libraries. Music and poetry were his two master passions. The rest of his life he contended against poverty and the ravages of consumption.

He was one of the marvellous flute-players of America, and as a flutist won his way everywhere, and soon obtained a position in the Peabody Orchestra. He was greatly attracted to such music, and formed a scheme for travelling orchestras so that young people might be educated to an appreciation of the finest symphonies.

He read and studied and wrote so diligently that he was soon known in Baltimore as a man of letters. He loved quaint and curious bits of literature and embodied them in books for boys. Among them were " The Boy's King Arthur," " The Boy's Percy," and " The Boy's Froissart." He also wrote excellent critical studies on English verse and the English novel.

Like Timrod and Hayne, Lanier is filled with the spirit of the Southland.   His poetic themes are love, Nature, and faith, and in remarkable feeling for tone and colour, expressed in felicitous words.   His poems are among the rarest in our literature, and a few extracts are chosen: —

> " Music is love in search of a word."

> " His song was only living aloud,
>   His work, a singing with his hands."

> " Thou'rt only a grey and sober dove,
>   But thine eye is faith and thy wing is love."

His " Corn " which is full of " green things growing " has often been counted his master-song, for when it came out in " Lippincott's," in 1874, it drew attention to his other poetry.

We seldom find a Southern robin in literature; but Lanier, in "lyrical outburst," writes his "Tampa Robin": —

> " The robin laughed in the orange-tree;
>   ' Ho, windy North, a fig for thee:
>   While breasts are red and wings are bold
>   And green trees wave us globes of gold,
>   Time's scythe shall reap but bliss for me
>   — Sunlight, song, and the orange-tree.
>
> " I'll south with the sun and keep my clime;
>   My wing is king of the summer-time;

My breast to the sun his torch shall hold;
And I'll call down through the green and gold,
Time, take thy scythe, reap bliss for me,
Bestir thee under the orange-tree!"

Would we know of Lanier's euphony, read a stanza from his " Song of the Chattahoochee," which ripples and flows along like Tennyson's " Brook ": —

"Out of the hills of Habersham,
Down the valleys of Hall,
I hurry amain to reach the plain,
Run the rapid and leap the fall,
Split at the rock and together again,
Accept my bed, or narrow or wide,
And flee from folly on every side,
With a lover's pain to attain the plain,
Far from the hills of Habersham,
Far from the valleys of Hall."

In his " Ballad of Trees and the Master," Lanier shows his power in religious verse. In this he reverently touches the life of our Lord, in his dramatic presentation of the scenes in Gethsemane and on Calvary; while his noblest poem, " The Marshes of Glynn," manifests in sweeping and rhythmic metre, his earnest faith in God. In all Lanier's writings, one detects his intense love of beauty and his attempt to correlate music and poetry.

He received the appointment of lecturer on English literature in Johns Hopkins University, Baltimore, but he could not hold it long on account of failing strength; and he travelled much but he grew weaker and weaker. The glow of sunrise had ever been in his poems —" Sunrise " was his swan-song, and thus it ended: —

> " The sun is brave, the sun is bright,
> The sun is lord of love and light,
> But after him it cometh night "—

and his short, troubled life closed on September seventh, 1881.

The names of Timrod, Hayne, and Lanier, will have lasting place in every anthology of American men of letters, by reason of their pure and elevating gifts, and the sadness and courage of their lives.

Lanier believed implicitly that his Southland would be redeemed; but he could not in most eager vision have prophesied the wondrous evolution of the New South. Here plough and mill and factory are busily at work. Public schools are established all over the land, and everywhere cities are rapidly growing. And what wonderful strides have been made in literary progress — enough to satisfy the most wide-awake reader. Our story does not concern living authors, else we should dwell upon the fascinating masters of the story that perhaps first caught their genius for construction from Edgar Poe. Vivid and romantic pictures there are of quaint " Old Creole Days ";

"The Grandissimes" is replete with episode and mirth; "Dr. Sevier" is delicate and artistic.

Lovable "Uncle Remus" introduces us to "Brer Rabbit," "Brer Fox" and "Brer B'ar," who fascinate us alike with folk-lore and philosophy. "In Ole Virginia" we read of plantation life during the war. Who does not know "Marse Chan" and "Meh Lady"?

Another lures us away into the remote wilds of the Tennessee mountains, and lets us into the secrets of a gloomy and powerful race; and then we may emerge into the broad sunshine of the Kentucky "blue-grass region"— listen to the song of the cardinal, and revel in the witchery of meadows and hempfields, sunny skies, and wild forests, as pictured in the sketches of its literary artist. Maurice Thompson speaks of the South as the land

> " . . whose gaze is cast
> No more upon the past."

XXIX

WESTERN LITERATURE

VERY like the New England colonists were the self-reliant pioneers of the West, working shoulder to shoulder, with push and energy, following the trail over the aboriginal mountains or through the dense woods, fighting Indians or wild beasts, mining for gold, or building camps and towns — and their assertive, democratic character is seen in the books of their authors as in the speeches of their political leaders; and while in the South, we have the note of the lyrist or the romancer, in the West, we may gather tales of bold and picturesque adventure.

With scant traditions and few high schools, the busy West made a tardy beginning in literature, but its growth has been unchecked, until to-day as we follow the sweep of civilisation across our broad land, we find an unbroken line of authors. We study the lives of some of these to learn what has been accomplished.

First, there is Bret Harte (1839-1902), who is a kind of historian of an early era, for his renown rests on his making California life — in phases both good and bad — known to the world in the days of the modern Argonauts. The son of a Greek professor of Albany, New York, he was deemed a precocious rather than a scholarly boy; but even at seven, he pored over Dickens, just because he liked his way of saying things. As he older grew, visions of golden air-castles floated before him as he marvelled at the almost unbelievable stories that came to the East — of the finds of California — stories that lured many a youth to the then distant Pacific coast.

When he was fifteen, his father having died, he took his mother and started West to pick up a fortune ready to his hand. What unusual scenes must have opened on the eyes of both mother and son when they reached California, coming as they did from dignified, conservative Albany! For they were at once face to face with novel and chaotic social conditions; this sparsely-settled land of majestic mountains, primeval forests, rugged canyons, and flashing sea-coast, had been suddenly altered into a very wildwood of freedom.

Few women were to be seen; but thousands of men in red shirts and high-topped boots were digging for gold; some of them heroic men, delving with restless, homesick energy for a hoard just large enough to transport their families thither. Rugged workmen, too, there were; and vagabonds and fugitives from justice — and they varied the digging by gambling and duelling and much easy sword practice.

But Harte did not, at once, enter into his " El Dorado." After a time his mother married again.

He made many ventures, he policed the safes of the " Wells and Fargo Express Company " from bandits; he was, in turn, collector, druggist, school-teacher, and secretary of the mint, and finally from being a printer, he graduated into editorial work, and was one of a group of young journalists — among them was Mark Twain — all full of hope in the future; and Harte was later made editor of the newly-started " Overland Monthly."

His various occupations had taken him all over the country, and with rare mimetic quality and keen sensitiveness for the spectacular, he had collected materials for many short stories, and *these* were *his* gold mines which he profitably worked for years. They were not like those of Dickens but written in the same sympathetic spirit — and with Irving, Poe, and Hawthorne, he is conspicuous among our creators of the short story. His style is individual and he has an astounding vocabulary. Most of his characters are apprehended with realistic humour and pathos, from *real* life.

After several of Harte's books had been published and welcomed, it was suggested that they would be even more telling, if he would try romance. Then " The Luck of Roaring Camp " appeared. Its characterisation was so rough and unusual that it was severely criticised, but it attracted notice everywhere, and " The Atlantic " immediately asked for another story after the same manner. This gave Bret Harte reputation for his tales, while " The Heathen Chinee," somewhat later, made his name as a humourous poet.

At this period, Chinese " cheap labour " was the war-cry and " He went for the Heathen Chinee! " and immortalised him. Many other poems of Harte's are very popular; so, as well, are his prose tales, for he was an incessant writer. He had no rival in his descriptions of old California sights and sounds. Sometimes he delivered lectures; the one most often heard was " The Argonauts of Forty-nine." But slow of thought and speech, he cared little for lecturing.

A man of strong impulse, he was weak in character; he was true to a present friend while ignoring an absent one. He was uncertain in keeping appoint-ments and most improvident in financial concerns; there was a vein of satire in his editorial columns that grew more evident; he did not hold his own in the world of letters; and after a few years, he lost favour in San Francisco. He came East and wrote for " The Atlantic " and other periodicals. He lived an irregular life, always beyond his income, and finally, in 1878, left his family to accept the consulate at Crefeld, Germany, and was soon transferred to Glasgow, Scotland; but he was " a wandering comet " — he did not meet his duties squarely — and was presently removed from the consular service.

However, as a polished gentleman and a man of

letters, he was taken more seriously in England than elsewhere. England liked his books, placed them on her book-shelves, and highly estimated their author. And in England he spent his later years and died, in 1902, at Camberly, Surrèy. And Woodberry says: —

" He had no rival and left no successor. His work is as unique as that of Poe or Hawthorne."

From Bret Harte's career, it is pleasant to review that of Eugene Field (1850-1895), for he is the laureate that the Middle West has given to children. His first leaning towards literature came to him when as a little boy in St. Louis, his grandmother made him write sermons, and paid him ninepence for every one that he wrote. He was very carefully educated but he could not graduate at college, for his father died and the money gave out. But he was soon hard at work at journalism and finally settled in Chicago, engaged on the editorial staff of " The Daily News."

He describes as follows the romance of his life: —

" A little bit of a woman came
Athwart my path one day;

. . " " . .

That little bit of a woman cast
Her two eyes full on me,

SAMUEL L. CLEMENS

FRANCIS BRET HARTE

EUGENE FIELD

HENRY CUYLER BUNNER

And they smote me sore to my inmost core
And they held me slaved forevermore,
Yet would I not be free.

.   .   .   .   .   .

And I'm proud to say that I bless the day
When a little woman wrought her way
Into this life of mine!"

And in Chicago, this winsome man and his family were perfectly idolised. He was the leader of " The Saints' and Sinners' Club," the " Saints " being three Chicago clergymen. He illustrated manuscripts for his friends and in many directions interested them in literature. He treasured his books, using the gentlest touch in opening and closing them. He was a gatherer of rare editions: —

" Such as bibliophiles adore —
Books and prints in endless store —
Treasures singly or in sets."

His poems and prose later have won alike the hearts of grown-ups and children; but especially to the latter, he dedicated exquisite lines — and how they, in return, lavished upon him their affection. To assist in his work, he kept in his library a curious collection of toys and trinkets and dolls and animals; and " each spinster doll, and each toy animal and each tin soldier, had a part to play in some poem." The best-known of his works are " A Little Book of

Western Verse," and "A Little Book of Profitable Tales," and a variety of juveniles appear in these. Who that has read it can ever forget "Little Boy Blue"? Or who can overlook the moral so pathetically emphasised in that "little peach of emerald hue" that dawned on the sight of Johnny Jones and his sister Sue?

> "John took a bite and Sue a chew,
> And then the trouble began to brew,—
> Trouble the doctor couldn't subdue,
>   Too true!
>
> Under the turf where the daisies grew,
> They planted John and his sister Sue,
> And their little souls to the angels flew,—
>   Boo hoo!"

Field hoped to write a "Modern Mother Goose," founded upon Indian folk-lore, but this he was unable to do.

He was a universal joker, and he had great power of adaptation, even to taking the epitaph on Shakespeare's tomb and fitting it as follows to his own portrait, and as an advertisement for his works: —

> "Sweete friends, for mercy's sake forbeare
> To criticise ys visage here;
>   But reade my bookes
>   Which, spite my lookes
> Ben fulle of mightie plaisaunt cheere."

Another like Bret Harte, to preserve contemporary

life in the West, was Samuel J. Clemens, so familiarly known as Mark Twain, the celebrated humourist, standing perhaps above, and separate from the other two. Born in Missouri, he spent his boyhood in Hannibal. Possibly he would not have called this so feelingly "a loafy, down-at-the heel, slave-holding Mississippi town," if he could have imagined that, in 1912, his first home would be presented to the city by Mr. and Mrs. George A. Mahan; and accompanied by a bas-relief portrait, and a memorial tablet, which bears these words : —

"Mark Twain's life teaches that poverty is an incentive rather than a bar, and that any boy, however humble his birth and surroundings, may by honesty and industry accomplish great things."

Samuel's father died when he was but twelve, and he left school to become a printer, a vocation which he pursued in different places for eight years; and printing the words of others led him to the desire of being an author himself, and yet his strongest ambition was to serve as pilot on the Mississippi; and when the opportunity came, he gladly quit printing, and hoped to live a pilot and die at the wheel, but during the war, the river lost its commerce.

He next went to visit Nevada, the land of outlaws, mining-camps, and murders. He did not escape the mining fever and journeyed to California — then wandered away to the Sandwich Islands. In San Francisco, he reported for a newspaper; his humourous sketches brought him into notice, and he began to lecture. Later, he travelled in Europe, Egypt, and the Holy Land. Then as partner in a publishing-house that failed, he lost every cent of his well-earned fortune; and like Walter Scott, in similar emergency, he assumed the whole debt and wrote untiringly until he had paid every penny of the firm's indebtedness. In his last years, Mark Twain lived in Hartford, Connecticut. where he and his wife entertained delightfully, and yet a later home was at Redding, not very far distant.

The bare facts of this life do not sound literary, but few Americans hold a more secure place in the affection of readers of all classes than Mark Twain; and we have hurried over the plain facts that we may take a second view from a literary standpoint, and first as to his early scholarly preferences, and these they were: " I like history, biography, travels, curious facts and strange happenings, and science; and I detest novels, poetry, and theology." His views certainly changed in time — at least in regard to novels.

In the beginning, he wrote much for boys: for following in the steps of T. B. Aldrich's " Bad Boy," his " Tom Sawyer " and " Huckleberry Finn " embody experiences of his boyhood. " Tom Sawyer " is a tale of his days spent at a wretched Western school, and into it, are woven Indians and witches and charms, a maiden, a bit of camp life — all actual scenes en-

acted by wide-awake boys; while " Huckleberry
Finn "—" The Odyssey of the Mississippi "— holds
the interest by the novelty of its incidents.   Perhaps
the vital one is when Huck debates with himself
whether it is his duty to save Jim, the runaway slave,
or to deliver him to his master.   " Huckleberry
Finn " is Mark Twain's classic.

His " Stories of the Mississippi Valley " form an
amusing fragment of his own autobiography.   Over
and over he heard the sounder cry out " mark twain! "
as the lead drops two fathoms, and in this quaint,
practical phrase originated his pen-name.   He had a
knack as a pilot of picking up all sorts of specimens of
human nature, and presenting them to the reader; and
the " Father of Waters " itself, here and elsewhere
in his books, inspired him as the Hudson inspired Irving.

After his extensive travels, he wrote his " Innocents Abroad," and afterwards his " Tramps
Abroad"; the former specially is inexpressibly funny
with the pretensions of some of the " Innocents " in
their absurd situations — and as long as the world
laughs, it will be popular.   It has been published in
several languages, and rewarded its author with fame
and fortune.

" Pudd'nhead Wilson " is a slave story with a most
philosophic hero.

Twain's " Jumping Frog "— known to everybody
— was written in San Francisco.   Bret Harte said

that it never could be so funny to anyone as to him when Mark Twain repeated it in his drawling tones. There is much beauty and a stern sense of justice in his " Personal Recollections of Joan of Arc." His English stories, " The Prince and the Pauper," and " A Connecticut Yankee at King Arthur's Court," are placed against carefully studied backgrounds.

To call Mark Twain just a humourist would be as one has said to describe Shakespeare as a strolling-player. Back of his humour are always the philosopher and reformer. He loved to hit hard at hypocrisy and every insincerity, and admired noble character. As to his emphatic style, he had a saying: " As to the adjective, when in doubt, strike it out! " And yet with Franklin, Holmes, and Lowell, his humour was most genial, even though the underlying purpose was clear.

Many Clemensesque experiences might be recorded, did space permit. The accompanying one is pleasing or trying, which ever we choose to think it:

One morning going to breakfast before his wife, he discovered at her plate a bulky envelope bearing foreign stamps. His curiosity overcame him; he opened it to find a detailed account of his own death and burial in Australia,— and a note of condolence to Mrs. Clemens. The description was so touching that it moved him to tears, and later when he was in Australia, he visited the tomb of the impostor who had impersonated him there.

And in closing, just one reference to his unswerving love to his family, as evinced when he had the following epitaph by Robert Richardson placed over his daughter's grave : —

> "Warm Summer sun,
>   Shine kindly here,
> Warm Southern wind
>   Blow softly here,
> Green sod above
>   Lie light, lie light,
> Good night, dear heart,
>   Good night, good night."

He founded at Redding, a public library, and since his death Mr. Andrew Carnegie has made this self-supporting, to be known for ever as " The Mark Twain Memorial Library."

Of Mark Twain, Rev. Dr. Henry Van Dyke has written : —

" Those who know the story of his friendship and his family life know that he was one who ' loved much ' and faithfully, even unto the end. Those who know his work as a whole know that under the lambent and irrepressible humour which was his gift there was a foundation of serious thought and noble affections and desires."

And out of the new West have come other writers. Among them, Edward Eggleston, the editor, novelist, and itinerant preacher, who, in his Hoosier stories, has made us acquainted with picturesque characters and log-cabin life. And if we would seek a master-bard, " The Poet of the Sierras " has long stood apart like a mountain peak, giving to the world from time to time glimpses of wild beauty and rugged grandeur as he has written of Western scenery and people; and he yet lives to reminisce of the early California days. And now some of our best poets and historians and novel-writers are in the Western States. As truly as " Westward the course of Empire holds its way "— so truly, " Westward the course of literature *shall* hold its way."

WYNKEN, BLYNKEN, AND NOD

(Dutch Lullaby.)

" Wynken, Blynken, and Nod one night
    Sailed off in a wooden shoe,—
Sailed on a river of crystal light,
    Into a sea of dew.
' Where are you going, and what do you wish?'
    The old moon asked the three.
' We have come to fish for the herring-fish
    That live in this beautiful sea;
    Nets of silver and gold have we!'
        Said Wynken,
        Blynken,
        And Nod.

The old moon laughed and sang a song,
    As they rocked in the wooden shoe,
And the wind that sped them all night long
    Ruffled the waves of dew.

The little stars were the herring-fish
  That lived in the beautiful sea —
'Now cast your nets wherever you wish,—
  Never afeared are we!'
So cried the stars to the fishermen three:
      Wynken,
      Blynken,
      And Nod.

All night long their nets they threw
  To the stars in the twinkling foam,—
Then down from the skies came the wooden shoe,
  Bringing the fishermen home;
'Twas all so pretty a sail it seemed
  As if it could not be,
And some folks thought 'twas a dream they'd dreamed
  Of sailing that beautiful sea;
But I shall name you the fishermen three:
      Wynken,
      Blynken,
      And Nod.

Wynken and Blynken are two little eyes,
  And Nod is a little head.
And the wooden shoe that sailed the skies
  Is a wee one's trundle-bed;
So shut your eyes while mother sings
  Of wonderful sights that be,
And you shall see the beautiful things
  As you rock in the misty sea,
  Where the old shoe rocked the fishermen three:
      Wynken,
      Blynken,
      And Nod."

— Field.

XXX

A GROUP OF EASTERN AUTHORS

IT takes many lives to form a rounded literary tale, and the following chapter contains a few vignettes of others who claim mention in our book; most of them have died so recently that we could not, if we would, place them in fair perspective. Prominent among these are Taylor, Crawford, Hale, Stockton, Whitman, Stoddard, Stedman, and Aldrich.

Bayard Taylor (1825-1878), was a Pennsylvania boy of Quaker family, of whom a phrenologist early foretold that his vagabond instincts would control his life; and with a hundred and forty dollars, a few newspaper promises, his knapsack and wunderstaff, he started out at nineteen to fulfil the prophecy; he spent two years in Europe, tramping over three thousand miles, and learning to live on six cents a day. This sojourn his biographer calls his " University education."

On his return, his letters to " The New York Tribune " and other papers were collected into a volume, and readers were enthusiastic over the pluck displayed in " Views Afoot." One has wondered what he might have accomplished if he had owned a bicycle — for with feet attached to pedals, " Views A-Bicycle " would have multiplied his opportunities a hundred-fold. Then when the gold fever of '49 caught the East, he followed the Argonauts to California as correspondent of the " Tribune," and took in Mexico on the way back.

In later trips, he wandered from Iceland to Cape of Good Hope, and in the East as far as India, China, and Japan, always with pen in hand, mastering languages, wearing native dress, and as far as possible assimilating native customs. So his travel books are glowing pictures of actual things, but they are utterly devoid of the historical setting that would have enhanced their value. At one time he was secretary of the United States legation at St. Petersburg, and he died in 1878, while on a mission to Germany.

In his writings, he emphasised his love for his early home, Kennett Square, Pennsylvania, by building there his stately residence " Cedarcroft "; and it is with this that his novels are associated. " The Story of Kennett " is by many ranked his best book. He acquired extensive knowledge of German classics, and among his translations, that of Goethe's " Faust " is most faithful and sympathetic. He was, also, an interesting lecturer on a wide range of themes, but he cared not to be noted either as traveller or lecturer, and his aim was to be a famous poet.

This ideal he never reached; he had lyrical genius and has written a fair amount of verse — but he may not be ranked great; for his versatility hindered concentrated effort, and besides he wasted talent on what was commonplace. His finest dramatic poem undoubtedly is " The Masque of the Gods." His " Centennial Ode " was read at Philadelphia, in 1876. Among his longer poems is " Lars: a pastoral of Norway "; in his lyrics is " The Song of the Camp," in which are the familiar lines: —

> " The bravest are the tenderest,
>   The loving are the daring."

His " Bedouin Song," is thought by some to hold its own among our choicest love lyrics.

This self-made man was master of a score of languages, and shared fellowship with authors the earth around, and he wrote more than fifty books. He is remembered, however, as poet and translator.

Marion Crawford (1854-1909), the son of a sculptor, was born in Rome, and spent so much of his life there and in other foreign cities, that in Italy he was taken for an Italian — in France for a Frenchman — in Germany for a German. One of the most prolific of writers, he published in twelve years twenty-five books — his daily output of words being sometimes six thousand.

His style was free from mannerisms; and always the cities where he lived, the streets and people and houses, grew into his pages, and he fearlessly painted existing conditions. And a wide circle caught the

EDWARD CLARENCE STEDMAN   BAYARD TAYLOR

THOMAS BAILEY ALDRICH   WALT WHITMAN

spirit of his intellectual and artistic novels, and as he owned, " they became in his hands a marketable commodity." To characterise his numerous works would be entirely beyond our scope. His first, " Mr. Isaacs," is full of Oriental colouring. " The Cigar-Maker's Romance " is, perhaps, most perfect in form; while the " Saracinesca Trilogy," with the scenes laid in modern Rome, has hosts of readers.

Edward Everett Hale (1822-1909), for his optimistic devotion to his native city, has been called " A Bostonian of Bostonians." For more than fifty years, he was a prominent Unitarian minister, and he also showed wonderful versatility as a lecturer, writer of essays, history and biography, and a master-craftsman of short stories. In these, like De Foe, he made fictitious subjects appear real.

The best illustration of his art is " The Man Without a Country." In this, an officer who is being tried for treasonable conduct curses his native land; on this account, he is condemned to spend his life forever at sea, and never in any way to hear the United States mentioned, or to read a word concerning it. This story, with its grave moral, was quoted the world over as true; and appearing as it did in the time of the Civil War, it did much to quicken the patriotism of both soldiers and sailors.

And Edward Everett Hale identified himself with many philanthropic projects. His Waldensian story, " In His Name," was widely read; while his " Ten

Times One is Ten," proposing the formation of circles of " King's Sons " and " Daughters " has carried immense force everywhere, for its motto is: —" Look up and not down; Look forward and not back; Look out and not in; and lend a hand."

Francis Richard Stockton (1834-1902), another writer of brief stories, resembles Edward Everett Hale, in that he, too, made fiction seem reality, and yet in his whimsical romances, he stands quite alone. His fantastic characters, set in the oddest kind of plots, encounter ridiculous and bewildering experiences; and all are treated with such seriousness and quiet dignity that as we breathlessly watch absurd people do absurd things, for the moment everything becomes true. Among Stockton's creations are " The Casting Away of Mrs. Lecks and Mrs. Aleshine," " The Hundredth Man," and " The Lady or the Tiger? "

Young people are not usually fascinated with the problems which Walt Whitman, with keen directness, presents in his writings; but his name is so noteworthy among our men of letters that we obey the summons to glance at his life and work as we pass along. The literary world is always trying to decide which of the problematic authors — Emerson, Hawthorne, Poe, or Whitman — ranks highest — and Whitman (1819-1892), makes the greatest challenge of them all! Some regard him a second Homer, and in their Whitmania are absorbed in Whitmanesque literature; while

others are sure that he is but an impostor, forcing his
" Whitmanesque stuff " upon our bookshelves.

This isolated and eccentric genius was a native of
West Hills, in " fish-shaped " Long Island, and after
his family moved to Brooklyn, he often returned to his
early home to wander with the fishermen or clam-
diggers, or hay-cutters, or herdsmen; and one of his
chief pleasures was to declaim Shakespeare or Homer
to the sea-gulls or the surf — for it goes without saying that he was a literary youth and read everything.
After gaining his education in the Brooklyn public schools, he was a teacher and editor in different towns in the island; and in Brooklyn he
was a painter and carpenter, and a writer of editorials.

With a passion for crowds, inspiration came to him
as he watched the busy tide, surging up and down the
city streets, and he often haunted ferry-boats, omni-
buses, and theatres, and his companions were drivers,
pilots, and deck-hands. Presently, a strong desire
was in him — no less than to put on record his own
distinctive personality, and it should be unlike that of
any other American that ever wrote. He changed
his name Walter to " Walt "; assumed an unconventional garb; wore a rough beard; stuck his hat on one
side of his head; and said what he chose. Naturally
such audacity did not pass unheeded.

He began to write his " Leaves of Grass," which
was intended to be an appeal to the masses, but he

little realised that its profundity was far too great for his purpose.

Whitman, like Whittier and Thoreau, never went abroad but travelled widely in the United States and Canada — very often as a pedestrian. Once he halted in New Orleans for a time to do editorial work. For nearly three years during the Civil War, he was a volunteer hospital nurse, and he lived on the coarsest fare that he might give the boys luxuries; and thousands of those for whom he cared testified to his tender ministrations. The war stirred his inmost soul, and in his " Drum-Taps " is a more human touch than in any other of his poems.

His dirge written on the death of Lincoln is a *perfect* dirge; and Donald G. Mitchell, after reading it, said: —

" If he gathers coarse weeds into his ' Leaves of Grass,' we forget and forgive when he doffs his cap in reverent and courtly fashion to ' My Captain.' "

Defiant of all laws of conventional life he freed himself from literary trammels, and felt himself a reformer, preaching democracy and comradeship. He is better known as a poet than as a prose-writer, and with colossal self-confidence announced: " I celebrate myself and sing myself." The title " Leaves of Grass " was given to his collected poems which as he said were made of " words simple as grass." In these idealistic gems scattered here and there, he discloses his intense fondness for Nature.

In sympathy with every class but the aristocratic, he knew little of society. He had, however, devoted literary friends to whom he was " The good grey poet "— among them, Bryant, Burroughs, and Stedman; and the last honoured him with a whole chapter in his " American Poets " and thus eulogises him: —

> " Blythe prodigal, the rhythm free and strong
>   Of thy brave voice forecasts our poet's song."

England sees in Whitman our future poet, and this is because of the warm appreciation of Swinburne and Tennyson and Symonds.

The venerable poet spent his last days in Camden, New Jersey, in a dingy little house, whose library held " the storage collection of his life." In the town, he was called " Socrates," or as one has dubbed him, " Mr. Socrates." Everybody knew him — and expected his kind word — for, after all, he possessed a curious kind of sociability. Burroughs says: —

> " He is like a mountain; as you get away from him in point of time and perspective, the features soften down and you get the true beauty."

Richard Henry Stoddard (1825-1893), was a poor Massachusetts boy, who was taken to New York as a child, and there found his education in the public schools. Next he worked in a foundry and studied poetry at night, for he had a rich fancy, with a fascinating love of the beautiful. He studied so diligently in classical and modern poetry that he became an excellent critic; and somewhere he tells how he wrought his own songs —

> "Like the blowing of the wind
>   Or the flowing of the stream
>   In the music of my mind."

Through Hawthorne's favour, he obtained a position in the New York custom-house, and served later in the dock department and public library; and presently he was able to abandon official duties and to devote himself to his loved literature. For the rest of his life, he was known as journalist, and editor — and what he preferred most — *poet*. His prose works consist largely of criticism and biography, but from first to last he *was* a poet, and in his style, influenced by Wordsworth, Shelley, and Keats.

His " Songs of Summer " was published in 1856. Two stanzas are quoted: —

> "The sky is a drinking-cup,
>   That was overturned of old,
>   And it pours in the eyes of men
>   Its wine of airy gold.

> We drink that wine all day,
>   Till the last drop is drained up,
> And are lighted off to bed
>   By the jewels in the cup!"

His " Book of the East " is tinged with the brightness of the Orient.

Stoddard is perhaps not popular, but admired by critical lovers of poetry, because his instincts are sure. He was imbued alike with the wisdom and the strength of the self-educated man; but he fostered the literary spirit of his day in New York, working in friendship with other authors, specially with Taylor and Stedman, and for himself he offers this apology: —

> " These songs of mine, the best that I have sung,
>   Are not my best, for caged within the lines
>   Are thousand better, if they would but sing!"

Edmund Clarence Stedman (1833-1908), came from Hartford to New York, and here entered into journalistic work. During the war, he served as newspaper correspondent. His most popular poems which belong to his earlier years are war ballads and lyrics. His others manifest artistic and humourous rather than creative gifts. Among them are the eloquent tribute to Hawthorne, already quoted, and many in a vein more light, such as " Toujours Amours " and " Pan in Wall Street." On the last subject Mr. Stedman could write feelingly since for thirty-six years he was the " Banker-Poet." His renown rests on the magnificent books of clear and incisive criticism which he has left, and from which we have several times made extracts. These are included in his invaluable volumes: " Victorian Poets," " Poets of America," " A Victorian Anthology," and " An American Anthology."

The " Banker-Poet " was a man of the world, delighting in the acquaintance of men in different walks in life, and a leading factor in literary centres, ever ready to assist younger men of letters. He will be remembered long as a cordial and optimistic scholar with wide knowledge of literature.

High among the authors that succeeded the old New England group must be ranked Thomas Bailey Aldrich (1836-1907). " The Bad Boy " of Portsmouth, New Hampshire, he spent his summers here, and his winters in New Orleans. As a youth, he was hurried into his uncle's office in New York, for he had betrayed an instinct for rhyming and it was feared that he *might* become a poet. Notwithstanding this precaution, there appeared before he was twenty a slender volume of poems. This was followed by his dainty " Babie Bell," which, copied far and wide, would alone have made its author known.

And now came the conflict between counting-house and bookish workshop, and the latter won, and Aldrich commenced editorial and journalistic writing in

New York, and also became a member of the group of notable Metropolitan poets, including Stoddard, Stedman, and Taylor.   In 1870, he removed to Boston, and there his elegant Mount Vernon Street home was distinguished for the generous hospitality of its host.

For ten years, he was the clever, mirthful, and methodical editor of " The Atlantic Monthly."   He was a perfect workman, embroidering his themes to the minutest detail.   We estimate his tales and poems as we would a miniature of artistic finish.   One of his characteristics was to hold a story till it was completed to his full satisfaction.   George Parsons Lathrop, in the following quotation from Aldrich, illustrates this point: " I've got a story under way that promises well.   But just as my people were in the midst of a flourishing conversation, they stopped. No one of them would say a thing, and there they sit, while I've been kept waiting a couple of weeks for the next speech."   Indeed, Aldrich always wrote when the mood was on him rather than in careless haste.

His " Story of a Bad Boy," told in romantic vein, admits us to the secrets of his own youthful escapades, and it is now not only a juvenile classic, but invests the old Portsmouth house with historic charm.   Indeed, Portsmouth days and Portsmouth ways enter into some of his other prose works.   His reminiscences of trips abroad are embodied in his graphic and amusing book, " Travels from Ponkapog to Pesth." Among the shorter tales are " Marjorie Daw " and " Two Bites at a Cherry."

Aldrich describes a poet as one who

> " deftly weaves
> A tissue out of autumn leaves,
> With here a thistle, there a rose,
> With art and patience thus is made
> The poet's perfect cloth of gold."

and in this "perfect cloth of gold" his verse is woven. Here is a description from " Friar Jerome's Beautiful Book "— the volume that " was not writ in vain "— and it is a rare picture of an illuminated page: —

> " Here and there from out of the woods
> A brilliant tropic bird took flight;
> And through the margins many a vine
> Went wandering — roses, red and white,
> Tulip, windflower, and columbine."

Aldrich was also a maker of sonnets and of delicate quatrains — those " Four line epics one might hide in the hearts of roses."

Sometimes he is called " The Poet of Ponkapog," because many of his poems hailed from this country home not far from Boston; again some would dub him " The American Herrick "; and his flawless

EDWARD EVERETT HALE

FRANK R. STOCKTON

WILLIAM DEAN HOWELLS

F. MARION CRAWFORD

lyrics possess the Herrick gem-like polish, but not the soul that shines through those of the English bard — yet rarely are the two combined.

Everything from Aldrich's pen was eagerly awaited; so we may think him one of the few who wrote too little, for seven or eight volumes comprise his works, and they are commended as especially desirable for young people.

And there are others — and they are legion — whom we might add: Donald G. Mitchell, our beloved " Ik Marvel," who bequeathed us his " Dream Life " and " Reveries of a Bachelor "; Richard Grant White, the noted philologist and Shakesperean critic; Thomas Wentworth Higginson, anti-slavery agitator and author; Sidney Porter, whose nom de plume was "O Henry," was a clever short-story writer; Henry Cuyler Bunner, many years the dignified and humourous editor of "Puck," whose short stories have had wide distribution; and Richard Watson Gilder, the editor and "poet of the soul."

And literature like politics could not have existed without the newspaper of which Thomas Jefferson once said: " I would rather live in a country with newspapers and without a government than in one with a government without newspapers." So just a word in praise of Horace Greeley, who was potent in the thought of his time, and who founded " The New York Tribune."

To-day publishers are seeking new forms of invention, for there is no end of curiosity shown by the audiences that wait expectant on their work. And fashions change; yesterday automobile romances held attention — to-day, " High Times in an Aëroplane "; while psychology, sociology, economics, romanticism, classicism, and realism, are all compelling themes in poetry and prose; and the poet finds his inspiration even in the city streets where flowers bloom in florists' windows, on the market-stall, and in crevices.

Strong Nature friendships are being established. We may ramble in " Fresh Fields," with our essay-naturalist; try " Fisherman's Luck " on " Little Rivers "; learn the characteristics of wild animals and birds and roadside flowers; and with " Sharp Eyes " pry into Nature's tiniest secrets. And as for science, what discoveries has its literature proclaimed; and America in the short story as constructed by Irving, Hawthorne, Poe, and Bret Harte, has made one of her noblest contributions to literature, and never was our land better equipped with story-tellers than to-day.

The widest field, however, is monopolised by the novelist. Crawford, in his day, called the novel " a pocket theatre," and the novelist, " a public amuser "; but now the best novel may be either psychological, realistic, or problematic, and demand the serious attention of the most serious reader. Mr. Howells, the alert novelist, essayist, and editor, and dean of our literary guild, who has been true to his traditions says, in comparing the past with the present, that there has been no hour of his literary past when he has had the least fear for the literary future, and he adds : —

"All of human life has turned more and more to the light of democracy, the light of equality, if you please. Literature, which was once of the cloister and the school, has become more and more of the forum and incidentally of the market-place. But it is actuated now by as high and noble motives as ever it was in the history of the world, and I think that in turning from the vain endeavour of creating beauty and devoting itself to the effort of ascertaining life, it is actuated by a clearer motive than before. . . .

"To the backward glance, the light of the past seems one great glow, but it is in fact a group of stellar fires. Perhaps it is as some incandescent mass that the future will behold this present when it has become the past."

NOCTURNE

"Up to her chamber window
A slight wire trellis goes,
And up this Romeo's ladder
Clambers a bold white rose.

I lounge in the ilex shadows,
I see the lady lean,
Unclasping her silken girdle,
The curtain's folds between.

She smiles on her white-rose lover,
She reaches out her hand
And helps him in at the window —
I see it where I stand!

To her scarlet lip she holds him,
And kisses him many a time —
Ah, me! it was he that won her,
Because he dared to climb!"

— Aldrich.

XXXI

WOMAN IN AMERICAN LITERATURE

PART FIRST

IN order to give our story a gentle ending, we just glance at the part played by woman in American literature. For the feeble twitterings of the songstress were very early heard — even from the colonial day when Anne Bradstreet lightened the harshness of pioneer life by the consolation of poetry. These "first breathings" were a combination of high thought, fantastic conceit, and sentimentality, graced by poetic touch.

Tender-hearted Lydia Huntley Sigourney belonged to the "Knickerbocker Group"; and her one aim in her fifty-six volumes of verse and prose was to do good. It is difficult now to realise how much her solemn lines were quoted in her own day. Her memorial tablet in Christ Church, Hartford, bears Whittier's words: —

> "She sang alone ere womanhood had known
>   The gift of song which fills the air to-day;
> Tender and sweet, a music all her own
>   May fitly linger where she knelt to pray."

Among prose-writers, were sentimental and con-

335

ventional novelists, whose stately, slow-moving characters acted conventional parts. " Charlotte Temple," for example, written by the playwright and novelist, Mrs. Rowson, was stiff and absurd — the heroine always " bedewed with tears." Then there was " The Wide, Wide World," whose lachrymose heroine literally absorbed the *wide, wide world.* " The Lamplighter" was more normal in its pious setting. But these and other old tales, with chapters capped with morals, won phenomenal success when they were issued, while now-a-days we count them as bits of departed grandeur over which Holmes chants the requiem : —

> " Where, O where, are life's lilies and roses,
>   Nursed in the golden dawn's smile ?
> Dead as the bulrushes round little Moses,
>   On the old banks of the Nile.
>
>   .   .   .   .   .   .
>
> Where are the Marys and Anns and Elizas
>   Living and lovely of yore !
> Look in the columns of old Advertisers,
>   Married and dead by the score."

In this era of stilted ideals and flowery exaggeration, one very remarkable novel, " St. Elmo," penetrated every corner of our land as hundreds of material monuments give evidence of the enthusiasm which it aroused; for there were " St. Elmo " coaches and steamboats and hotels and towns! The novel was written by Augusta Jane Evans, a Southern lady, whose " Beulah " had already won success.

In " St. Elmo," Miss Evans catches her heroine, Edna Earl, a girl of twelve, a stern little moralist, standing at dawn, outlined against Lookout Mountain; a duel and a wreck quickly follow — and in time Edna Earl becomes another Jane Eyre, and St. Elmo Murray, another Rochester. And Arthur Bartlett Maurice, the critic, claims that beneath the pompous phraseology, there lurks a real story, inspired by such lofty ideals and passionate sincerity, that, though written over half a century ago, the book remains an early chapter in the code of life — and " St. Elmo " like " Uncle Tom's Cabin " stands apart.

And what reading was offered boys and girls of the earlier times? In colonial days, they were probably fascinated with the prodigies of Mather's " Magnalia." Then " Robinson Crusoe," " Pilgrim's Progress," " Gulliver's Travels," " The Arabian Nights," and the novels of Scott and Cooper — alike held their fancy; while Jacob Abbott's " Histories " and " Rollo Books " were everywhere sought, for they conveyed wisdom and moral instruction in readable form.

And in turning from the statuesque women-writers of a by-gone age to the flesh-and-blood interpreters of our own, we shall find a new world opening out before the children as before those of larger growth.

We recall a few names of women who have made healthful impress upon literature — among them, Louisa M. Alcott, Mary Mapes Dodge, Helen Hunt Jackson, Celia Thaxter, and Sarah Orne Jewett.

To make a brief sketch of Louisa M. Alcott (1832-1888), we must in imagination retrace our way to intellectual Concord, which through her has given a contribution to children's literature. On a hillside stands " Old Orchard House," teeming with memories of four clever, wide-awake little women. Here it was that " Joe scribbled, May wrestled for fine words; here Beth's little cottage piano stood, and May mothered them all when dear Mrs. Marsh was away." We know them each one, and remember what an instantaneous welcome all received when they made their first courtesy to the public; and it was just because they were so real and natural, and proclaimed a gospel of simple living and happy work.

These were their maker's masterpieces; but at the mention of her name, other wholesome children, both boys and girls, come trooping into our memory. Jusserand says: " A tale is the first key to the heart of a child,"—and what a magical key Miss Alcott held! Her life was a struggle for she was very young when it was discovered that she — rather than her visionary father — must be the family bread-winner.

At eight, she wrote her first poem; it was dedicated " To a Robin," and her mother encouraged her to keep on, assuring her that she might in time become a second Shakespeare. Fired with this modest ambition, the child continued to write on such subjects as dead butterflies and lost kittens, even until the story mania set in; and in order to gain subsistence, she also did sewing and went out to service, and presently her newspaper articles began to be accepted; and the little desk now stands in the parlour where Louisa turned her observation into manuscript, sometimes working all night by the light of a single tallow-dip.

And while the family struggled for daily bread, over the way in the " School of Philosophy," Dr. Alcott, " Socratic Talker of his Day," was dispensing his " Seer's-rations " of mystical wisdom. Rose Hawthorne once said that " the only point at which Dr. Alcott ever met the world was in his worship of apple trees! "

Emerson was the truest friend that Dr. Alcott ever had; and to Miss Alcott he was " The Beloved Master," who, by the simple beauty of his life, and the wealth and uplift of his works, helped her to understand herself. She went to the war as a volunteer nurse and nearly died of fever. She spent years of discouraging toil, before the success of " Little Women " gave her place in the world of letters.

She died in 1888, in the " Thoreau-Alcott " home in Concord, and is buried in Sleepy Hollow Cemetery not far from her " Beloved Master," upon whose grave, at his burial, she had laid a lyre of yellow jonquils.

Mrs. Alcott once announced that she " had been married twenty-nine years and moved twenty-seven times," and several homes in Concord attest the truth of her remark; but it is " Old Orchard House " that the Woman's Club of the town has set apart to be the shrine of Louisa M. Alcott. Four rooms are devoted to memorials; the rest is a vacation home for working-girls, in tribute to one who sacrificed her life in the service of others.

The story of our next authoress, Mary Mapes Dodge (1838-1905), presents a striking contrast to that of Louisa M. Alcott. Daughter of Professor Mapes, the distinguished writer and scientist, she passed a happy childhood in her New York home. She never attended school but with her sisters studied under tutors. There were no children's magazines, but she feasted on ballads and Scott and Bunyan and Shakespeare. It seemed as if she had always loved to write, and as a maiden, she assisted her father in preparing learnéd pamphlets.

There was granted her a happy married life of a few short years, and then she was left a widow with two young sons, and she was at once their comrade, rearing them tenderly and wisely. Feeling that she must needs do something for their support, she took up literature, writing essays and stories for grown-up readers; and she improvised bed-time tales for her

CELIA L. THAXTER

SARAH ORNE JEWETT

HELEN HUNT JACKSON

MARY MAPES DODGE

boys which she presently determined to offer to other children as " The Irvington Stories."

About the time that these were published, in 1864, she became absorbed in Motley's " Dutch Republic," as well as in many books concerning quaint and valiant little Holland and Dutch history. She commenced to weave a story and soon " Hans Brinker " was published. Every chapter as she wrote was submitted to the criticism of two Hollanders who lived near her, and the tale was so true to life that Dutch boys were sure that Hans Brinker had skated on the canal; and once when her own young son went into a book-store in Amsterdam and asked for something to read, the clerk brought it forth as the best juvenile story in Holland; and it was translated not only into Dutch — but also into French, German, Russian, and Italian.

With Harriet Beecher Stowe and Donald G. Mitchell, Mary Mapes Dodge became editor of " Hearth and Home." In this she proved so successful with the " Juvenile Department " that the editors of " The Century " asked her to edit a juvenile magazine, and in 1873, " St. Nicholas " came into being, christened by Mrs. Dodge. Her ideal for a children's magazine was to make it strong, true, and beautiful; it must be full of life and eager impulse, and its cheer, the cheer of the bird-song; and to the fulfilling of this ideal, this brilliant and attractive woman devoted the rest of her life. Young readers felt the spell of enthusiasm and always sought her stories.

Among her editorials, the witty little preacher, " Jack in the Pulpit," held his audience spell-bound. Many were her rhymes and jingles, and among her pleasing tales " Donald and Dorothy " and " Pluck."

Through personal friendship with noted authors, she secured from them many contributions, and even fascinating " Lord Fauntleroy " made his first bow to the public as a serial in " St. Nicholas."

For older people, Mrs. Dodge wrote poems and prose tales; among the latter was " Theophilus and Others," and among the " Others " was amusing " Mrs. Maloney on the Chinese Question."

Mrs. Dodge was constantly sought by her coterie of special friends, and one evening every week she was the genial hostess in her New York home, over-looking Central Park. And Onteora cast its spell over her as over many professional men and women, and it was here in her rustic home that she died; and this " lover of little ones up to the end " was mourned by children to whom she has left a memorial of far-reaching influence, even the juvenile classic which she sent forth touched with the finest thought and fancy of her day; and Richard Watson Gilder wrote:

" Many the laurels her bright spirit won;
    Now that through tears we read ' The End,'
  The brightest leaf of all — now all is done —
    Is this: ' She was the children's friend.' "

XXXII

IN 1880, there appeared in " St. Nicholas," a story headed " The Naughtiest Day of My Life." This was a confession written by Helen Fiske Hunt Jackson (1831-1884), describing an escapade as a child when with another little girl she ran away from her home in Amherst, Massachusetts, to Hadley, four miles distant. The whole village of Amherst, even to college professors, joined in the search, and late at night the children were brought back; and in merry, impulsive mood, Helen walked in exclaiming: " Oh, mother, I've had a perfectly splendid time! " This is a most characteristic anecdote of the childhood of brilliant, impetuous Helen Fiske, daughter of Professor Fiske of Amherst College.

She was married at twenty-one to Captain Hunt of the army, and with her social and winning nature, enjoyed the wandering life of a military household; later her husband, now Major Hunt, was killed in Brooklyn, while experimenting with an invention of his own for firing projectiles under water. Two years more, and her handsome, precocious son Bennie died of diphtheria, and before he passed away, he made his mother promise not to take her life. Stunned by the blows that had followed in swift succession, Mrs. Hunt for a time shut herself away from the world, and finally her solace came in the form of literature.

In her home in Newport, Rhode Island, she studied rhetoric and literary methods and gradually acquired careful construction. After years, her poems began to be admired. These are on Nature, home-life, and abstract themes. They are meditative rather than joycus, and in their glow and intensity rank very high. Emerson considered them the best of those written by American women, and used to carry them in his pocket to read to his friends.

How expressive of her colour-sense and delicate ear for melody are her lines: —

> "Chestnuts, clicking one by one,
> Escape from satin burrs; her fringes done,
> The gentian spreads them out in sunny days;
>
> The summer charily her reds doth lay
> Like jewels in her costilest array;
> October, scornful, burns them on a bier."

And perhaps the sorrow that clouded her own life found expression in "The Spinner," from which we take extract: —

" Like a blind spinner in the sun,
  I tread my days;
I know that all the thread will run
  Appointed ways;
I know each day will bring its task
And being blind, no more I ask.

  . . . . . .

But listen, listen, day by day,
  To hear their tread
Who bear the finished web away,
  And cut the thread,
And bring God's message in the sun,
' Thou, poor, blind spinner, work is done.' "

Of restless and adventurous temperament, Mrs. Hunt travelled much on the Continent. In her " Bits of Travel," she immortalised a German landlady; and while the latter did not enjoy having her love-story given to the world, she called the writer who had sojourned with her " the kindest lady in the world."

" Bits of Talk " followed " Bits of Travel," and these with other things signed with the pen-name " H. H." had very many readers, doubtless because the author's personality was so wrought into every word.

" H. H." had early asserted that she would never be a woman with " a hobby "; but after listening to lectures in Boston and New York on the wrongs of the Indians, her soul was stirred to its depths and from this time she consecrated her life to a single purpose — she would emancipate the Indian — as Harriet Beecher Stowe had emancipated the negro. She travelled over the West, carrying cheer to them in their adobe villages as she listened to their tales and pledged herself to do what she could, and they many times saluted her as " Queen."

To make her facts accurate, she spent three months working in the Astor Library, New York, and then published her " Century of Dishonour." At her own expense, she sent a copy to every member of Congress. The work exhausted her, she went to Norway for refreshment; and on her return received an appointment from the President to investigate the needs of the Indian. Again she searched into her problem and her report was clear and vigorous.

She was interested, also, in early Spanish Missions, and these were told of in magazine articles. In 1884, " Ramona," her best novel, came out. It is a powerful work, its moral revealing her interest in the red man, and it has now, in 1913, reached its ninety-third printing!

After years of strenuous labour, her health was failing, and she removed to the West. She married a Mr. Jackson, a Quaker, and a banker of Colorado Springs, and here she made a beautiful home and ten years of life remained. Here she cherished her human friendships, and her love for flowers which she gathered by the carriageful from " her garden "

— as she fondly called a peak of the Cheyenne Mountains.

Her vigour never returned and her last moments were full of suffering. Shortly before she died, she said: " My ' Century of Dishonour ' and ' Ramona ' are the only things I have done of which I am glad now; they will leaf out and bear fruit — the rest is of no moment." She is buried four miles from Colorado Springs, near the summit of Mount Jackson which was named in her honour. She had begged that her grave be unadorned " with costly shrub or tree or flower "; it is simply a mound over which " The sweet grass its last year's tangles keeps." Her novels, sketches, and essays will live, but longer than any of them will be read her poems so full of gleam and gentleness.

Our next writer is Celia Laighton Thaxter (1836-1894), and to find her literary world, we must in fancy transport ourselves to the Isles of Shoals, off the coast of Portsmouth, New Hampshire, a cluster of eight rocky elevations with " frantic crags," which, according to Hawthorne, " are tossed together lying in all directions." Celia Laighton's birthplace was Portsmouth; but when she was five years old, her father, owing to some political disaffection, withdrew for ever from the mainland, bringing his wife and children to these desolate islands, ten miles out in the Atlantic, and here he became keeper of the White Island light.

Celia has described the first landing on the lonely rock, in the autumn sunset — the light-house like a tall black-capped giant gazing down upon them — while a few goats feeding at its base looked at them as they entered the little thick-walled stone cottage, from whose deep-seated windows she later made many pen-pictures.

Shells and rocks and waves were playmates of this little maiden and her brothers, Oscar and Cedric. They watched the sea-fowl soaring aloft or gliding over the water; vessels scudding over the dark blue sea; stealthy islanders paddling along the ledges, or stretched out on the wet sand looking for wild-fowl. They watched, also, the lighting of the lamp and as it sent afar its rays, they wondered how many hearts it nightly gladdened; and birds and flowers were very companionable, and " Peggy's Garden " in its brilliant glow became famous.

The child rowed and made rag-carpets and tended the sick; and as she older grew, more and more her heart went out towards the little Norwegian colony of fisher-folk. She heard the " good-byes "; saw the sailing away of the fleet, and the sudden squall that sent the small boats swaggering before it; and she would go to the little cluster of women assembled at the headland and comfort them with words of cheer; and her later tales and poems were set in the framework of a sea, " that sparkled, or sang, or foamed, or threatened."

As a rosy-faced maiden of sixteen, Celia was married to Levi Thaxter, a Browning student, and a missionary to the fisher-folk of an adjoining island; and then she was spirited away to the new world of Boston which suddenly opened before her fascinated vision. There were pictures and lectures and concerts and operas and theatres. Mr. Thaxter, with his studious nature, did not care for these things, but his girl-bride entered into all with a delighted surprise.

She never had really thought about admission to the field of literature until, unbeknown to her, a friend sent one of her poems to " The Atlantic " and it was accepted; she was glad and grateful, and her genius unfolded as she began to write. Her literary output is not large, but what she did is full of exquisite lyrical expression as " The Singer of the Shoals," and " The Singer of the Sea." Among her noted poems are " An Old Saw," " The Burgomaster Gull," " Tacking Ship Off Shore," and the trustful " Sandpiper." Among her tales is " The Spray Sprite " that danced in the breakers, and talked and laughed with the loons, and then did patchwork to the end of her days; and another tale describes Madame Arachne, and how as a child she peeped through the light-house window and watched the adventures of the wary dame; and " Island Garden " and " Among the Shoals," and letters and poems, are all pleasant reading.

Mrs. Thaxter spent much of her later life at Appledore, the largest island of the group, where her brother's home for an occasional guest had developed into a hotel; and this desolate island —

"With rifts and charms and storm-bleached jags,"

became a favourite resort for artists, musicians, and men of letters, lured thither by " The Singer of the Shoals." Among others, Whittier came and Hawthorne and Ole Bull — and " The Singer " received them dressed always in black and white and grey with sea-shells for her ornaments; and she entertained them with her music, her verses, or her charming conversation. Here she died and was buried; and the White Island light-house has disappeared and been replaced by another, more powerful but less picturesque.

On a clear day, the Isles of Shoals are distinctly visible off the coast of Portsmouth, and not far from the town in another direction is South Berwick, Maine, the home of another authoress, whose early environment like that of Celia Thaxter formed the subject of many a later tale. This was Sarah Orne Jewett (1849-1909), who, as a delicate child, was consigned to an out-of-door life in this quaint, seaboard town. She spent her days driving about the country with her doctor-father; she became intimate with his patients, and learned so much about ministering to the sick that she would have liked to be a physician.

Her wise father was a man who hated all affectation and insincerity, and with rare tact he taught her how to cultivate right powers of observation; and when she confided to him her desire to become a writer, he advised her not to describe people and things in general but just as she saw them — and the more she looked, the more interested she grew. South Berwick was full of bronze-faced lumbermen and sailors and old sea-captains; among the latter was her grandfather, and she always loved to hear him spin his yarns because he was " a perfect geography in himself."

Sometimes she lingered about the country-store to catch the shrewd and nautical conversations, and when she was about fifteen, city boarders with artificial ways began to invade the town, and from them she gained yet another viewpoint. So through her father's showing the way, she acquired marvellous insight into human nature, thus gathering material for her striking character sketches. Sometimes she visited her aunt in Exeter, who lived in a big house, adorned with unbroken china plates, and huge jugs by the fireplace.

The early Berwick home is yet standing, associated alike with a doctor's office and an author's den, with antique portraits and mahogany furniture, and a library overflowing with books; its setting, an old-fashioned garden stocked with fragrant posies. Somewhere in her reminiscences, Miss Jewett says:—

"Berwick always seems a little sad even to me! in the wane of winter the houses look at each other as if they said: 'Good Heavens, the things that we remember!' but after the leaves come out they look quite prepared for the best, and quite touchingly cheerful."

It was through her sympathetic portrayal of New England life that Miss Jewett became known in Boston society; and her most intimate friendship was with Mrs. James T. Fields.

Miss Jewett regarded literary work experimental, its vitality lying in the something that " does itself," and she adds: " There are stories that you write and stories that write themselves in spite of you!" She composed very rapidly, perhaps three thousand words a day, and her tales are lighted with touches of delicate fancy; there is in them the fragrance of woods and the murmur of pines and of tides; portraits of courtly New England dames, and boys and girls romancing in country ways. We find these all, in her dozen or more books, among which the following are prominent: " Deep Haven Sketches," " The King of Folly Island," " A Marsh Island," and " A Country Doctor "; while of " The Country of the Pointed Firs," Rudyard Kipling once said to her: " I don't believe you ever really knew how good that work is! "

Miss Jewett divided her time between Boston, Berwick, and Manchester-by-the-Sea, living there much with Mrs. Field. A woman of great dignity and sweetness of character, it brought cheer to look into her bright, piquant face. Very typical of her selfless spirit is her remark to a friend: " Oh, do let us always tell people when we like their work, it does so much good! "

In our brief sketch, we have quoted liberally from her own words, for somehow she has unconsciously told the world just the things that the world wants to know. In closing, we make extracts from her letters which have been edited by Mrs. Field. Many of these were written to Celia Thaxter whom she always addressed as " Sandpiper." After Longfellow's death, she eulogises him as follows: " A man who has written as Longfellow wrote stays in this world always to be known and loved, to be a helper and a friend to his fellow-men."

In another, she speaks of Dr. Holmes as " bearing his years cheerfully and drawing old friends closer, as he lets the rest of the world slip away little by little "; again, of Phillips Brooks's death and of the more than Sunday-like sleep that fell over the city during his funeral. An intense admirer of Tennyson, she emphasises the separateness of his life, comparing him to " a king of old of divine right and sacred seclusion." And in expressing her delight at meeting him, she writes: " If anybody had come

and said: 'See Shakespeare with me!' I couldn't
have felt any more delighted than I did about Tennyson; it was a wonderful face, and he was far and
away the greatest man I have ever seen!"

Among other literary women, there is Elizabeth
Stuart Phelps Ward, who wrote with philanthropic
purpose, calling attention to various forms of social
disorder; while her venturesome imagination displayed in "Gates Ajar" and like subjects, opened
before the world the very soul of the New England
woman.   And there is Julia C. R. Dorr, noted for
her graceful songs and travel sketches; and Mrs.
Whitney, whose juvenile stories made special appeal
to the maiden: —

> "Standing with reluctant feet
> Where the brook and river meet;"

while for over fifty years, Margaret E. Sangster was
counted an inspirer of home life.

Alice Morse Earl threw about colonial days the
spell of her own enthusiasm, alluring one to an interest in a coffee-pot, a bit of lustre, or a tattered
calash; and in her gracious company we stray "into
old-time gardens, ponder over sun-dials of yesterday,
dance at plantation feasts, grow acquainted with the
children of New Amsterdam, or follow the fashion
of two centuries of belles and beaux."   And Emily
Dickinson must not be omitted, and that "soul

diary " which she wrote just for her own entertainment in her life of seclusion at Amherst; and since her death her poems have been generally read, and they contain fragmentary passages of high inspiration that are more and more praised as time passes.

Harriet Prescott Spofford is unique in this group in the hues with which she paints her " Amber Gods," " New England Legends," and other fancies. She links the past with the present; for as " Mistress of Deer Island," she presided over her river-girt home. And of these women and of others of whom we might speak, the best ideals are becoming classics while the weak ones are being winnowed out.

To-day women are most active in the realm of letters, grappling boldly with profound problems and " isms " of every cult. There are laureates of the new women and her modern possibilities. The most popular subject is realistic fiction. Woman has thus far made her literary mark, and the question naturally arises: " What will be her status at the end of another hundred years? "

THE SANDPIPER

" Across the narrow beach we flit,
    One little sandpiper and I,
And fast I gather, bit by bit,
    The scattered driftwood bleached and dry,

The wild waves reach their hands for it,
    The wild wind raves, the tide runs high,
As up and down the beach we flit,—
    One little sandpiper and I.

Above our heads the sullen clouds
    Scud black and swift across the sky;
Like silent ghosts in misty shrouds
    Stand out the white lighthouses high.
Almost as far as eye can reach
    I see the close-reefed vessels fly,
As fast we flit along the beach,—
    One little sandpiper and I.

I watch him as he skims along,
    Uttering his sweet and mournful cry,
He starts not at my fitful song,
    Or flash of fluttering drapery.
He has no thought of any wrong;
    He scans me with a fearless eye:
Staunch friends are we, well tried and strong,
    The little sandpiper and I.

' Comrade, where wilt thou be to-night
    When the loosed storm breaks furiously?
My driftwood fire will burn so bright!
    To what warm shelter canst thou fly?
I do not fear for thee, though wroth
    The tempest rushes through the sky;
For are we not God's children both,
    Thou, little sandpiper, and I?'"

                                        — *Celia Thaxter.*

356

POPPIES IN THE WHEAT

(Copyright 1892, by Roberts Brothers)

" Along Ancona's hills the shimmering heat,
A tropic tide of air, with ebb and flow
Bathes all the fields of wheat — until they glow
Like flashing seas of green, which toss and beat
Around the vines.   The poppies lithe and fleet
Seem running, fiery torchmen, to and fro
To mark the shore.   The farmer does not know
That they are there.   He walks with heavy feet,
Counting the bread and wine by autumn's gain,
But I,— I smile to think that days remain
Perhaps to me in which, though bread be sweet
No more, and red wine warm my blood in vain;
I shall be glad remembering how the fleet,
Lithe poppies ran like torchmen with the wheat."

—*H. H.*

ADDITION OF 1922

XXXIII

NATURE-LOVERS—ESSAYISTS—HISTORIANS

FIRST we glance into the lives of three nature-lovers, withdrawing them from the many who would conjure us.

John Burroughs (1837-1921) the friend alike of children and grown-ups, is called "The Foremost Nature-lover since Thoreau." He was born on an ancestral farm near Roxbury, in the Catskills—"the odd child" in a large family—for with the same environment as his brothers and sisters he was the only one to whom appealed the magic of nature and books.

From early boyhood he studied the doings of birds and insects and flowers, and so wise did he become that in later years specimens were sent him from all the world around for identification.

He was a school-teacher at seventeen and next was employed first in Washington and then in New York State, but business proved irksome. After 1874, he made his conventional home at "Riverby," West Park, New York, calling himself "a literary naturalist" and his occupation "grape culture."

His holidays are more fully associated with "Slab-sides," an ivy-covered cabin further back among the hills. Here he lived simply, wrote his books, communed with Emerson and Whitman, and entertained the men, women and children that visited him, because they wished to see the author of "Wake Robin," "Winter Sunshine," and other books that had brought to them the lure of wood and stream. His is the story of a quiet life but there are bits of travel interwoven. Once with Mr. Roosevelt he visited Yellowstone Park and Alaska. One day Mr. Roosevelt said to him, "Did you take notes?" And Burroughs replied, "No, everything that interests me sticks to me like a burr"; and it was three years later that his "Camping and Tramping with Roosevelt" was published. He never wrote about anything that he did not fully like, and without study.

Another inspiring bit of travel was that when in the great Arizona Desert he met the "Tall Grizzly Scot," John Muir, Western explorer and geologist. How together they must have glorified the wonders of mountains and glaciers and forests and rivers of the West and Southwest and of the Hawaiian Islands—and how Burroughs loved to listen to Muir's racy conversation.

Just one more glimpse of our naturalist. We find him an elderly man, seated in "Woodchuck Lodge" near his birthplace, busy with his pen and happy in reminiscences of early days. And not far from the "Lodge" on "Boyhood Rock," we to-day read a memorial tablet on which is inscribed:

NATURE-LOVERS

John Burroughs—1837-1921
"I stand amid the eternal ways
And what is mine shall know my face."

W. H. Hudson (1852-   ). This is a naturalist
with a New England mother and an English father,
but his name is added to this book of American
authors because he is so remarkable. The privilege
is claimed of introducing him to our American youth
—thousands of whom have never heard of him—but
they may wisely cultivate his acquaintance.

Naturalist and novelist, he may be placed beside
John Burroughs, for like Burroughs he helps us
solve nature's secrets. Galsworthy calls him "the
most valuable writer that our age has produced."

In the region of the thinly settled pampas of
Argentina, he was born in a low, rambling house
sheltered by twenty-five ombre trees, each a hundred
years old; and among the branches of one of these
the restless, inquiring group of little Hudsons constructed a play-house.

It is in his "Far Away and Long Ago" that we
read the story of Hudson's childhood and youth in
South America. It is almost legendary in its dream-
like episodes and feeling for beauty, for from earliest years the influence of nature upon him helped
his mental and spiritual development.

He would lie in the sun-dried grass to see the
evolutions of the long, black Argentina serpent, or
again looking up study the habits of the huge bat

wrapped in buff-covered wings, or watch a flock of flamingos—"angelic-like creatures"—sweeping by, and like Burroughs he must, from a mere child, have felt in his very soul the melody of bird-song.

Grown to man's estate he has for many years shown himself a magical writer whether in South America or up and down England. His genius for interpreting nature-life is marvellous, with an exquisite love of beauty. He combines in his books anecdotes, bits of story, and romance.

Among his books are "An Old Thorn"; "The Purple Land"; "Idle Days in Patagonia"; "Birds in Town and Village"; and "Adventures among Birds."

Marvellous poems have been written by nature-lovers. Rev. Dr. Henry Van Dyke is Princeton professor, preacher, essayist, diplomat, prose-writer and poet—but it is as a nature-lover that we quote two stanzas of his splendid ode, "God of the Open Air."

ODE

God of the Open Air

I

"Thou who hast made thy dwelling fair
  With flowers below, above with starry lights
And set thine altars everywhere,—
  On mountain heights,
In woodlands dim with many a dream,
  In valleys bright with springs,

And on the curving capes of every stream:
  Thou who hast taken to thyself the wings
    Of morning, to abide
Upon the secret places of the sea,
  And on far islands, where the tide
Visits the beauty of untrodden shores,
Waiting for worshippers to come to thee
    In thy great out-of-doors!
To thee I turn, to thee I make my prayer,
  God of the open air.

VI

By the breadth of the blue that shines in silence o'er me,
By the length of the mountain-lines that stretch before me,
By the height of the cloud that sails, with rest in motion,
Over the plains and the vales to the measureless ocean,
(Oh, how the sight of the greater things enlarges the eyes!)
Draw me away from myself to the peace of the hills and
  skies."

—Rev. Dr. Henry Van Dyke.

Among essayists as among nature-lovers it is difficult to make selection. The name of Agnes Repplier (1857-) is that of a most gifted essayist. She is a native of Philadelphia and of French ancestry and has spent much time in European travel.

She writes upon a great variety of current topics and from many points of view. She is never afraid to preach high ideals and her criticisms—marked by common sense or sparkling with wit—are always clever and helpful. Lately her practical articles on education have evoked much discussion.

Many little volumes have been published as the products of her pen, among which the one entitled "Essays in Miniature" is specially charming. Miss Repplier's frequent contributions to magazines possess lively interest for the reader.

Samuel McChord Crothers (1857-) is also an essayists who stands forth prominently. He was born in Illinois—became a clergyman—and after several pastorates has been settled in Cambridge, Massachusetts, since 1895. He has written several books of essays, many of which are full alike of charm, humour, and wisdom.

Perhaps the collection dearest to the heart of the young book-lover is either "The Gentle Reader" or "The Pardoner's Wallet."

We have already glanced into the lives of historians from early colonial times. Now from a modern viewpoint, two of the most scholarly are John Fiske and Woodrow Wilson.

John Fiske (1842-1901) was born in Hartford, Connecticut. A precocious boy and a ravenous reader, he devoted himself to legend and science and psychology and history, and with rare play of fancy he would tell a story. He was but a youth when he commenced to collect a library. As a student in Harvard College he had much trouble with his tutors owing to his revolutionary ideas.

He wrote books on a variety of topics, but research into the evolution of history was the study of his life, and he had vast knowledge on this subject. Early periods of American history with all their conflicts were to him as interesting as the World War of the twentieth century would be to the writer of to-day.

"The Discovery of America" is his best book. He began it with the fables of a Western Continent, leading thence to the discovery of Columbus.

His "Beginnings of New England" is most artistic in workmanship; it contains a real portrait gallery of the founders. His style is vivid and perspective good.

John Fiske was also a profound but noted university lecturer.

Woodrow Wilson (1856-). Coloney Harvey, in 1911, described Woodrow Wilson as "a highly Americanized Scotch-Irishman, descended from Ohio, born in Virginia, developed in Maryland, married in Georgia, and now delivering from bondage that old Democratic commonwealth, the State of New Jersey."

Son of a Southern gentleman, one of his earliest impressions as a boy, was hearing on the street the shouting that Abraham Lincoln had been elected and that there would be war. As a youth he had a passion for the study of history and politics. He went through Princeton College and later was its renowned president—then Governor of New Jersey —and for two terms President of the United States.

But it is as a writer—not a statesman—that he is named here. His state papers, diplomatic messages and proclamations, have been noted for their clear, forceful, and flexible style, always maintaining the traditions of the best English culture.

He has had a habit of jotting down anywhere a note or two in shorthand, from time to time, and then with the inspiration seized him, of seating himself at his typewriter and shaping his thoughts, sentence by sentence.

Among Mr. Wilson's books are "The Theory and Practice of Government"; "Division and Reunion"; and greatest of all, his five-volume "History of the American People." Loving Democracy, he holds up fine ideals. It is a typical history for a true American to read.

CHAPTER XXXIV

NOVELISTS

IN this hurrying age the novel and short story are leading forms of literature, and publishers are constantly alert for good plots. The names of novelists are legion, each one striving to interpret life in some form. A few write the sort of thing that the world but little notes or long remembers. Others make clear and direct appeal to the reader's sentiment. We select illustrations from among novelists most honoured.

Henry James (1843-1916) may easily be called "The Father of the Modern American Novel," because of his original methods of thought. He was born in New York City and educated abroad and lived in England most of his life.

He wrote many novels, short stories, and essays. They are full of minute analysis, in which, with much imagination and grace of style, are contrasted the characteristics of people in the Old and the New World. He was truly an "Apostle of Realism," and his novels are international.

He had very distinct individuality and wrote with such psychological instinct that his works do not generally appeal to the young; but we add his name because he is so distinguished and has impressed so many thinkers in both England and America.

Among his best known books are "The American"; "The Lesson of the Master"; "The Madonna of the Future"; and "The Wings of the Dove."

Mrs. Atherton—Gertrude Franklin Horn—(1857-   ) is the g. g. niece of Benjamin Franklin, and a native of California. She is an extensive traveller and has had a broad and fearless outlook upon life. She writes with firm grasp upon her subject and independently of literary rules.

Her novels and short stories, with California for a background, relating to its early history, are valuable as records, especially the attractive volume, "The Splendid Idle Forties," describing picturesquely the vanishing life of the "Golden States," while in another—quite as realistic—is depicted the earthquake tragedy of a later day.

Mrs. Atherton emphasises her political views in "Senator North,' in which a whole scheme of national problems in Washington is ably discussed.

Her most lasting monument, however, must be "The Conqueror." In this, with strength and passion and illuminating glimpses of his contemporaries, is narrated the life of Alexander Hamilton.

More recently, Mrs. Atherton has spent much time abroad, and one of her contributions to War literature is "A Book of Essays" dedicated to "Eternal France."

Alice Brown (1857-) is a favourite New England writer of novels, short stories, and plays. As a child she lived on a New Hampshire farm, and after graduating at Exeter Academy she taught, and while teaching studied her pupils, and later some of them became her story people.

After one of her trips abroad she wrote a book entitled "English Impressions"; and in connection with another trip, in collaboration with a friend, she published a booklet on Robert Louis Stevenson.

She possesses rare knowledge of the characteristics of New England women and the customs of the country and has remarkable mastery of dialogue. These she embodies skilfully and realistically in her plots, which, in later years, seem to show the influence of Henry James.

Among her attractive novels and convincing short stories are "The Prisoner"; "The Story of Thyrza"; "Tiverton Tales"; "Meadow Grass"; and "Vanishing Points."

Besides prose works she has with poetic vision traced "The Road to Castaly," fountain of the gods, and this has received nation-wide attention; and when sixteen hundred and forty-six plays were submitted anonymously for a prize, Miss Brown gained it—and ten thousand dollars it was—for her "Children of the Earth." Her home is now in Boston.

Mrs. Deland—Margaret Campbell—(1857-)

was born in Allegheny, Pennsylvania. Her parents dying in her infancy she went to live with an aunt in Manchester in the same State. Delightful descriptions come to us of her childhood days, for reading and inventing stories she dwelt in a land of fancy. Ever since she has shown wonderful interest in child-life.

She gives an amusing account of her days at school, emphasising the accomplishments then taught. One of her earliest literary ventures was scrawling bits of verse over everything. These with others were later woven into "The Old Garden."

Mrs. Deland is one of the most popular and versatile of modern novelists, but we have space to mention but three or four of her works. In them she manifests alike a sense of humour and pathos. She always represents truth as higher then beauty, and she loves to deal with moral and religious problems.

This latter trait is shown forcefully in "John Ward, Preacher," and "The Awakening of Helen Richie"; while in "The Iron Woman" are portrayed fine gifts of observation and construction, making it one of the impressive novels of the age.

A most fascinating book is "Old Chester Tales." Manchester is "Old Chester," and the figures of men and women that might have lived there are drawn with living distinctness, while Dr. Lavendar is the link that binds them together. He is one of the unique types in American literature. Quaint and alluring "Old Chester" will live as will the English "Cranford" and other towns about which romances cluster.

In 1918, Mrs. Deland went to France to work in an army canteen and afterwards she wrote her "War Essays." Her latest publication is "The Vehement Flame." Her present home is in Boston.

Mrs. George C. Riggs—Kate Douglas Wiggin— (1857-   ). This authoress makes universal appeal to the hearts of the young. She was born in Philadelphia and as a clever and interesting child was devoted to reading. She spent her girlhood years in New England, graduating at Bowdoin College. Then the family removed to California.

With rare insight into the hearts of children she loved to tell them stories, and this faculty developed into deep interest in free kindergartens. Through her influence these were organised in California and were soon known throughout the West. Educational movements of every kind receive her attention and personal effort.

She is an optimist with fertile imagination and she has the gift of transforming the common into the beautiful.

Her first book that captivated the world was "The Birds' Christmas Carol," written in 1888. Then followed "Timothy's Quest" and "Rebecca of Sunnybook Farm," both strongly evincing her understanding of New England character; and the three "Penelope" books, whose setting was laid in the British Isles. "Penelope" is her grown-up heroine.

Perhaps Mrs. Riggs's most delightful venture is "The Old Peabody Pew." At present New York City is her residence.

Owen Wister (1860-   ) is a Philadelphian by birth. He is a graduate of Harvard College and has given his views of the life of a college boy in his "Philosophy Four."

He does not, like many others, write up one region, but is versatile in conception with wide range of vision. His earlier books were short stories of ranch life, and then stringing Western episodes together he produced his most romantic and popular work, "The Virginian," delightfully written, and holding the attention from beginning to end.

With powerful imagination he pictures fierce, struggling lives and cruel deeds. The hero is a Wyoming cow-puncher—a youth of strange dialect, and withal such a crude sense of justice and heroism that he can inspire the love even of the demure little New England school-teacher. We are given a glimpse of an old phase of American life that is historically valuable.

"Lady Baltimore" presents a striking contrast to "The Virginian" and shows the influence of Henry James. The plot is carefully constructed and of exquisite workmanship. It recalls the new life in the South with the remains of old Southern dignity and custom.

The scene of the story is laid in Charleston, South Carolina, and "Lady Baltimore," by the way, is a delicious kind of cake.

Among other things, Owen Wister has written a "Biography of General Grant," and his "Pentecost of Calamity" is his contribution to the World War. He is also a sportsman and botanist. He resides in Philadelphia.

Hamlin Garland (1860-   ) is the son of a pioneer and spent his childhood in the Middle West when it was only a frontier, and in his novels and short stories he has used as a background the home and the life of his boyish days.

In his "Son of the Middle Border" he describes feelingly the stern drudgery of farm and camp and mine, and he colours his descriptions in a most unusual way. His style is not elegant, but eloquent in its realism.

His "Daughter of the Middle Border," very recently written, is a romance of the same early day, portraying the same rugged, unconventional life.

Two of his best short stories are "Among the Corn Rows" and "The Creamery Man." He has written much and is unequalled in his special field, so that one wishing to study frontier life in early times should read Hamlin Garland.

Mrs. Wharton—Edith Newbold Jones—

(1862-   ) was born in New York City and among her educators were tutors, travel, and wide reading.

On marrying Mr. Wharton she removed to Boston but in later years has lived very much abroad. From a child she has always held high social and literary ideals. She was one of the truest disciples of Henry James, whose letters show the intimate sympathy and admiration that existed between them.

In satire she sometimes rivals Thackeray. In novels and short stories she writes with keen insight and intensity. Her art betrays a wonderful finish and in her descriptions is shown real understanding of human nature. Her heroes and heroines may be aristocratic, yet many of them have but little heart and are menaced by unhappiness.

Among Mrs. Wharton's finest novels are "The House of Mirth" and "The Age of Innocence," the latter a story of New York society fifty years ago; among her novelettes, "Madame de Trêymes" and "Ethan Frome."

Her gentle humanity has been most truly evidenced in her service for devastated France. One of the very best of our War stories is "The Marne," most artistically written in 1918. What a devoted hero is Troy! and how feelingly the author's love for France is expressed when she says:

"Every stone that France had carved, every song she had sung, every new idea she had struck out, every beauty she had created in a thousand fruitful years, was a tie between her and her children."

Later she writes with renewed admiration, "French Ways and Their Meaning."

Winston Churchill (1871-), a native of St. Louis, is now living in Cornish, New Hampshire. His historical romances, upon each of which he has spent years, with intense regard for accuracy of statement, make him one of our most trusted novelists—his setting of history rather than his plot being his strong point. His works are panoramic, each one being a succession of episodes placed in a great era of American history.

One of the first is "Richard Carvel," a tale of a colonial aristocrat in the time of the American Revolution with Paul Jones as hero—and it refuses to be forgotten.

Another is "The Crisis," a story of the Civil War, and Abraham Lincoln appears. "The Crossing" gives graphic pictures of the Middle West with border warfare and Indian massacre.

For his next plot, Mr. Churchill turns to New Hampshire and "Coniston" represent the doings of a political "boss"; while "Inside the Cup" is a religious novel in which church and social affairs have part.

These are perhaps the author's best. He has few colourful women but his men are very characteristic. He is extremely popular because he has really made the American historical novel famous.

Ellen Glasgow (1874-   ) is a Virginian by birth, and nearly all of her novels, written with power and pathos, have their setting in Southern Virginia, the region with which she is most familiar.

Among them is "The Miller of Old Church." "Old Church," like Mrs. Deland's "Old Chester," is a unique town, and the novel will preserve the record of the gentle breeding and old-time courtesy and hospitality of the typical Southerners that came in touch with the sturdy miller.

Her "Romance of a Plain Man" represents life in the new South after the Civil War—the beginning of the reconstruction period. Barriers are breaking down between the working-classes who are struggling to rise and prove the dignity of labor, and the poor aristocrats who have to meet them.

Miss Glasgow's recent novel, "One Man and His Time," is written like her others in an epic spirit— epic because one man is prominent and a problem is worked out. This is also a cleverly wrought novel of courage.

The gift of story-telling is, as one has said, "inborn in Ellen Glasgow."

She has no peer as a novelist, interpreting the South in its transformation period. Her home is in Richmond, Virginia. She walks in her garden and thinks out her plots—then writes behind locked doors, her dog her only companion.

Ernest Poole (1880-   ) is one of the most

promising of the younger authors. A Chicago boy, he early showed fondness for writing. He graduated at Princeton College and has spent some time abroad as a magazine correspondent. In 1805 he visited Russia to study conditions there. On his return he lived for years in Greenwich Village, New York City.

He has always been interested in university settlement work, specially in New York messenger- and news-boys. Great docks and warehouses have held for him curious attraction and wherever he goes he visits the docks. So easily he has proved himself a specialist in writing "The Harbor," which appeared in 1915. The first part of the book makes wonderful revelations of the lives of longshoremen—the latter part turns to social reforms.

The setting seems to be Brooklyn, New York, but the materials are really drawn from a Chicago dockyard during a strike.

In 1917 he won the "Pulitzer Prize" for his novel, "The Family," awarded because the writer had striven to portray the best type of American manhood.

Mr. Poole was abroad during the War and in 1920 the novel "Blind" told his story of "the blinding, vast tornado, with the deep changes that it wrought."

His books are few, but he writes and rewrites each one several times before considering it perfect enough to offer his publisher—proving the oft-repeated saying: "Genius is the capacity for taking infinite pains."

DRAMATISTS

It was not until the latter part of the nineteenth century—during the period when poetry and romance voiced the aspirations of the literary—that drama first took form in the United States. An early and unique example is Longfellow's "Closet Drama."

Real plays had been supplied from abroad, but now came into notice two American writers—Clyde Fitch and Augustus Thomas. They devised modern situations, introduced current songs and fashions, and illustrated city life of the day, composing lines—not for the reader—but for definite actors and actresses. These were sometimes thrilling but never profound.

Clyde Fitch (1865-1909) wrote sixty-nine realistic plays, in which the plots were natural and consistent. Some of them, like "The Climbers," were amusing satires on city folks. Others were historical, as "Nathan Hale," "Barbara Frietchie," and "Beau Brummel." The last was highly popular when produced and is still quoted.

Augustus Thomas (1859-1891) also used up-to-date material and told his story well. His first plays were a series named after different States, as "Colorado" and 'Alabama," picturing life in the West and Southwest. He dramatised the novels of other authors.

Among his later plays, "The Witching Hour" and "The Harvest Moon" are best known.

Both Fitch and Thomas had far-reaching influence on the increasing group of succeeding dramatists, who have evinced more marked originality.

William Vaughn Moody (1869-1910) was alike a poet and dramatist in both prose and verse. A son of the Middle Border, after graduation at Harvard College he travelled in Europe, taught for years in the University of Chicago, and died prematurely just as his genius was ripening.

Some of his exquisite lyric poetry is perhaps difficult to understand, but there are superb lines running through it all; for example, we quote from "Heart's Wild Flower":

"What are the dearest of God's dowers to the children of
     his blood?
 How blow the sky, the wilding flowers in the hollows of
     his wood?"

And again, the lines in "An Ode in Time of Hesitation":

"Soon shall the Cape Ann children shout in glee,
   Spying the arbutus, spring's dear recluse;
   Hill lads at dawn shall hearken the wild goose
   Go honking northward over Tennessee."

Mr. Moody's two forceful prose dramas, "The Faith Healer" and "The Great Divide," have both been successful upon the stage. His cycle of poetic drama was unfinished at the time of his early death. Its Promethean theme is the unity of God and man.

Richard Hovey (1864-1910) was, like William Vaughn Moody, a forerunner of the School of Modern American Poets and Dramatists. Like Moody, too, he was born in the West and became in time professor in Barnard College, New York City. Again, like Moody, he attempted a cycle of poetic drama, his subject being the Arthurian legends—but he, also, died before his musical cycle was completed.

With the Canadian poet, Bliss Carman, he wrote "Songs from Vagabondia." Besides, he composed battle-hymns which were suggested by the Spanish-American War.

His early poems showed his love of life and comradeship—his later ones soared into spiritual realms. They all abounded in beautiful and picturesque lines. His premature death was a great loss to the world.

Charles Rann Kennedy (1871-   ) was originally an Englishman, but has become a naturalised American. He has married a well-known actress, Edith Wynne Matthison, and she takes leading parts in her husband's plays.

Mr. Kennedy has created yet another style of unique drama. He is familiar with Greek forms, and his plays are written in strictest conformity with the three dramatic unities.

They have symbolic themes, are full of seriousness and poetic fervour, and are arranged for few actors. They should be studied in order to understand their moral force. Probably the most popular on the stage is "The Servant in the House."

Mrs. Lionel Marks—Josephine Preston Peabody—(1874-   ) was born in New York City but her home is now in Cambridge, Massachusetts. She has shown in many ways her strong interest in social progress. Her poetry is noted for imagination and the spiritual tone of her pure lyric verse. This is sometimes a bit mystical.

Among her well-known poems are "The House and the Road," beginning

> "The little road says 'Go'
> The little house says 'Stay' "—

and her "Ever the Same," a tribute to "The same little rose."

The titles of some of her volumes are "The Wayfarers" and "The Singing Leaves"; also "The Harvest Moon," which is dedicated to the women of France. It is perhaps in poetic drama that she has best revealed herself and with what various purposes have different dramatic authors worked. Mrs. Marks's effort has been to recall Shakespeare's day and Shakespearean form of plays, and with this in-

tent she has written "Marlowe," the plot centering about the old song:

"Come live with me, and be my love."

Her masterpiece, however, is "The Piper," and it won a prize offered by the Stratford-on-Avon "Memorial Theatre." It was produced there and afterwards in New York City. It presents the beautiful message that love gives us always the best things.

Percy MacKaye (1875-). His dramatisation of Chaucer's "Canterbury Tales" and "Jeanne d'Arc" are most realistic, for the actors in setting and costume and conversation are so in accord with their day.

Then Mr. MacKaye has devised a new dramatic art which is called "Community Masque." In this he combines drama, pageant, and civic festival, in picturesque way, and he interests whole towns and cities in taking part in act and chorus.

We may name "Sanctuary," a Bird Masque, first given in Cornish, New Hampshire, in honour of President and Mrs. Wilson; "A Civic Masque" in St. Louis, representing the one hundred and fiftieth anniversary of the founding of the city; "Caliban," or Masque in New York, in 1916, in celebration of the "Shakespeare Centenary." Great enthusiasm is exhibited by masses of people in these artistic ventures.

These are but brief illustrations of the work of

various kinds of playwrights to show the trend of drama in the United States. New writers with new plays are constantly receiving notice.

One thing that has greatly aided the work has been the founding of a course for the study of dramatic composition by Professor Baker of Harvard College, himself a noted writer.

His successful venture was followed by that of Professor Brander Matthews of Columbia College, the honoured critic and scholar.

Just now there is a struggle for more freedom of production. A protest of amateurs against professionals would prove that literary merit is worth more than money, and small theatres are springing up in different cities for the bringing out of plays. Is it possible that we may yet discover a modern Shakespeare?

CHAPTER XXXV

POETS

THE latter part of the nineteenth century saw the passing of the singers of the old New England group of poets and it seemed, at first, as if there would be none to take their places.

But presently there was a reawakened zeal for poetry of an unconventional type that has appeared almost a revolt against that of an earlier day. A new school of young and vigorous singers arose; some members exploited Walt Whitman's conceptions; one was Promethean in his venture; another revived Arthurian legends; while yet others, recalling Wordsworth's and Coleridge's lyrical ballads, became "Imagists," surprising the literary world with their "vers libre." They were not so particular as the New England group about rhythm and metre.

Daring to be original, with true realism many have studied life rather than books; sometimes climinating every ornament, they have reflected the spirit of the age in field and mine and factory. Indeed, every kind of environment has been touched upon.

And there are also poets with vivid imagination and soul power, who, with artistic beauty, have written poems of place or childhood or love or war or patriotism.

POETS

The wonderful developments in periodical literature have greatly assisted both poets and short-story writers; and so many books of poems are appearing that it is difficult to estimate their literary value—for not all poetry is immortal.

We have space for only a few of the leaders, representing the trend of their work, while there are scores who rightly find space in a larger volume. But which may live in the "Hall of Fame"—who may tell?

Edwin Markham (1852-   ) was born in Oregon and as a young man worked in California at farming and herding cattle and the blacksmith's trade. Later he became superintendent of schools.

One day a picture by Millet fascinated him, and he wrote some lines that at once made him famous as "The Laureate of Labor." Jessie Rittenhouse—herself a well-known poetess—has said:

"Edwin Markham in his 'Man with the Hoe' sounded the humanitarian labour note in America, in the early dawn of the twentieth century."

Now he took up writing as a profession, becoming a notable figure, both as poet and lecturer.

In studying his life one wonders if his own lines have not been his inspiration:

> "For all your days prepare,
>   And meet them ever alike;
> When you are the anvil, bear—
>   When you are the hammer, strike!"

Mr. Markham is a special favourite of the young, not only because he tells a poetic story so clearly but also for his humour, optimism, and colourful description.

His volumes, "The Shoes of Happiness" and "Gates of Paradise," are full of delightful readings. From his "Lincoln and Other Poems" we withdraw "Lincoln," for great honour has recently as always been accorded this wonderful bit of hero-worship.

Lincoln's life was long ago honoured at his birthplace by a glorified log-cabin, and later on the banks of the Potomac by a Greek Temple, most perfect of architectural structures. On Memorial Day, May 30, 1922, this was dedicated by President Harding, in the presence of "The Blue and the Gray"—a vast assembled multitude paying tribute—and here Mr. Markham read from his amended "Lincoln":

> "A man to hold against the world,
> A man to match the mountains and the sea."

The concluding stanza is as follows:

> "And when he fell in whirlwind, he went down
> As when a lordly cedar green with boughs
> Goes down with a great shout upon the hills,
> And leaves a lonesome place against the sky."

Mr. Markham's home is now at West New Brighton, Staten Island, New York.

Edith M. Thomas (1854-) was born in Chatham, Ohio, and as a girl, writing for local papers, she elicited the attention of Helen Hunt, who encouraged her to contribute to current magazines. She has written excellent prose essays, but she is a genuine poet devoted to classic forms. Her lyrics and sonnets, treating of love and life and nature, show her delicate touch, and some of them are exquisite. The World War at first shocked her, but it also inspired her to write poems of comfort and courage.

Among her many little volumes—which are literary treasures showing her careful workmanship—are "The Round Year," "Fair Shadow Land," "A New Year Masque," "The Inverted Torch,"—while among her very pleasing poems are "The Soul of the Violet," "Frost To-night," "The Compass," and "Grandmother's Gathering Boneset."

Miss Thomas's home is now in New York City.

Madison Julius Carwein (1865-1914) is ranked as one of the most gifted of American poets. He was born in Louisville, Kentucky, and lived there most of his life. He began to write verses while attending the high school, reciting them from the chapel rostrum.

The freshness and beauty of the poems of the "Kentucky Lyrist" as they came out in local papers early won special praise from Aldrich, Howells and other eminent critics, and through their kindly reviews he gained in time an international reputation.

Mr. Carwein led a strictly literary life. His output was tremendous—in all, thirty-six volumes.

A painter of nature with an exquisite sense of the beauty of tree, cloud, bird, flower and brook, and with romantic imagination, he followed the mood of every season, immortalising in tuneful verse the soft, Southern landscape. Many of his haunts are still shown in and around Louisville.

Litsey, leader of the younger writers, called Carwein "The Kentucky Woodland Thrush."

Among his numerous publications are "Blooms of the Berry," The Garden of Dreams," "Myths and Romances," and "Nature Notes and Impressions."

THE GIPSY

Deep in a wood I met a maid,
   Who had so wild an air
Her beauty made my heart afraid,
   And filled me with despair.

She wore a gown of gipsy dyes,
   That had a ragged look;
The brown felicity of her eyes
   Was like a mountain brook.

Around her hair, of raven hue,
   Was bound a gentian band,
And from each tree the wild birds flew
   And fluttered to her hand.

The crow sat cawing in the thorn
   As if it, too, would greet

Her coming; and the winds of morn
  Made music for her feet.

Barefooted down the wood she came
  Bearing a magic rod
That left the leaves it touched aflame
  And aster-starred the sod.

I spoke to her! "Tell who you are!
  So fair, so wild, so free!
A being from some other star?
  Or wildwood witchery?"

She smiled, and, passing, turned and said:
  "You do not know me, then?
Why, I am she you long deemed dead,
  Autumn, returned again!"

—Madison Julius Carwein.

By permission of John P. Morton and Co., Louisville, Kentucky.

Edward Arlington Robinson (1869-). His home town, Gardiner, Maine, is the "Tilbury" where many of the scenes of his poems are laid. He thus has immortalised it as Mrs. Deland immortalised "Chester."

He has experimented in different kinds of poetry, among them free verse. Among his realistic portraits are his "Squire"—"Gentleman from Soul to Crown"—and the optimistic, irresponsible "Captain Craig."

He sees the characteristics of common people and illumines them in his lines. He was a special favourite with Theodore Roosevelt. His best poems, "The Master," is a tribute to Abraham Lincoln. It is found in his finest collection of poems, "The Town Down the River."

Amy Lowell (1874-) is a native and now a resident of Brookline, Massachusetts. She belongs to a literary family of which James Russell Lowell was a member. She spent her girlhood days in general reading and wide travel and for eight years studied forms of poetry.

Then this woman of rare mental gifts began to write and volumes of prose criticism and verse have come from her pen. Working with fellow-poets, a new creed has been propounded. They believe that poetry must be dedicated to beauty, and while now and again they adhere to classic forms they depart entirely from the views of the nineteenth century New England group and this new poetry is called "vers libre" or "free verse."

Miss Lowell, as a lover of experiment, has—with her fellow-workers—thus introduced novel and striking forms. Among these is "polyphonic—prose-poetry." The word "polyphonic" means "many-voiced," and refers to the many voices of poetry. The word "prose" is interpolated simply to explain the manner in which this free verse is printed.

Miss Lowell defines "polyphonic—prose-poetry"

as "The finest, most elastic of all forms—for it follows all the rules that guide other forms and can go from one to the other in the same poem with no sense of incongruity." In all the "imagist poetry" a clear image must be outlined and rhythm created to embody it. Some of the images are formed of gentle lyrics; in others horror is invoked to portray them.

A poetess of intense personality and surrounded by an impressionist circle, Miss Lowell has made the achievement of these later years a creative literary period.

Among her works are "Sword Blades and Poppy Seed," "Tendencies in Modern American Poetry," and "Can Grande's Castle." The title of one of her books, "A Dome of Many-coloured Glass," suggests her wide variety of conceptions. Apart from her originality, she has surely come into special touch with Wordsworth, Coleridge, Keats, Tennyson, Browning, Poe, and Whitman.

Her volume, "Pictures of the Floating World," published in 1919, ignores old poetic forms.

POLYPHONIC-PROSE-POETRY

But there is something more wonderful yet. Set your faces to the Piazzetta, people, push, slam, jam, to keep your places. "A balloon is going up from the Dogana del Mare, a balloon like a moon or something else starry. A meteor, a comet, I don't really know what; it looks, so they say, like a huge apricot, or a pear—yes, that's surely the thing—blushing red, mellow yellow, a fruit on the wing, garlanded with streamers and tails, all a-whirl and a-flutter.

Cuts the strings and she sails, till she lands in the gutter. "How do you know she lands in the gutter, Booby?" "Where else should she land, unless in the sea?"

"You're a fool, I suppose you sat up all night writing that doggerel." "Not at all, it is an improvisation." "Here, keep back, you can't push past me with your talk. Oh! Look! Look!"

That is a balloon. It rises slowly—slowly—above the Dogana. It wavers, dips, and poises; it mounts in the silver air, it floats without direction; suspended in movement, it hangs, a clear pear of red and yellow, opposite the melting, opal-tinted city. And the reflection of it also floats, perfect in colour, but cooler, perfect in outline, but more vague, in the glassy water of the Grand Canal. The blue sky sustains it; the blue water encloses it. Then balloon and reflection swing gently seaward.

One ascends, the other descends. Each dwindles to a speck. Ah, the semblance is gone, the water has nothing; but the sky focusses about a point of fire, a foamless iridescence sailing higher, become a mere burning, until that too is absorbed in the brilliance of the clouds.

You cheer, people, but you do not know for what. A beautiful toy? Undoubtedly you think so. Shout yourselves hoarse, you who have conquered the sea, do you underestimate the air? Joke, laugh, purblind populace. You have been vouchsafed an awful vision, and you do nothing but clap your hands.

From "Can Grande's Castle."

—*Amy Lowell.*

By permission of Messrs. Houghton, Mifflin and Co.

Robert Frost (1875-) was born in California and has lived long in New England and for two or three years in England.

Poetry to him is a living language and he possesses an unusual selective memory. His first volume, "A Boy's Will," perhaps represents incidents of his own early life as a young poetic artist. Two other volumes, "North of Boston" and "Mountain Interval," are dramatic pictures of the more serious side of New England life, with its grim forces working amid familiar scenes. They are also tinged with the natural beauties of the land.

It is difficult to choose from many other poems which display fresh creative spirit and truthfulness of insight. In "The Death of the Hired Man" are the following lines:

"Home is the place where, if you have to go there,
They have to take you in."

*   *   *   *

"I should have called it
Something you somehow haven't to deserve."

In "Mending the Wall," it is proved that "Good fences make good neighbors." "The Woodpile," with its striking closing passage"; "The Birches," "The Pasture," "After Apple Picking," "The Runaway"—are all pictorial in form.

Mr. Frost's present address is Ann Arbor, Michigan.

THE RUNAWAY

"Once when the snow of the year was beginning to fall
We stopped by a mountain pasture to say "Whose colt?"
A little Morgan had one forefoot on the wall
The other curled at his breast. He dipped his head
And snorted to us; and then he had to bolt.
We heard the miniature thunder where he fled,
And we saw him or thought we saw him dim and grey
Like a shadow against the curtain of falling flakes.
"I think the little fellow's afraid of the snow.
He isn't winter-broken. It isn't play
With the little fellow at all. He's running away.
I doubt if even his mother could tell him 'Sakes,
It's only weather.' He'd think she didn't know.
Where *is* his mother? He can't be out alone."
And now he comes again with a clatter of stone,
And mounts the wall again with whited eyes,
And all his tail that isn't hair up straight.
He shudders his coat as if to throw off flies.
"Whoever it is that leaves him out so late,
When everything else has gone to stall and bin,
Ought to be told to come and take him in."

—*Robert Frost.*

Mrs. Ernest Filsinger—Sara Teasdale—(1884-) was born in St. Louis and from a child her chief interest has been poetry. She has written very frequently for magazines. In 1918 a prize was awarded her for her "Love Lyrics" by the "Poetry Society of America."

Just to quote a line here and there from different poems must allure us to seek further into her graceful conceptions,

In one we find

    "Blue waves whitened on a cliff";

in another,

    "Scent of pine trees in the rain";

Then we may listen to

    "The woodthrush twirling three notes";

Again there are

    "Holy thoughts that star the night";

Yet again,

    "Shadowy fields of Indian summer";

and lastly,

    "The winter snow-hushed and heartless."

Among **Mrs. Filsinger's** published volumes is "Helen of Troy and other Poems." Her home, like many of our authors, is in New York City.

Alan Seeger (1888-1916), student, traveller, and soldier-poet, enjoyed a very brief but brilliant career. He was born in New York City and some of his boyhood was passed in Mexico. Even as a child he loved to write. His poem, "The Deserted Garden,' shows his fascination for the picturesque Mexican colouring.

After graduating at Harvard College he spent four years in Paris, living a kind of Bohemian life among students. He had the gifts of song and romance and wrote there most of his "Juvenilia." Referring to his fondness for the gay city he said:

"One crowded hour of glorious life
Is worth an age without a name."

Later came the World War, and joining the "Foreign Legion" of France he threw himself heart and soul into the great adventure and some of his letters and poems are either prophetic or commemorative. One begins:

"I have a rendezvous with Death";

Another is the

"Ode in Memory of the American Volunteers"

who

"Fell in the sunny morn and flower of their young years,"

and who had

"That rare privilege of dying well."

In one of the furious advances, his squad made a daring rush. He was wounded and now follows his famous achievement, for as he lay dying he cheered on, his comrades by singing a marching song. His life was given—but the victory won!

On May 21, 1922, high tribute was accorded Alan Seeger in France. In the little town of Landricourt-Sous-Coucy, impressive ceremonies marked the dedication of a church-bell, presented by the "Poetry Society of America" in honour of an American poet.

Katharine Lee Bates (1859-   ) was born in Falmouth, Massachusetts, and graduated at Wellesley College, and for years has been a member of the faculty. She has travelled and studied much abroad. She is a versatile writer in prose and poetry, alike for children and older readers.

Among her numerous works are "College Beautiful and Other Poems," "Lectures on English Religious Drama," "Stories of Chaucer's Canterbury Tales"—retold for children, "In Sunny Spain," and from "Gretna Green to Land's End."

In appreciation of her scholarly culture as teacher, lecturer and author, honorary degrees have been conferred upon her.

We remember how Francis Scott Key and Julia Ward Howe at once attained international fame by a single, patriotic poem; and the name of Katharine Lee Bates is added, for her "America the Beautiful" is also sung on public occasions all the world around, and the following is her description of its inception.

In 1893, she was with other Eastern instructors teaching in a summer school at Colorado Springs, right under the purple range of the Rockies. Among the expeditions taken was one to Pike's Peak. There in one ecstatic gaze over the vast sea-like expanse, the opening lines of the hymn floated into her mind, and before leaving Colorado, the four stanzas were pencilled in her note-book. Later she revised the poem, making its phraseology more simple and direct, and she adds:

"That the hymn has gained in all these years such a hold upon the people is clearly due to the fact that Americans are at heart idealists, with a fundamental faith in human brotherhood."

AMERICA THE BEAUTIFUL

"O beautiful for spacious skies,
 For amber waves of grain,
For purple mountain majesties
 Above the fruited plain!
  America! America!
 God shed his grace on thee
And crown thy good with brotherhood
 From sea to shining sea!

O beautiful for pilgrim feet,
 Whose stern, impassioned stress
A thoroughfare for freedom beat
 Across the wilderness!
  America! America!
 God mend thine every flaw,
Confirm thy soul in self-control,
 Thy liberty in law!

O beautiful for heroes proved
 In liberating strife,
Who more than self their country loved,
 And mercy more than life!

POETS

America! America!
May God thy gold refine
Till all success be nobleness
And every gain divine!

O beautiful for patriot dream
That sees beyond the years
Thine alabaster cities gleam
Undimmed by human tears!
America! America!
God shed his grace on thee
And crown thy good with brotherhood
From sea to shining sea!"

—*Katharine Lee Bates.*

AFTERWORD

Edward Garnett—an apostle of interpretative criticism—makes the following prophecy:

"I believe firmly that American literature will count many great original achievements within a couple of generations. All the pith and sap of a great literature are there, and a ferment of spiritual force which sooner or later must burst into flower.

"There is the mingling of many races out of which a great world literature must grow, but it must be founded on a true American spirit."

America has found herself and in many ways presents her claim to the soul of the world. Think of her scientific wizardry—how the President's voice by wireless circles the earth! Can our imagination lead to what in the coming years may be the achievements of our American authors?

We pause just here in our brief and simple "Story of American Literature," for we may not attempt to interpret the unrounded lives of any of the younger living authors, many of whom are already striking an individual note.

CPSIA information can be obtained
at www.ICGtesting.com
Printed in the USA
BVHW09s0029090718
521063BV00007B/96/P